THE COMPLETE HISTORY OF
SATURDAY NIGHT FEVER

MARGO DONOHUE

CITADEL PRESS
Kensington Publishing Corp.
kensingtonbooks.com

CITADEL PRESS BOOKS are published by

Kensington Publishing Corp.
900 Third Avenue
New York, NY 10022

All Kensington titles, imprints, and distributed lines are available at special quantity discounts for bulk purchases for sales promotions, premiums, fund-raising, educational, or institutional use. Special book excerpts or customized printings can also be created to fit specific needs. For details, write or phone the office of the Kensington sales manager: Kensington Publishing Corp., 900 Third Avenue, New York, NY 10022, attn Sales Department; phone 1-800-221-2647.

10 9 8 7 6 5 4 3 2 1

First Citadel hardcover printing: September 2025

Printed in the United States of America

ISBN: 978-0-8065-4392-5
ISBN: 978-0-8065-4394-9 (e-book)

Library of Congress Control Number: 2025935038

The authorized representative in the EU for product safety and compliance
is eucomply OU, Parnu mnt 139b-14, Apt 123,
Tallinn, Berlin 11317; hello@eucompliancepartner.com

For Lester

Contents

Interviews[*]

Julie Anderson: Sister of choreographer Lester Wilson. November 7, 2023.

John Badham: Director. September 24, 2023.

Joseph Cali: Actor, Joey. February 18, 2024.

James Carpinello: Actor, Tony (1999 Broadway musical). October 17, 2023.

Ed Cermanski: Musician/member of the Trammps. November 1, 2023.

Anita Louise Combe: Actor, Stephanie (1998 London musical). September 14, 2023.

Robert Costanzo: Actor, paint store customer. October 11, 2023.

Erica Damsky Loiacano: Bay Ridge resident during the filming. August 16, 2023.

Dennis Danehy: Son of street dance pioneer Don "Campbellock" Campbell (the Lockers). January 5, 2024.

Diane Day Crump-Richmond: Assistant to Lester Wilson and former *Dance Fever* dancer. February 5, 2024.

Denny Dillon: Actor, Doreen. August 8, 2023.

---

[*]All interviews have been edited for length and clarity.

Yvonne Elliman: Singer of "If I Can't Have You." January 17, 2024.

Simon Fanshawe: Journalist who interviewed Robert Stigwood late in his career. November 27, 2023.

Joanne Farrell: Actor, Stephanie (1999 London Musical). September 28, 2023.

Lorraine Fields: Assistant choreographer for Lester Wilson. October 10 and November 6, 2023.

Jimmy Gambina: Trainer for John Travolta and fight coordinator for *Saturday Night Fever*. October 14 and 17, 2023.

Macarena Gandarillas: Dancer, choreographer, and friend of Lester Wilson. January 4, 2024.

Freddie Gershon: Former president of the Robert Stigwood Group. November 24, 2023.

Kristian Gravenor: Journalist based in Quebec. December 7, 2023.

Noel Hankin: Club owner of The Best of Friends, Inc. (TBOF) social club. Author of *After Dark: Birth of the Disco Dance Party*. September 11, 2023.

Betsy Harris: *Solid Gold* dancer who worked with Lester Wilson. January 16, 2024.

Michael Hausman: Head of production for Robert Stigwood. March 26, 2024.

Shawn Hausman: Production assistant on the *Saturday Night Fever* set. November 22, 2023.

Adrienne King: Actor and background dancer. January 5, 2024.

Randal Kleiser: Director of *The Boy in the Plastic Bubble* and *Grease*. March 6, 2024.

Nan Knighton: Playwright of *Saturday Night Fever* musical book. September 11, 2023.

Shanta Kumari: Homeowner for *Saturday Night Fever* interiors. August 17, 2023.

Alex Marchak: Dancer featured in the 1977 film. February 27, 2024.

Kevin McCormick: Executive producer. September 19, 2023.

Joy McMillan: Assistant to Robert Stigwood. November 15, 2023.

James McMullan: Photographer and artist of the original *New York* magazine feature (and cover). December 1, 2023.

Pete Menefee: Dancer and costume designer. February 28, 2024.

Richard Montoya: Dancer who worked with Lester Wilson. February 21, 2024.

Charonne Mose: Dancer who worked with Lester Wilson. January 6, 2024.

Paul Nicholas: Producer and writer for the *Saturday Night Fever* musical. September 18, 2023.

Orfeh: Actor, Annette (1999 Broadway musical). October 5, 2023.

Bruce Ornstein: Actor, Gus. August 8, 2023.

Paul Pape: Actor, Double J. August 10, 2023.

Lisa Peluso: Actor, Linda, Tony's sister. January 15, 2024.

Donna Pescow: Actor, Annette. February 13, 2024.

Arlene Phillips: Writer/choreographer of the original *Saturday Night Fever* musical. September 1, 2023.

Paige Price: Actor, Stephanie (1999 Broadway musical). August 28, 2023.

Zack Reed: Partner of Lester Wilson. January 23, 2024.

Denise Rusinak: Dancer whose father owned the 2001 Odyssey nightclub. January 15, 2024.

Sue Samuels: Dancer, instructor, and cofounder of JoJo Smith Dance Studio. Trained John Travolta and Karen Lynn Gorney in early production. January 10, 2024.

Jason Samuels Smith: Son of JoJo Smith, and a Tony Award–winning dancer and choreographer. January 10, 2024.

Martin Shakar: Actor, Frank Jr. July 5, 2023.

David Shire: Composer and music adapter for the soundtrack. November 2, 2023.

Yelena Sionova: Homeowner of *Saturday Night Fever* location. August 17, 2023.

Peter Stanfield: Journalist and British rock author. February 19, 2024.

Ron Stigwood: Assistant to Robert Stigwood as well as his nephew. October 29, 2023.

Ann Travolta: Actor, Lenny's Pizza gal. January 22, 2024.

Robert Upchurch: Singer/member of the Trammps, "Disco Inferno." November 3, 2023.

Alberto Vasquez: Actor, gang member. September 27, 2023.

Ben Vereen: Actor, dancer, and friend of Lester Wilson. April 26, 2024.

Frankie Verroca: Background actor. March 1, 2024.

Larry Vickers: Dancer and colleague of Lester Wilson. February 15, 2024.

Geneva Vivino: Stage name Karen Burke, dancer in *Saturday Night Fever* competition scene. April 8, 2024.

Patrizia von Brandenstein: Costume designer. September 5, 2023.

Erica Wexler: Daughter of screenwriter Norman Wexler. November 15, 2023.

Darrell Wright: Dancer and friend of Lester Wilson. February 24, 2024.

Jeff Zinn: Actor/stand-in for John Travolta. October 23, 2023.

FEVER

John Travolta's trailer in front of the 2001 Odyssey,
May 1977. *Photo courtesy of Alex Marchak,
who was a dancer in the movie.*

Day 1: March 14, 1977

Sitting in his trailer, the star of *Saturday Night* (the original title of the film) can hear the shouts of thousands of kids outside. They want a glimpse of their favorite "Sweathog" from the hit TV show *Welcome Back, Kotter*. John Travolta embodied the character of Vinnie Barbarino with his tousled hair, dimpled smile, and overall doofus likability that attracted millions of viewers each week.

Six foot two inches in his platform shoes, Travolta trained with the boxer who turned actor Sylvester Stallone into *Rocky*. Six miles of daily running followed by calisthenics took more than twenty pounds off his frame, and his new, slim physique looked amazing in gabardine pants and silk shirts. His makeover from "cute" to "hot" would be one of the most striking images as he transformed into Tony Manero.

"*Barbarino! Come out!*" they screamed, and jumped onto the roof, trying to peek through the windows. Travolta's sister Ann, who has a small role as the Lenny's Pizza server, remembers asking her brother if he was okay. She told me he smiled at her. "Not nervously but more excited about the possibilities." Yes, the actual shaking of the trailer was unnerving, but the kids were psyched to have *the* Barbarino in their midst. "*Do the Barbarino dance!*" They sang his character's self-glorifying "Barbarino song" as they imitated his hip-swirling routine that they saw every Thursday night on ABC TV. When do they have famous people come over the bridge toward Brooklyn? The fans were helping to set the tone of the shoot. *And* they sent the message that his star was on the rise.

It is hard to fathom now, but there was a time when Travolta was *not* a movie star. That he was just another actor who could sing a little, dance a little, and handle light comedy. (He played Doody in the touring company of *Grease*.) That he would become the embodiment of modern dancing as well as the face and the look of the 1970s.

His television fame brought thousands of fan letters each week and his show was on top of the Nielsen ratings. In 1976 alone he released his self-titled first record; appeared on *American Bandstand*; starred in his first movie, *Carrie*, and the top-rated TV movie *The Boy in the Plastic Bubble*. Travolta's face was featured in all the teen magazines as well as in *People* magazine, which marked his transition to more adult characters.

The twenty-three-year-old was dating Diana Hyland (who was eighteen years older and played his mother in the aforementioned TV movie) and was hot enough of a property that none other than Robert Stigwood, the Australian impresario of RSO Productions (producers of *Grease, Tommy,* and *Jesus Christ Superstar* and the manager for Eric Clapton and the Bee Gees), offered him a three-picture deal for $1 million. An unheard-of sum for a television personality at the time, as feature films were much more impressive than anything on "the boob tube."

Perhaps this was the reason the production of *Saturday Night* did not think to hire more security than the few off-duty police officers who showed up in Bay Ridge that morning. The film's previous director, John G. Avildsen, received accolades for *Rocky*, which looked like it would be a lock for several Oscars (it was) and was less impressed with Travolta after each meeting. Who was this chubby kid? Where was the sex appeal? Why do we have to make his character so mean? He would soon be fired by Stigwood.

The new director, thirty-eight-year-old John Badham, was hired only three weeks before, with the star in place but very few locations committed. Executive producer Kevin McCormick (twenty-three years old) was busy buying clothes off the rack for his actors while trying to navigate the streets of Brooklyn for filming permits. He was also in charge of keeping fifty-one-year-old Norman Wexler, the volatile screenwriter (*Joe, Serpico*) whose script would often be quoted as the cast's favorite, on time with his many revisions. The chain-smoking, gun-toting scribe with severe mental health issues (he once bit a flight attendant on a cross-country flight) was a "handful" but took seriously the job of telling a gritty story truthfully.

Leading up to the first day of filming were weeks of excitement and almost unbearable stress. The $3 million dollar budget was microscopic compared with movies of comparable scope. Paramount made it clear that this production would be cheap and fast. This gritty story led by a sitcom heartthrob and with music by the Bee Gees was almost a joke to Michael Eisner (the president of Paramount Pictures from 1976 to 1984) and Barry Diller (the chairman and CEO of Paramount Pictures from 1974 to 1984.) The future titans of Hollywood made it clear that *Saturday Night* would get only a minimal amount of attention.

The firing of Avildsen was destabilizing to the cast and crew. And who was playing the lead actress? Karen Lynn Gorney? The soap star? Could she even dance? In the meantime, the leads and many members of the cast were given dance lessons with future dance legends JoJo Smith and Lester Wilson. First cousins from Queens who each would be responsible for the street dance elements of the movie.

The *New York* magazine article, imperiously titled "Tribal Rites of the New Saturday Night" was written by former UK journalist Nik Cohn in the summer of 1976. When he was in his mid-thirties, Cohn was looking for stories to maintain his freelance career and hopefully sell a screenplay to Robert Stigwood. Though an ally of the queer and trans community, he chose instead to focus on the heterosexuals-only discos in Italian neighborhoods, with their loud shirts and even noisier racism giving life to its residences on the weekends.

Cohn supposedly received $100,000 and first dibs at the screenplay for the rights to the story (which he later admitted was a fabrication of his imagination). He quickly realized he was no Wexler and abandoned the idea of being a part of the production. Who would care about this little disco movie anyway? Wasn't this music supposed to be dead?

It seems that very few people believed in the film that would come to define a generation. They underestimated the appeal of Travolta and his legions of worshippers, who would gladly skip school just to have a peek at him. That he could never disguise himself well enough before entering the 2001 Odyssey club featured in the article and film. The clubgoers would pick him out and tease, "You better represent us good!" He always responded with perfect manners and charm that he indeed planned to represent them well.

New to the crew was the forty-something Michael Hausman, who had recently collaborated with director Miloš Forman and would go on to have an illustrious film career. Stigwood hired him to cover the coordination of the whole production. Not fluent in the lead's career, he decided to check out the sitcom and was less than impressed. "I said, this guy's got this big hair and a duck's ass in the back. You know? Who the hell gives a shit about him? There's not gonna be any security problem. And so we went to the location, which was right next to an elevated subway line. There was an entrance, and you can go up. It was right there," he admits to me.

Erica Damsky Loiacano was ten years old and on the bus for school that morning and recalls when her bus driver told the kids, "You know they are filming a movie with John Travolta up on Eighty-Sixth Street near Lenny's Pizza. Really? So, none of us stayed on the bus that day. Basically, we just hung around the entire day watching and just having a good old time."

So, on that first morning when they attempted to begin the film shoot with Travolta's Tony Manero getting his two slices of pizza, thousands of fans disrupted the workday. Director Badham had no choice but to shut down the set before noon. He told me, "No matter where I aimed the camera, you could see people hanging into the frame. Their yelling could be heard for miles."

Loiacano remembers, "We were at Twentieth Avenue on Eighty-Sixth Street. People were standing on the subway platform, an elevated subway platform. Everybody is hanging over the side, you know, waiting. The trains could not even go by. I know they were just watching the filming. We were all watching the filming, and it took forever, because they could not get rid of us!"

Kevin McCormick realized that going out into the neighborhoods ahead of time, trying to secure locations and releases, garnered up excitement for the movie. "From then on we had to create fake call sheets and set up filming at all hours to try and fool the fans," he claims. Sometimes they succeeded.

By contrast, according to Badham, the nighttime shoot later that day at the dance studio where the character of Tony would woo one woman and cruelly dump the one "in love" with him was a "relative breeze" as the Faces (the name of the gang that follows Tony Manero) picked up the star standing out front. There was little dialogue (except for the rampant cursing), and they were able to keep the spectators to one side.

The Faces were Joseph "Joe" Cali (Joey), Paul Pape (Double

J.), Bruce Ornstein (Gus), and Barry Miller as Bobby C. All except Miller were in their mid-twenties (Miller was twenty), and for these theater-trained actors, this was their first movie experience.

Their first scene with Travolta, according to Cali, was "hairy" because the crowds were getting rowdier every time they saw Travolta enter the car driven by the wholly unqualified Miller—a Los Angeles native who was not comfortable behind the wheel. "He couldn't drive for shit," affirms Cali. The news of the movie being overwhelmed by locals brought even *more* excitement to the set.

As the crowd multiplied from the hundreds to the thousands, Travolta noticed a break in the barricade. As Cali tells it, "They come running down the street at the car. John is freaked. Oh, my God. We tell them to get down. We are screaming at Barry. 'Fucking hit it! Get out of here!' So, we had to just drive, and the PAs [production assistants] are on the walkie-talkies. They were all freaked because we disappeared. We drove out because John would have gotten mauled."

"It was like that scene on *The Godfather* when he is in Cuba. Beating on the car. I always remember that scene. That is what it felt like when the fans broke through. They are gonna have to be careful from now on because he was such a huge star," Cali recalls.

The thirteen-week shoot would be full of controversial casting decisions, the death of Hyland, more f-bombs and cursing than in any previous Paramount film, the early beginnings of one of the most popular soundtracks of all time, and a "smog machine" and slippery lighted floor that made dancing in the club almost torture. This is a movie that was released in a PG version soon after to allow kids to see it and has a television-friendly appeal known to most people who would be shocked to see what the "real film" is about.

In its original, R-rated form, *Saturday Night Fever* (the eventual title given by Stigwood and derided by the suits at Paramount as sounding like a venereal disease—one of their many bad decisions) is a rough film to sit through. There is the blatant racism of its characters, homophobia, misogyny, a rape scene, a suicide, and a priest who leaves the priesthood. It is a story about people who feel helpless to leave their situation while fearing their prospects may get only dimmer.

There are also stories to tell behind the scenes: the mafia shakedowns, on-set romances, the shooting of the club sequences that sometimes required camera sleight of hand (and dance doubles) to enhance performances, on-set drug use, fights between the star and director, stunt scenes gone awry, and a dance instructor who takes the credit for the film's choreography though he never spends one day on the set.

The Robert Stigwood Organisation (RSO) (and their tough president and chief operating officer Freddie Gershon) would negotiate the number of screens to feature the movie (about $10,000 per screen at the time). RSO told Paramount they would cover that cost for more points on the film, which made Stigwood millions in a few weeks. It is rumored that George Lucas tried to negotiate a similar deal for *The Empire Strikes Back*.

Stigwood's career hit the stratosphere with the release of the *Saturday Night Fever* soundtrack, featuring the Bee Gees and other top disco acts, and released a full one month before the film's release. The way movies and soundtracks were marketed after this enormous success changed Hollywood.

Then along came the crash of disco, brought on by an exasperated audience tired of everything turning disco, including the Muppets, the Rolling Stones, and even Ethel Merman. That, along with hundreds of rock stations changing formats overnight to this new dance sound—the overkill caused a hate spiral.

Stigwood would also face this backlash with box office disappointments such as *Sgt. Pepper's Lonely Hearts Club Band*, starring the Bee Gees and Peter Frampton (really!) and the Travolta/Lily Tomlin romance stinker *Moment by Moment*.

He was the architect of his most vivid dreams while also living a closeted life. A natural seducer of people, he would spend his twilight years in isolation after trying to make the magic happen again with a musical theater version of the film in the late 1990s.

Saturday Night Fever is one of the great successes of the 1970s, with its box office take of $237 million, Travolta's Academy Award nomination for Best Actor, the soundtrack that sold over forty million copies (the top-selling album of all time until Michael Jackson's *Thriller*), and its selection for preservation from the National Film Registry.

As the Bee Gees said at their 1997 Rock & Roll Hall of Fame induction, they were the "enigma with a stigma." Their great fame came at the cost of being attached to a movement that seemed to take over (and overwhelm) the culture. *Saturday Night Fever*, having survived the fashions going in and out of style and the truly awful Sylvester Stallone–directed sequel *Staying Alive*, became the classic it is known for now. And here is where we get to finally hear the best stories from most of the players. Get your white suit and platform shoes ready!

CHAPTER 1

Robert Stigwood

Impresario (im-pre-sa-rio):

1. A person who organizes or manages public entertainments.
2. A person who organizes and often finances concerts, plays, operas.

The frequency of the word *impresario* used to describe Robert Stigwood is almost staggering when you do even light research into the life of a very complicated man who was at turns warm, shy, charming, and generous, and then in equal parts standoffish, blunt, and cutthroat. He was an expert in finding talent and organizing projects to bring fun to people's lives.

One of the titans of the disco generation—a producer, manager, entrepreneur, and filmmaker—he was also terribly withdrawn and prone to avoiding close interactions. You could find him at Studio 54 enjoying the company of the beautiful people, and in a second he was gone. Flying off to one of his properties or holed up on his yacht, responding to very few callers.

He preferred to be called Robert, though his friends, family, and frenemies have several other nicknames, such as "Stiggy," "Stinkweed," and "Stig." Even at the height of his power, when he made millions each week; owned a fleet of Bentleys and yachts, a home in Bermuda, not to mention his gorgeous mansion in the English countryside; and presided over a staff

Robert Stigwood on the cover of the
July 31, 1978, issue of *Newsweek*.
Serge Mourant/Alamy Stock Photo.

of more than 150 people, the founder of RSO (the Robert Stigwood Organisation) thought of himself as a fortunate man who
could inspire other imaginative people to their best potential.
He took risks and believed in his vision.

Robert Colin Stigwood (born in 1934) was from Adelaide,
Australia, growing up near future Fox News titan Rupert Mur-
doch. At the age of eighteen, Stigwood toyed with the idea of
becoming a Catholic priest and went to Sacred Heart College.

He described to *Newsweek* in 1978 that one night he "had a party and changed his mind" on anything ecclesiastical.

The fact that he wound up living most of his life as a closeted gay man added to his many reasons not to pursue a religious path for his career. His engineer father was successful, and his mother (who would go on to marry five times) was elusive. Stigwood was teased for being "artistic" and not being a serious enough man. He wanted money, success, and adulation but he was not going to find it competing with his family in Adelaide.

After writing ad copy for a few years, he hopped off to London, promising his friends he would return a millionaire one day. Though he had only a few dollars in his pocket (as he often recalled), Stigwood managed to find his way around London. He softened his accent to sound a little more British. A member of the bourgeoisie. A bon vivant with a head for new ways to make lots of money for everyone.

He would gain and lose a fortune as a talent agent for commercials in the UK, among many career avenues, before settling on the record business. For a time, it seemed he would be a lock to manage Apple Records (and its biggest act, the Beatles) when the Beatles' manager, Brian Epstein, died of a drug overdose. Paul McCartney was very vocal with his personal distaste for the up-and-coming mogul and his affection for the Bee Gees. Stigwood decided to create RSO with the backing by Polygram B.V. Records and a roster that included the brothers Gibb as well as Eric Clapton as a solo artist and a member of Cream, Derek & the Dominos, and Blind Faith.

In 1967 and 1968, Robert worked on the London stage, managing the productions of *Hair* and *Oh! Calcutta!*. After falling in love with the productions on Broadway, Stigwood brought them over to the West End, hiring future stars Tim Curry and Elaine Paige. Both shows featured nudity, which had been banned for over one hundred years according to the 1843 Theatres Act, which required all scripts to be approved by the Lord Chamberlain of the Household. Stigwood was one of the community leaders who were able to overturn the Theatres Act. He also had a piece of the profits for both shows in his portfolio.

In addition to those successes, Stigwood became aware of a concept album, *Jesus Christ Superstar*, created by Tim Rice and Andrew Lloyd Webber. Their previous musical, *Joseph and the Amazing Technicolor Dreamcoat*, had underperformed at the box office, and they felt an album featuring RSO talent would be an instant hit. Stigwood was not interested in producing their album, but he offered Murray Head (who was in a production of *Hair*) and teenage Yvonne Elliman as vocalists.

When the double record was released in 1970 in the UK, Head's title single was received with a collective "meh." However, the US audience quickly embraced it, and soon it was rising up the *Billboard* charts. Elliman's "I Don't Know How to Love Him" (the seventeen-year-old was originally under the impression she would be playing Jesus Christ's mother rather than Mary Magdalene) had the rare distinction of being a hit on the charts at the same time a cover recorded by Australian Helen Reddy was an international success.

Always one to think big, Stigwood immediately became fixated on a Broadway version of the musical. His first job was to shut down the hundreds of unauthorized versions happening around the globe with the help of top lawyer John Eastman, the brother of Linda McCartney. The beginnings of his reputation as a tough negotiator began at this time, as they showed no fear of bad publicity, sending cease-and-desist orders to high schools, churches, and local theaters that were putting on their own productions without paying the licensing fee. They even sued a nun in Sydney—and won.

It's no surprise to find out one of his favorite movies was *The Producers*, about two men (played by Gene Wilder and Zero Mostel) who try to create a Broadway flop to defraud investors. Stigwood's idea was to take those lofty ideas, bring them to the stage, own the rights and publishing, and make large sums of money.

In 1997, Lloyd Webber told the reporter Simon Fanshawe for the *London Times* that though he and Rice are called the innovators of the modern musical, it had all been invented by Stigwood. "He taught us how to do it."

I spoke with Fanshawe, a culture journalist in London for over four decades, with a fondness for the London stage. "What Robert understood was that once you have a production, you have an album. You had, in other words, you had the thing. And what you did was you took the thing and you franchised it. Consequently, now if you see *Les Misérables* in Tokyo, Sydney, London, or New York, or wherever, it is exactly the same show."

While auditioning actors in New York in 1971, one in particular caught his eye—seventeen-year-old John Travolta from Englewood, New Jersey. The recent high school dropout who hit the Broadway auditions along with his older sisters, Ann and Ellen, tried out for a part in the chorus. Though he was too young, Stigwood printed his name on a large yellow pad. There was something special about that gangly kid with the shy smile.

Although *Jesus Christ Superstar* was given middling reviews at the time, its ensuing success helped cement Stigwood's reputation as a tastemaker. Whatever caught his fancy, he would pursue it with a passion, negotiate to give himself the most profits possible, and spend a giant sum on marketing.

In 1973, Stigwood was brought in to help bring the Who's *Tommy* to the big screen, with Ken Russell as the director. The 1969 rock opera was a startling success for the band as they leaned away from their pop sound to work with a full orchestra. After performing it several times live, the band was ready to have it adapted for film and needed a producer who understood the material and how to get mainstream press attention.

Most studios passed, due to the "drug content," but Columbia Pictures (with its new executive, Peter Guber, as an enthusiast) offered a tiny budget of $3 million to produce the feature-film adaptation of the rock opera. Stigwood invested some of his own money in the production and insisted that the movie stars Oliver Reed, Ann-Margret, and Jack Nicholson be used, along with his friend Paul Nicholas, who played the lead in the original London staging of *Jesus Christ Superstar*. Also along for the ride was freshly out-of-rehab Eric Clapton, as well as Elton John and Tina Turner.

Leaving the day-to-day set work to Beryl Vertue (who, as the co–executive producer, was able to sweet-talk Ike Turner into letting Tina leave for London for a monthlong shoot, which was a show of her fearlessness), Stigwood hired Ann-Margret's agent, Allan Carr, to manage the film's marketing with a $150,000 budget. The world premiere was at the Ziegfeld Theaters in March 1975 with a special trip to the newly opened Fifty-Seventh Street subway station, where the guests partied until dawn.

It became a massive success with a $35 million box office and a number one album. According to Stephen Dando-Collins's *Mr. Showbiz: The Biography of Robert Stigwood*, he impressed not only the movie studio but also Pete Townshend, who noticed how quickly the band was paid their share. "Stigwood's accounting to us was very fast," he said.

Stigwood was driven not by future speculation but by what he noticed around him. He was either drawn into something or he had no interest. This was a man who was guided by his own personal instincts and desires. He would hear a band and sign them on the spot. He saw a TV program he liked and then would try to get an American version sold.

In many ways, he had more of a head for publicity than business. In the future, when the Gibbs brothers dominated the charts, he would often appear in interviews with them. He often posed with them on red carpets, and they rode in his limos to premieres. It is difficult to find any press surrounding the film or soundtrack that does not mention Stigwood and his genius for putting talent together.

Over and over, his former friends and colleagues talk about his "vision." Stigwood could see things no one else would catch. He had the audacity to reach for the widest audience. To ask for the top stars to join his projects. And he did this with his gift for seduction.

Nan Knighton, a poet and playwright who would go on to work with Stigwood in the late 1990s for the *Saturday Night Fever* musical, informed me that he had a rather interesting party trick. She told me, "I was at his house with two other friends when he hypnotized me. I thought it was a joke at first, but I was able to remember the name of my first-grade teacher, my old phone number at age five, et cetera. In retrospect, it made sense to me he could hypnotize. It was simply one more aspect of his instinctive ability to pick up on the pulse of everything around him."

On top of his taste for fine wines and liquors, he was an excellent cook used to whipping up five-course meals at the drop of a hat, and kept his home cozy with warm fires, something to smoke or snort, lush surroundings, and his ability to talk to anyone about any subject on earth. When reporters interviewed him, he wound up asking them more questions than answering what they asked him.

When he could afford a staff, guests were made comfortable

with their favorite food and wine. Bedrooms would be kept spotless, and meals would be prepared and then cleaned up with nary a visit from a housekeeper or butler. It seemed to happen by magic.

Stigwood was not one to go to an office every day and live a monotonous life. To deal with him meant taking day trips to Bermuda, having three-hour lunches, and taking his calls from wherever on earth he chose to be that day. You prefer face-to-face conversations? He was too busy would be the answer. The meeting will take place only at the home office—he will be calling you from his yacht.

His former head of productions, Michael Hausman, told me during his first meeting with Robert in 1977 about his reputation for avoiding in-person appointments. "He was actually very shy and almost impossible for people to meet. I was one of the very few fortunate people able to visit with him personally. And he was interviewing me, or I am not sure."

He could be incredibly awkward at times and used this as a cover to not have to be present for all business doings. The word *secretive* is raised frequently in my interviews by people who knew him best. It could have had something to do with having to keep his private life (which was illegal in most places throughout much of his life) on the back burner by only trusting some people in his inner circle.

In the early part of the 1970s, Robert moved his business to New York City to avoid the heavy taxes in Britain. Eventually settling at the San Remo at 145 Central Park West, on the twenty-sixth floor, with neighbors James Taylor and Carly Simon, he was known to entertain lavishly with many young men whose public displays of affection on his balcony caused quite the stir for the rather staid Upper West Side neighborhood.

Stigwood would also set up the apartment to audition actors, mostly attractive young men. Joseph Cali (Joey C. in *Saturday Night Fever*) recalls having a meeting with Robert a few months after the movie's premiere.

"I get this note, I remember after the movie opened, to meet Stigwood at his apartment. And at the time they were casting *The Pope of Greenwich Village*. I go up to his apartment. And he had some business meeting, and then he came to talk to me. And he offered me some coke, and I got the deal right away—'the casting couch.' I had this offer in front of me, you know, because he was a major powerful producer.

"I did not give a shit about that part of my career. I said, 'You know, hey, Robert. It has been so incredible working for you, but you got the wrong guy.' You know? Right. I love you. You are great. You are incredible, but I gotta go," Cali says, laughing, as he recalls this story.

Cali was teased by his friends for years for not "going for it," but overall, he has a fondness for working for Stigwood. "He put two and a half million into the actual movie production and the other half into promotion, into marketing, which was just fucking genius."

John Maggio, the director of the Stigwood HBO documentary *Mr. Saturday Night*, told *The Ringer* podcast in 2021, "He had this insane entrepreneurial spirit. He was a gambler, and he ended up showing up in the music scene in the sixties in London. And he just fit right in because he was a total showman. He was right there in that moment in London, that crazy sixties moment, and people loved him. He was a total hard-ass, the way managers used to be back in the day."

Maggio also told *The Ringer* that in the mid-1970s Stigwood loved discos and knew the best spots around the world. "He did a lot of stuff behind the scenes, which is, in fact, one of the reasons why he discovered and knew disco was gonna be so hot, because he was going to the discos in Paris. He was going to underground discos in New York. He was going to Rio. So, he saw the phenomena early on before other people did."

When he was not entertaining, Stigwood was looking for TV properties to bring to the US. His head of TV, Vertue, brought *Till Death Us Do Part* and *Steptoe and Son* to future genius Norman Lear, who made *All in the Family* and *Sanford and Son* huge sitcoms. He made a tidy profit from them.

His biggest issue was finding interest in the Bee Gees. After some hits in the late 1960s, their career was in a nosedive. Robert had promised to make them not only international pop stars (meaning *big* in America) but also movie stars. In 1970 he tried to get a TV special featuring Robin and Maurice Gibb's improbably named album *Cucumber Castle* to air in the United States.

After a couple of years of a break, all three brothers reunited to create a more funky, urban sound. According to David Meyer's *The Bee Gees: The Biography*, Ahmet Ertegun, the cofounder and head of Atlantic Records, recommended that Stigwood hire the producer Arif Mardin to work with the band. Mardin's past work included recordings with Aretha Franklin, David Bowie, and Ringo Starr. He encouraged the band to embrace a more R&B image and sound.

The 1975 release *Main Course*, recorded at Eric Clapton's favorite location in Miami, 461 Ocean Boulevard, would change their lives. After years of recording in England and France, the Florida sunshine and laid-back attitude were the antidote to their doldrums. It would bring out the hits "Jive Talkin'" and "Nights on Broadway." With Barry's falsetto and Robin and Maurice's perfect harmonies, the top-notch musicianship showed that disco was a style of music just beginning to catch on.

Children of the World (1976) featured the number one song "You Should Be Dancing" which would be immortalized in one of John Travolta's biggest dance sequences in the movie. After a successful comeback, the band headed to France to mix a live album and await Robert's next big idea.

Kevin McCormick was a twenty-three-year-old New Jersey native who found himself in London assisting Stigwood and subsequently moving back to the States to help start up the movie division at RSO in New York City. Describing this time, he explains, "Once he [Robert] was out of England, once he had this new agenda, it was really an incredible thing to watch, because I've seen it with certain artists, over time, where there's just this incredibly fecund period where, like a magician, he's pulling rabbit after rabbit out of a hat. Robert was a gut player. He has that thing that the Australians have. They are sort of pirates from an island, you know, whether it is Rupert or, you know, they take big bets on themselves and others. And they are very litigious."

By 1976, the RSO's office at 135 Central Park West was busy with projects when Stigwood announced to his team that after watching John Travolta on *Welcome Back, Kotter*, he was convinced the actor was now ready for film stardom. Travolta quickly signed a three-picture deal for $1 million.

This was met with quite a bit of curiosity by the press at the time as TV stars (and especially sitcom actors) were considered of a lower class than stage and film thespians. Sure, he was famous now, but how long would it last? Only teenage girls cared about him! None of this fazed Stigwood. He knew Travolta had the "it" factor. Now it was time to find him three movies.

McCormick remembers, "He signs a three-picture deal. He does not have a deal at a studio, so it is all meant to be independent mass movies. And then *Saturday Night Fever* was the first property we bought, and then *Grease* came along. And then we made *Moment by Moment*, which did not work. They would make a lot of money out of it, anyway."

Grease was a given, as Travolta had played Doody on Broadway and was eager to be the lead and add new music to the soundtrack. However, according to his contract, Stigwood could not begin a film adaptation until the Broadway version finished its run—in 1978.

During this time, Stigwood had an assistant, Joy McMillan, who was in her early twenties—tall, chic, with long red tresses—who was often photographed with her boss because of her sheer hotness. Stigwood never announced his sexual orientation but was often described as a "bachelor who is married to his work." He depended on McMillan to keep him on schedule and be on top of production for both *Saturday Night Fever* and *Grease,* which meant she had seen her boss under wonderful circumstances and almost unendurable stress.

In an email, she shared her thoughts: "Robert (we called him Stiggy) was the most extraordinary person I have ever known. He was brilliant, he had incredible business sense, he was charming, had a great sense of humor, tough, sensitive, and extremely generous to those in his inner circle. He had a great love of life and adventure, and he absolutely loved sharing it with everyone he knew."

His detractors at the time seemed to resent his way of doing business, which was calling in from all over the world and avoiding in-person networking. Stigwood had ideas, assembled the right team to manage them, and for a while made more money than he could have ever dreamed of.

He wooed entertainment lawyer Freddie Gershon with lavish trips and unerring hospitality to become his president at RSO Records in New York. Gershon remains in awe of how well Stigwood ran his company.

"Robert had nothing to do with all the people you meet in Hollywood who run the studios. I am talking about every one of them from Fox through MCA through, all these studios, because they are all hired to run other people's assets," Gershon told me. "They never built those companies. They are not entrepreneurs or risk takers. They had no vision."

In 1976, Robert took a meeting with Nik Cohn, who had moved to New York with his now wife, the artist formerly known as Arfur—Pamela Marchant. He was writing feature stories for *New York* magazine and was hoping to sell him the rights to one of his stories. McCormick, one of Robert's most trusted tastemakers, told him he would keep him in mind as they were searching for a part for John Travolta.

Stigwood stated whatever might be the first film for John would have to have a musical component that would include the Bee Gees and others on the RSO label. Cohn said he would think about it.

CHAPTER 2

The Scribes of Saturday Night

Nik Cohn and Norman Wexler

B orn in 1946 to an academic father and a Russian mother, Nik Cohn was shy, awkward, and often questioned about his religion. To be an Irish Jew in the 1950s and 1960s was not exactly a path that led to fitting in with his peers.

Nik Cohn spent his teenage years in Northern Ireland like many of his peers, obsessed with American rock music as well as the style expressed by the "teddy boys" and the "mods" of London. Both were a subculture of the British youths after World War II who embraced rock and roll and believed in the old adage that "the clothes make the man." After years of rationing fabrics during the war, retail executives saw an opportunity to sell flamboyant suits with tapered trousers and flashy jackets in the image of stylish men (called "dandies") in the Edwardian period. They did not attract the customers who served their country, but rather the younger generation who were forming gangs dived into sale bins to buy up as much stock as possible.

Teenagers throughout the UK took on the clothing as a way to create a flashier identity that went with the dangerous sexiness of rock music made popular by Elvis Presley, Little Richard, and Buddy Holly. To round out their appearance, special attention was given to longer, greased-up hair and having the perfect shoes in which you could dance all night.

Nik Cohn, author of the 1976
New York magazine article "Tribal
Rites of the New Saturday Night," 2001.
Agence Opale/Alamy Stock Photo.

The term *juvenile delinquent* became a fashionable way to describe the 1950s youth movement. Teddy boys were the English equivalent to "greasers" in America and were presented in the media as a scourge on society. In Anthony Burgess's novel *A Clockwork Orange* (published in 1962), the Droogs gang is based on the teddy boys of London.

The mods of the mid-1960s became popular in England with a more refined aesthetic of slim-fitting suits that resembled the high fashions coming out of Italy and France. They also drove motor scooters, did *not* grease up their locks, and encouraged women ("birds") to join them in their fun. According to Peter Stanfield, author of *A Band with Built-In Hate: The Who from Pop Art to Punk*, "Mod means modern. Mods are teenagers, sophisticated, urbane, not so much rebellious as contemptuous of the frantic adult that is so interested and horrified by them."

Cohn went to the local Protestant school, where he felt like an outsider, and had no interaction with teddy boys in the Catholic section of Derry. He told Karl Whitney of the *Irish Times* in 2016, "It set up a lifetime pattern of looking at tribes that I could never be part of." Bookish and uncomfortable with small talk, he found his heroes in the UK music and fashion magazines. The post–World War II world in London was different from that across the pond in the United States, where (white) Americans saw their futures prosper, with former veterans taking over the workforce and migrating out to planned communities in the suburbs. After the years of fear and rationing, the unspoken dictate was for Americans to be successful and cheerful.

The same was not true in England. The bombings had decimated cities, and rationing existed for years after the war. The motto was "Keep Strong and Carry On," and with a young Queen Elizabeth in charge, the teen movement tentatively broke out with the worldwide popularity of Elvis Presley. Early rock and skiffle music would inspire a new generation to pick up the guitar and learn harmonizing. The Beatles were the biggest example of the changing of the guard with popular music.

In 1964, eighteen-year-old Cohn left for England to begin a career as a writer. He liked the Fab Four simply fine. They were talented and wrote some catchy tunes. But he was obsessed with Little Richard. The Black, omnisexual, piano-playing singer with the killer squeal was pop perfection. Catchy, danceable, and just a hint of dirtiness existed in tunes like "Lucille" and "Keep A- Knockin'" made his heart soar. It was dangerous and illicit.

In his 1968 book of rock criticism (one of the first in journalism), *Awopbopaloobop Alopbamboom* (taken from the Little Richard classic "Tutti Fritti"), Cohn drew lines between Black and white music. From Elvis's boom to Jimi Hendrix. In it he describes the time he saw Little Richard in concert (his favorite performance of all time): "He looked beautiful—he wore a baggy suit with elephant trousers, twenty-six inches at the bottoms, and he had his hair back-combed in a monstrous plume like a fountain. Then he had a little toothbrush moustache and a round, totally ecstatic face."

And he took note of the mods and teddy boys who made up much of the scene in 1960s London. These were kids who loved music, clothes, and dancing. They spent a week's pay on the "right shirt" and hours getting their hair gelled and combed to perfection. Riding around the streets on Vespas and other motor scooters looking for "birds" (good-looking chicks) who either ratted or ironed out their hair. All fighting to look chic in the miserable English weather.

They smoked, drank, and took speed to keep up with one another. This was not a "jeans and T-shirt" crowd of rockers. Mods and teddy boys took time on their appearance. Spending their week either in school or at a boring factory job. Saving up their energy to party all weekend. Bands like the Who and the Yardbirds blazed from the speakers as they danced and fought and made up and fooled around. The suits were tight, and the skirts were short. Not exactly the most comfortable clothes for dancing, but they managed.

One London mod from his hometown of Derry, Chris, a childhood friend turned hoodlum, became a source of fascination for Cohn. The way the men moved and behaved commanded respect. They did not need to shout to be heard. Women were attracted to them, and men wanted to be close enough to catch the residual coolness. Friends of mods and gang leaders were known as "Faces," a most British expression.

As the 1960s entered the Age of Aquarius, the mods and teddy boys either adopted a newer look or just dropped the whole rock-and-roll dream altogether. Cohn was very grumpy about progressive rock and acid rock. Songs were now too long, and no longer about sex and fun.

By this time, he was an in-command music reviewer who had no qualms about giving bands like the Beatles and the Rolling Stones bad reviews. Hence, the reason Pete Townshend was so nervous about showing his rock opera, *Tommy*, to the persnickety journalist.

The basic story about a "deaf, dumb, and blind kid" was dubbed too dreary by the rock journalist Cohn, who simply told Pete Townshend after listening to an early version, "I just don't hear any hits." The two often met to play pinball and drink in their downtime. Townshend knew that Cohn was looking to make the sister of his girlfriend a novelty star.

Dressing like an early twentieth-century newsboy, "Arfur" was a teenager from Montreal named Pamela Marchant whom Cohn presented as a pinball genius who was also a mute (to hide her Québecois accent).

According to Townshend's 2012 autobiography, *Who I Am*, "Kit Lambert [the Who's manager] brought Nik Cohn, the young record critic from *The Guardian* to IBC to listen [to *Tommy*]. Nik and I had become good friends. One day, Nick brought Arfur, the real girl who was his inspiration to meet me. She was short with short dark hair, pretty, a rough cut in a tight-fitting denim jacket. We would play pinball furiously and competitively, and she slayed me on a machine with six sets of flippers."

After listening to the latest version of *Tommy*, Townshend recalls, "Nik said he thought the opera was pretty good, but the story was a bit humorless. Kit's face tightened as he heard Nick confirm his worst fears. 'Why did Tommy have to be a guru. It was all so old hat.' I tried to explain that Tommy was a kind of divine musician that he felt vibrations as music and made music in the hearts of his followers. Nik's expression made it clear

I was making things worse." Townshend countered, "What if Tommy was a pinball champion, and that is the reason he gathered so many disciples? 'Oh, well, in that case, of course, it would get five stars!' I wrote 'Pinball Wizard' the next day. I had an acoustic guitar and vocal on one track and an electric overdub and backing vocal on the other."

The most famous track from *Tommy* was written under duress to tempt Cohn into a five-star review, and it remains a song Townshend hates to this day. Cohn turned "Arfur" into "Tommy." Just as his 1967 novel, *I Am Still the Greatest Says Johnny Angelo*, about a burned-out rock star, inspired David Bowie to create Ziggy Stardust.

Then Cohn became bored with it all.

In 1975, Cohn took off with the younger Marchant sister for New York to work as a freelance writer for *New York* magazine. He told the *Irish Times* in 2016 that London "seemed dead, it was just as if I'd been locked in a tight little box and suddenly somebody had given me the keys to the world."

Editors Clay Felker and Milton Glaser founded *New York* in 1968, and with a circulation of almost two million per week, it was in competition with the likes of *Esquire* and the *New Yorker* for high-end readers and quality writers. The cult classic documentary *Grey Gardens*, by the Maysles brothers, was inspired by a cover story by Gail Sheehy in 1972 about the Beale mother and daughter.

Cohn was hired to write features on topics that intrigued him. New York City nightlife at the time was moving in two distinct directions: punk rock with clubs like CBGB and Max's Kansas City and more-dance-oriented night clubs. Being a fan of pop music and tired of British culture, Cohn sought out where fellow misfits gathered.

Noel Hankin, author of *After Dark: Birth of the Disco Dance*

Party, is one of the founders of the social club The Best of Friends (TBOF), a group of Black professionals in the 1970s who created a network of discotheques originally meant to appeal to the after-work midtown crowd. It immediately caught on, and they started branching out to the outer boroughs. Midtown's Leviticus was so popular that it became a subject of a *New York Times* article published on January 3, 1976, praising the new kind of clubs where people got dressed up and learned to dance.

According to Hankin, "our clubs were not at the fringe of town. They were right there. Park Avenue, 58th Street, 57th Street, 86th Street, 33rd Street, and right off Fifth Avenue. And it was exciting for young Black folks who never had any social activities in Midtown. So, for them, it was a step up in their environment to a great degree, and it was exciting. And dancing right after work. That was a thrill."

One of his regulars was a dancer named Tu Sweet, a Black queer entertainer who would, according to Hankin, "routinely light up the dance floor" with sometimes up to two partners, doing "innovative moves, spins, and gestures." He became an attraction on his own, catching the eye of Nik Cohn one night. Cohn wrote a piece about Tu Sweet, following him at a dance competition in early 1976. It was there that he learned about discos around the outer boroughs that had their own culture. He sensed a story and pitched it to *New York.*

Cohn's first attempt to visit the 2001 Odyssey night club, based in Bay Ridge, was a solo journey. He took a cab, as he was too frightened to take the subway after dark. The building at 802 Sixty-Fourth Street and Eighth Avenue had crude signage and seemed uninviting to outsiders. This was an Italians-only neighborhood, and the rumor was that the customers were loyal and liked to keep it to their own kind.

As Nik approached the building, a fight broke out at the

Artwork for the *New York* magazine article
"Tribal Rites of the New Saturday Night."
Reprinted with permission from artist James McMullan.

front door and spilled out into the street. The men in their gabardine pants, with thick Brooklyn accents, were soundly beating the tar out of one of the rejects of the club. This person promptly threw up on Cohn's shoes.

As revolting as this was, the writer noticed a man with black hair, in a silk shirt and tight pants, standing in the doorway watching all the action. He gave the air of someone who oversaw this mess. That his Faces were doing his bidding. That was the end of the night for the reporter, who fled back to the relatively "safe" at the time Manhattan.

The artist James McMullan was close friends with Milton Glaser and heard about Cohn's story idea. He was tasked with accompanying Cohn and Tu Sweet to different clubs in New York. With his camera and as the only person with a car, he ventured out to Queens with the rest of the trio to the first spot

Cohn wanted to check out. It was McMullan's job to conceive of the illustrations and look of the story.

"We went to the first club in Queens. It was a very Italian club, and Tu Sweet, at some point, asked a girl to dance with him. So, they went out onto the floor and did some dancing. And a group of these young Italian guys got up and were totally pissed off at this Black guy dancing with one of their girls. So, they tried to beat him up. The club bouncer managed to pull all these guys off, and I ran out, got the car, and drove it to the entry so that Tu Sweet and Nik could jump in, and we drove away," McMullan recalls.

After visiting three more clubs in Brooklyn, they called it a night. The next morning, Tu Sweet phoned to let them know he would not be returning for future journeys. Now a duo, Cohn and McMullan decided to venture out to Bay Ridge, where Cohn could give 2001 Odyssey another try.

That first night, Cohn attempted to make conversations with the clubgoers, but his shyness kicked into overdrive. His Irish accent, big splash of red curly hair, and dandy attire did not endear him to the crowd. So, he took to milling about on the fringes, writing notes to himself. McMullan walked around, taking photos and growling "I'm with the press" to anyone who glared at him.

Denise Rusinak's father, Charlie, ran the club, and the teenager worked the door at the time. She told me, "He [Cohn] contacted my dad and said, 'I am a writer, and I am working on a story about the borough. Blue-collar workers who work and live for the weekend. Spending their money on a new outfit and learning the latest dance moves.' He would come on a Friday or Saturday night to just sit and observe. And it was funny because he looked so different than everyone else. Like, the odd man out. Everybody was kind of suspicious of him."

McMullan found the groups of people fascinating. "What I sensed about them was that there was much more insecurity and loneliness than you would have thought just wandering around and not paying close attention. You can see from one of my paintings of the girl in the booth. She had been left out of whatever group was, decided to dance together, and there she was, and I felt a lot of that in there. It was an extraordinary situation, and the music was different," he told me.

When McMullan got back his black-and-white images, he conjured a new way to display what he saw with his art.

"I looked at all my photographs and began to do what I would usually do as an illustrator. What part of each photograph do I use? How do I combine them to make a story? And then I suddenly said to myself, 'Jim, this is the story. What you chose to photograph and your experience in the club.' The photographs reflected my experience in a very tangible way. Before, I used photographs very directly, and I did not try to combine information or change it in much of a way. I added color, which was a big deal, because the photographs are black and white," he explained to me.

The finished article detailed Cohn following a group of Faces who follow "Vincent." An Al Pacino lookalike, nineteen years old and working at a paint store to support his family. He has a brother in jail and lives in a cement high-rise. Vincent smiles all day at work but inside he is ready to explode. There are constant references to his headaches and temper. How his only real outlet is dancing, and he is not even all that sure he is good at it.

The story also features Cohn supposedly riding in a car with the Faces as they chase a rival gang member who tried to molest Vincent's younger sister. That he was included in their banal excursions around their neighborhood.

In *New York* they prefaced the ten-thousand-word feature

with "Everything described in this article is factual and was either witnessed by me or told to me directly by the people involved. Only the names of the main characters have been changed."

Published on June 7, 1976, "Tribal Rites of the New Saturday Night" caught the attention of New Yorkers of all stripes, including Kevin McCormick, who worked for producer Robert Stigwood at RSO Productions and was actively looking for material to be turned into a film project for John Travolta. "I knew Nik Cohn, through one of my colleagues, Bill Oakes. One of the first things I bought was an article that Nik had written for *New York* magazine. This sort of an apocryphal tale, in the same way that *Saturday Night Fever* was both. He said it was completely invented, but I am not sure that it was a hundred percent true."

The British rock journalist Peter Stanfield, who studies the work of Cohn, caught the comparisons of Brooklyn with Londoners of the past. In particular, he sees the mods and teddy boys throughout the piece. He explained to me, "If you look at the language he uses in the story, and it then gets used in the dialogue for the movie. It is not American. It is not an American vernacular. When he talks about the Faces, it does not belong to 1970s America. It belongs to mid-1960s Britain."

He also points out the obsession with clothes and appearance is like the mod experience, which might explain the story's appeal in the UK. The characters in the article spend an inordinate amount of time dressing up and grooming, something quite different from white male rock culture at the time. These Bay Ridge Faces are not dressing casually to watch Led Zeppelin at Madison Square Garden. They want to get dressed up and dance the night away at the clubs.

McCormick had spent the previous summer going to upstate New York with Stigwood to see Travolta in a local production of

Bus Stop. (The production was so overrun with screaming teenagers that they had to implement an age minimum of eighteen to enter the theater.) He knew the appeal John had and his desire to break the "Barbarino mold." When he read Cohn's feature, he made sure right away that Robert was aware of it.

Some of the future cast and crew of the film, including Bruce Ornstein (Gus), told me they were fans of "Tribal Rites" from its initial publication. "This was long before *Saturday Night Fever* was conceived. [After reading the article], I had no idea that this was going on. You know, this kind of stuff was going on in Brooklyn." Denny Dillon (Doreen) thought it was "wonderful." And the future director of the film, John Badham, said, "I read it when it came out and I told my agents at the time that it is not gonna be a simple adaptation. This was gonna need a grade-A novelist."

McCormick sent out the magazine to Stigwood, in the Hamptons, who immediately rang up RSO president Freddie Gershon, who remembers, "He said, 'Did you read *New York*? Did you read that thing about the kids in Brooklyn and how they give away their money and they are all little peacocks and grooming themselves for some ritual dance?'" Gershon read the story and liked it very much. Stigwood instructed him to make a deal with Nik Cohn right away.

Cohn was offered $10,000 for the rights and $100,000 to draft the first screenplay. Cohn signed quickly, but his attempt at a cohesive script eluded him. Stigwood instructed McCormick that he needed to find not only a studio and a director for the movie but also a proper screenwriter. Kevin had an idea of the perfect man for the job. He took a big gulp before mentioning Norman Wexler.

According to McCormick, the fifty-year-old screenwriter had only recently "gotten out of a mental institution," but he

Norman Wexler, screenwriter for *Saturday Night Fever.* Photo courtesy of his daughter, artist Erica Wexler.

was one of the best writers available. Raised in Massachusetts and Detroit, educated at Harvard, Wexler was a tall, intense man who loved to tell stories. Starting as an ad man in New York City in the 1950s, he dreamed of being a respected playwright.

His first break in show business came in 1969, when filmmaker John G. Avildsen (who started with "nudie" pictures at Cannon Films in the 1960s) hired him to write the screenplay for his first legitimate film, *Joe,* starring Peter Boyle and Susan Sarandon (in her film debut). The grim tale centered around a working-class man fed up with hippie culture. Released in the summer of 1970, *Joe* was a sensation around the country tired of college student protests and the culture becoming more vulgar.

Boyle (only thirty-four at the time) plays Joe, a World War II veteran who meets with an upper-class father named Bill (played by Dennis Patrick), whose teenager overdoses. Sarandon plays the daughter, Melissa, and while she is recovering in the hospital, the two men haunt Greenwich Village taking drugs and searching for Melissa's drug-dealing boyfriend.

In the end (spoiler!), they wind up in the country, with Bill using Joe's rifle to tear through a house filled with hippies. Shooting everyone, including his own daughter. The themes and graphic language (including multiple N-words, which disgusted the left-leaning Boyle) caused a sensation in theaters across the country, with audiences identifying with either Joe or the hippies. Or they were drawn into the spectacle of it all.

Boyle recalled being scared to walk the streets of New York afterward when learning about folks shouting at the screen that they were ready to take on Joe. Made for pennies, the film managed over $20 million at the box office, with round-the-clock screenings.

Diagnosed with bipolar disorder, Wexler would go through periods of intense highs, when he took incredible risks. For some reason he was at the site where Senator Robert F. Kennedy Sr. was assassinated and gave interviews to television crews stating he had argued with RFK's security as an FBI agent. There is no record of his ever being an FBI agent or working for the Kennedy campaign, but it was grist for him. To provoke people and get genuine reactions.

On a cross-country Pan Am flight in 1972, he got up in the middle of the flight holding up a copy of *Time* magazine with Richard Nixon on the cover and threatened to shoot the president. He was given a year's probation.

In 1973, he was nominated for an Academy Award for Best Screenplay for *Serpico*, starring Al Pacino playing the role of the real-life detective Frank Serpico. According to an upcoming documentary, *The Double Life of Norman Wexler*, directed by Jillian Edelstein, his intensity must have bothered Pacino, as when the two met later at an Actors Studio event, he started yelling for

Wexler to be thrown out right away. The writer laughed as he was escorted out.

In 1975, on yet another cross-country journey, a flight attendant accused him of biting her arm. He claims he was just trying to kiss her. Two months later he was arrested in Colorado Springs for attempting to buy "several guns." The prosecution in those cases allowed him to go free if he stayed in a psychiatrist's care.

It is probably not too shocking to hear that these acts put a strain on his marriage. Francine Longo was a successful ad executive who tried to protect their two teenage daughters (Erica and Maren) from his mood swings, but it was no use. His temperament (along with his need to bring handguns everywhere he went) made him undesirable in Hollywood. Karen Lynn Gorney told *Vanity Fair* in 2007 that he would bring chocolates and nylons to all the big New York talent agencies, trying to woo the secretaries to set up meetings with their bosses. His luck changed when he heard that Cohn was going to need help developing his first script.

Wexler charmed McCormick and Stigwood's twenty-one-year-old nephew, Ron Stigwood, just hired from Australia to learn the ropes of show business by his famous uncle. While Cohn's version was rather dour and focused on the commonality of the lower middle class around the globe, Wexler saw more optimism. He told the *Los Angeles Times* on June 12, 1977, "The film is about the possibility of reconditioning. Our hero has no known process through which he can open himself up, and he is suddenly presented with a chain of events which allow him to free himself."

Wexler's daughter Erica told me, "He did say that when he wrote the script, because he had a big brain, and he had a big social conscience, 'I'm writing this film, to give the message that with a bit of luck and tenacity, you can transcend your conditioning.'"

McCormick described to me how he felt when he picked

up Wexler's first draft: "The pages were great and very exciting. I took it to Stigwood, and he had this incredible reaction to it, which was that it was unwieldy. One hundred sixty-nine pages. [Most run between ninety and one hundred twenty pages.] Full of all sorts of incidents. And at that point, there was no music, but what it had was great characters and great scenes and a great pathos attached to it. Honestly, it is one of the things that I have learned over time in my career, there's certain things that you feel in your gut are the right things for you."

Working with Wexler meant McCormick had to visit him at his bachelor pad every day: "He was living in this apartment in Chelsea, which consisted of a bed, a table, and two chairs. And that was it. And he smoked nonfiltered cigarettes and drank coffee. He must have been on some mood stabilizer like lithium or something. Because you know that sort of haunted kind of solid look."

At the behest of his uncle, Ron Stigwood would often drop in to check on Wexler. He remembers, "Norman was a very big man and larger than life. He was a brilliant man, and like most brilliant people, there is that precipice that is easy to fall off. Norman was on the verge of that. I was asked to go down and pick up one of the drafts that he had written, and I noticed he had a small painting. He was impressed I knew it was from Friedensreich Hundertwasser. But he was very, very isolated."

Wexler spent his nights at discos around all the boroughs, soaking up the atmosphere. He witnessed couples dance and argue, friends converging in small banquets, DJs who had a pop star–like following, and the exclusivity of the neighborhood clubs. The 2001 Odyssey in Bay Ridge held a contest where he saw Black and Latino dancers being given the cold shoulder by Italians for having dared to enter *their* club. He also noticed how much better the dancing was by the so-called outsiders whose moves would get copied shortly after they left.

Wexler absolutely loved working on this script and felt he was most fortunate to have been nominated for a WGA Award for his screenplay. Erica told me, "Norman always said he was lucky. And if you know, as you get older, you realize so many things. Yes. You can have drive and tenacity, and there's ability, but the right things come together at the right time, all these random events. So, the screenwriter is the original creator, and he created something out of nothing. And without this script, there is nothing."

When interviewing the cast and crew, I was often told that Norman's shooting script was the best they had ever read in their careers. John Badham claims, "Norman Wexler, I do not think he ever was a novelist, but he is a great screenplay writer. He just brought everything. That is why I reacted so strongly to it when I first read it. It was just more than I ever could have hoped for. Not only great characters but great humor. Making me laugh constantly with the way the people dealt with each other. It was just wonderful."

Incredibly, *Inside the Actors Studio* host James Lipton, when he interviewed Travolta in 2003, mentioned he went to high school with Wexler and stated, "He was complicated in high school. Norman Wexler was greatly gifted, deeply troubled."

Travolta responded, "He did a lot of your work for you. I think great writing does half the work for the actor. It's when the writing is not so good that you have to really push up your sleeves and get to work. But great writing does half the work for you."

With the script getting into shape, it was time to hire a director. McCormick had heard there was a man working on a boxing picture that was getting some early buzz. He decided to meet him and see if he had any interest.

CHAPTER 3

The Johns

Avildsen, Badham, and Travolta

Two out of three ain't bad
—MEAT LOAF (1978)

With the screenplay being taken care of by Norman Wexler, Stigwood hired John Guilbert Avildsen (professionally known as John G. Avildsen) to direct the film. Wexler and Avildsen met at the chic D'Arcy Advertising Company in 1958. Both were storytellers with dreams of leaving the ad-man life and creating stories that made people feel more than just a desire to get a new car, razor blade, or baby shampoo. Wexler was hammering out plays on the weekend, while Avildsen was trained by his father to make movies.

Born in 1935 in Oak Park, Illinois, Avildsen's father worked as a mechanic and spent his downtime making movies with his 16mm Bell & Howell Filmo camera. The family would get dressed up in costumes, such as the future director playing "Baby New Year" in diapers and a top hat, and sometimes acted out elaborate stories. His English mother was an actor from Liverpool who could milk laughs from the most ridiculous premises and taught Avildsen the importance of paying attention to the audience.

Growing tired of agency work, where he made industrial

John G. Avildsen, the original director of *Saturday
Night Fever*. He was fired the same morning he
learned he was nominated for an Academy Award
for *Rocky*. (He won that award, for Best Director, in
1977.) *Zuma Press, Inc./Alamy Stock Photo.*

films for clients as diverse as IBM and Jeep, John learned to
direct and edit his work quickly. This became his "film school"
and his first pictures were "nudies" or "sexploitation" works that
dabbled in the newly expanding body confidence that was taking place in the late 1960s. They had titles like *Turn On to Love*
and *Guess What We Learned in School Today?*. They were cheesy,
but he gained enough experience to work for Cannon Films and
bring his playwright friend along for the ride.

Joe was made for $100,000, and Wexler's script was noted
in reviews as one of the sharpest looks at blue-collar racism.
John and Norman were so close that Wexler used the names of
Avildsen's wife (Melissa) in *Joe* and his son (Tony) in *Saturday
Night Fever*.

Joe would mark John Avildsen's first Oscar nomination for
best screenplay. The film became the top independent production of the year, and offers started coming in for all attached to
its success.

At five feet five, Avildsen radiated confidence and self-assurance on the set. Some actors loved this, such as Jack Lemmon, who specifically asked Avildsen to direct him in 1973's *Save the Tiger*, which won him his first acting Oscar since 1955's *Mister Roberts*. In his career, he would direct seven actors for Academy Award nominations, including Lemmon, Jack Gilford, Burgess Meredith, Sylvester Stallone, Talia Shire, Pat Morita, and Burt Young.

On the other hand, he could come across as imperious and just plain rude. Burt Reynolds said that he hated working with Avildsen in 1975's forgettable *W.W. and the Dixie Dancekings*, as the man had no interest in country music or the culture of Nashville, where the picture was filmed. He claims Avildsen did not even know that country star Mel Tillis had a stutter and admonished him in front of the crew for the way he was reading his lines. Reynolds also admitted that his anger at the director probably helped his performance.

Avildsen was fired from a few projects in his life, something that often happened during the initial setup of a film when people wind up with differing agendas. For example, with 1973's *Serpico*, based on the life of real-life whistleblower detective Frank Serpico, who fled the country after exposing the nefarious deeds of several New York City police officers. While the two became friends and Norman Wexler was hired to write the screenplay (his second Academy Award nomination), Avildsen balked at hiring producer Martin Bregman's girlfriend, Cornelia Sharpe, in the role of Serpico's girlfriend. He was let go and Sidney Lumet wound up directing.

His most famous work in 1976, when he signed to direct *Saturday Night Fever*, was *Rocky*. Created by and starring Sylvester Stallone, the two were at loggerheads throughout the production. Stallone (a conservative) saw Rocky as a young man working hard to achieve his goals and liberal Avildsen saw it as a boxer fighting the establishment. With a $1 million budget, they went on a twenty-eight-day shoot on location in Philadelphia with a non-union crew. Burgess Meredith played Rocky's trainer, Mickey, while Burt Young played Talia Shire's (Adrian) brother, Paulie. All would get acting nominations for multiple awards, but the big one was the 1977 Academy Award for Best Picture.

The film would earn over $117 million at the box office, and the *Rocky* theme by Bill Conti became an instant classic. Avildsen was on top of the world, though for many years Stallone resented how much attention the movie got for the action and direction rather than for his work as an actor. When asked about Avildsen's contribution to the Rocky canon, he would downplay it and say he would only discuss his work in the film. It made for uncomfortable interviews sometimes. Especially when the subject was ostensibly about Avildsen and/or *Rocky*. Stallone would eventually get over his anger.

Executive producer Kevin McCormick was met with many rejections from agents and studios in Los Angeles when searching for a director. He recalls hearing, "'Listen, kid. My clients do movies, they do not do magazine articles.' And I literally booked my passage back to New York the next day and thought I do not know what the fuck I am doing."

Then his luck changed. "And then the phone rang, and it was this guy. 'You're in luck. The guy you wanted to get to was in my office today, and he read the article, and he is interested in meeting, but you should see his new movie first. John will set up a screening for you all in New York," McCormick told me.

"So, we saw *Rocky* and hired John Avildsen before that film even opened. And then our movie was developed, and Avildsen wanted to be the director, DP [director of photography], and editor as well. I mean, he literally wanted to have multiple credits," Kevin remembers.

Having a feeling *Rocky* would be a huge hit, Stigwood at first catered to his new director's ideas for script changes. Even though he and Wexler were close friends, he was not above taking over the screenwriting with his own version, which made the lead character of Tony Manero more of a nice guy. The kind of person who helps old ladies with their groceries and warns kids about the dangers of drugs. And why was he so mean to his family? Stigwood chafed at making anything less than a gritty film.

According to Avildsen in the 2017 documentary *John G. Avildsen: King of the Underdogs*, he sensed a compulsion from Stigwood to include the music of the Bee Gees when he felt they were way past their prime. He was also not too keen on the idea of discos in general and thought of hiring dancers from Balanchine and having more focus on the love story.

Although he was hired for the gig, Avildsen was immediately met with resistance by the film's star. His first meeting with Travolta over breakfast at the Beverly Hills Hotel was the first stage of failure in his tenure as director. He looked down at the TV star and thought he had no sex appeal. Insisted that Travolta train with Jimmy Gambina, the boxing expert who had a role in *Rocky* (Mike) and helped set up the boxing sequences. This would help him lose the "baby fat" and they would worry about the dancing later. The star wanted to explore the script more seriously, but the director was adamant it would change to have a more positive outlook.

Then, after officially firing Norman Wexler, he started giving new pages to McCormick, who then passed them along to Stigwood. He recalls, "Avildsen was going through revolving doors with writers, and the script was getting worse every time. And the last thing he gave me in the new script, 'I have been thinking about the Bee Gees' music. I just think they are over. We need music that is more contemporary.' So, Stigwood called, and he said meet me at the airport tomorrow. So, I did, and I gave him the script."

Stigwood was furious about Avildsen's changes to the script. He instructed McCormick to set up a meeting at Stigwood's penthouse for ten the next morning, February 10, 1977. The executive producer recalls, "John and I were, like, twiddling our thumbs in the living room. Stigwood came in and he said, 'John, nice to see you. There's good news and bad news. The good news is you have just been nominated for an Academy Award, and the bad news is you are fired.' And that was the quickest meeting I have ever been in."

In the documentary, Avildsen blames his firing on the fact he was caught dating the "producer's boyfriend's girlfriend." Wexler told the *Los Angeles Times* on June 12, 1977, "Avildsen was moving in a Capra-*Rocky* direction, all involved in sweetness and light." The consensus is he was fired for wanting to change the film in a direction that Stigwood and Travolta hated. Wexler was brought back as screenwriter and McCormick had the task of finding a new director with three weeks left before production was set to begin.

Avildsen did not have long to wait for the better news in his career. On March 28, 1977, his film won best picture and best director at the Academy Awards. In the footage from the broadcast, Stallone appears grumpy for having his acting ignored. Avildsen would go on to direct *The Karate Kid*, *Lean on Me*, and *Rocky V*. He passed away on June 16, 2017, from pancreatic cancer.

Thirty-eight-year-old John Badham had an unusual background. He was a self-proclaimed "army brat" who was raised in England and Birmingham, Alabama, with a mother who starred in local TV shows and a stepfather who was a retired army general. With a scholarship to Yale, he worked on several musical productions as a stage manager and actor. It was at college that he first saw Orson Welles's *Citizen Kane*, which made him consider working in TV and film.

During his junior year, his nine-year-old sister, Mary, was cast as Scout in 1962's adaptation of *To Kill a Mockingbird*. Based on the Pulitzer Prize–winning 1960 novel by Harper Lee, the film starred Gregory Peck as Atticus Finch and Robert Duvall in his film debut as Boo Radley. Mary was nominated for an Academy Award, which gave her slightly jealous brother the urge to succeed on his own.

His résumé was packed with television, from *Night Gallery* and *The Streets of San Francisco* to 1974's *The Law*, with Judd Hirsch and Bonnie Franklin, which earned him a Primetime Emmy nomination for Outstanding Directing in a Special Program: Drama or Comedy. In 1976, he directed his first feature, *The Bingo Long Traveling All-Stars & Motor Kings* (a title I mangled several times during my first chat with Badham). The film, starring Billy Dee Williams, Richard Pryor, and James Earl Jones, takes place in the 1930s and is a fictional tale about Negro League baseball. It was scheduled for release in the summer of 1977.

In the meantime, he had been picked to direct the musical version of *The Wiz* with Diana Ross as the star. The hit Broadway show was an urban remake of *The Wizard of Oz*, and Diana Ross would be playing Dorothy. Badham could not figure out how to film Ross (thirty-four at the time) as a young girl and, feeling ill equipped to work around this conundrum, decided to get himself fired by offering a bizarre idea. In a production meeting he discussed shooting the entire film from Ross's perspective. Badham described to them, "We never see her—only her shoes, occasionally." He was booted right away.

Director John Badham (pictured here in 1995)
would take over the movie three weeks before
filming began. *coolaimages/Alamy Stock Photo.*

In February 1977 Badham was unemployed, separated from
his wife, and suffering from the worst flu of his life when his
agent called him about a new job. He had read about Avildsen's
firing in Liz Smith's column and wondered what was going on
with the project now called *Saturday Night.*

He told me, "My agent said, now do not read it till I make
a deal on this. Just do not worry about reading it. So, of course,
being the kind of person that just does the opposite of what your
mother tells you, I promptly started to read it, an hour later,
whenever I finished it, I was cured. My temperature was normal.
I am going around, this is great. Oh, boy."

He was hired immediately and soon had a tense first
breakfast meeting with Travolta, where he assured him the
film would be the vision they all thought was best. It would be
smart and gritty and would heavily focus on Travolta's dancing, which he had spent months working on. Travolta was eager
to know the status of the female lead. Amy Irving and Jessica
Lange were recently in consideration, but other commitments
(mainly Dino De Laurentiis, who picked Lange for the 1976

remake *King Kong* and would not let her out of her contract) and lack of chemistry with the meticulous star made it difficult to find the perfect Stephanie.

He also needed to hire the rest of the cast (only Travolta was locked in), finalize more than sixty locations for shooting (including the nightclub), and hire a choreographer, and then there was the Bee Gees part. When first meeting Stigwood, he handed him a cassette tape telling him, "There are three number one songs here." It was an early demo of the soundtrack, and Stigwood was wrong. There would be four number one songs on it.

Badham quickly flew to New York and got his first indication of what a low-budget film looked like—he was picked up by the production manager, Michael Hausman, at LaGuardia Airport. According to Hausman, "In those days, you could actually drive to LaGuardia Airport and park your car right at the curb and go to the gate to meet somebody. John Badham came out of the plane, and I introduced myself."

"We get to my car, which was a truck. It had a seat in the front and the back was a pickup. In front of my pickup was a limousine. And he started walking toward the limousine. And I said, 'No, John. Here is a garbage bag that we are gonna put your suitcase in, put it in the back of the truck, and I am gonna drive you to the hotel.' And for many years now, whenever he talked about making that movie, he said, that was Mike's way of telling me who is in charge and what it is gonna be like," he recalls with a laugh.

Scouting all the discos and familiarizing himself with Brooklyn were some of the tasks that wore him down, as the good clubs did not pick up energy until after midnight. The conclusion was that 2001 Odessey, the place where Nik Cohn's piece was created, would be the perfect location.

Badham explains, "I am going, and I am looking and watching all these people. And I realize that, of course, the 2001 Odyssey is the right kind of place where you could pay ten dollars to get in. The place was kind of grimy, but it is where the neighborhood kids came from. And they all danced like they had taught each other to dance. You know, brother and sister teams, and you could tell they were not professional dancers, which was a big part of the way we chose our background dancers, we wanted people that looked like they were from the neighborhood."

While the club was being updated, Badham then had to fill out his cast. For some of the actors, they had already been through the audition process with Avildsen, and they were nervous about collaborating with a new director who was not from New York.

Joe Cali was working with the beloved (and missed) casting agent Shirley Rich when he heard there was a change of director. "I got a call they wanted to bring me back and read again. And it was very weird, because Badham, to me, did not have a fucking clue about New York Italians. And it was a very weird vibe that he was now the director of the movie. But I went in, and I did another reading, did a big screen test, and I got cast. And they said I could play the part of Joey, which was in the Norman Wexler script."

Part of the cast consisted of stage, film, and TV veterans like Julie Bovasso (who was also a revered acting coach) as Tony's mother, Flo; Martin Shakar as erstwhile priest Frank Jr.; Val Bisoglio as Tony's father, Frank Sr.; and Lisa Peluso (Tony's younger sister, Linda), who at twelve was already a veteran of the New York stage and of dozens of commercials.

Peluso told me she basically insisted that she had to get the part as she was a huge *Welcome Back, Kotter* fan. "I was, like, this is my role. I am going to book this job. When I was in the

Actor John Travolta, 1975 publicity photo for the
TV show *Welcome Back, Kotter*, in which he played
Vinnie Barbarino. *Moviestore Collection Ltd./
Alamy Stock Photo.*

audition, I told them this role must be mine because I love John
Travolta. Anyway, they did hire me."

The young cast that was set to costar with Travolta, many in
their first movie role, felt a mixture of excitement and nervous-
ness about the opportunity. Paul Pape, who would play one of
Tony's henchman Double J., was originally from Syracuse but
had a family history in Brooklyn going back to the nineteenth
century. He scored the role after his first movie audition. Pape
remembers, "When I got it, I never looked at it as being any
kind of a big deal. I thought I am gonna be in a low-budget
movie with a TV star who had not crossed over into anything
big, and it's a great start for me." He would go on to have a few
scrapes with Badham but for the most part their relationship
was tension-free.

For Bruce Ornstein (Gus), Avildsen's firing was another chance to be in the movie. Ornstein said, "John Avildsen saw me and rejected me. And then he got rejected, and he was fired. John Badham took over, and I auditioned for John. It was very interesting, because there were so many young actors that were interested in this role. We were given a script and there was a group scene, and each one was assigned a different line to read.

"I am watching all these people do their thing. I was so involved listening to everybody else and just watching them that I did not realize that it was my turn. And I went, 'Oh, shit. Sorry!' I got a call about a week or so later saying I got Gus. So, the first day of rehearsal, I went up to John Badham, and said, 'Why did you cast me?' He said, 'Because you were the only one who was listening.' That's amazing. Okay. Good. I'll take it," he recalls.

Donna Pescow was cast as Annette, the lovelorn local girl who worshipped Tony. She told me, "John G. Avildsen originally was supposed to direct it. I had two auditions with him and then the callback, and then it went away. I guess a month or two later, they called me back in when they brought John Badham on. Which was probably right before they started shooting because I did not have a lot of time between getting the role and finding out and starting the role. That is why there were so many auditions, and I had no clue until I got the part about how big the role was."

The Bay Ridge native was a recent graduate of the American Academy of Dramatic Arts and worked hard to speak with a flat American accent. "And this wonderful, legendary casting director named Shirley Rich. She said, "I know you are from Brooklyn. Go back home and live with your family for a while. Get that accent back," said Pescow.

Other newbies included twenty-year-old Barry Miller as the pathetic Bobby C. in his huge platform shoes and with terrible driving skills. Denny Dillon as Doreen, who just loves to watch Tony dance, and Queens native Fran Drescher who memorably asked Tony, "Are you as good in bed as you are on the dance floor?"

The toughest role to fill was the main love interest—Stephanie Mangano. As described in the original Wexler script, "Stephanie, about twenty, about five foot seven, willowy, with an intense, attractive face, long black hair parted in the middle, and is in the process of re-creating herself. Eradicating the traces of her Bay Ridge origins and refashioning herself into a sophisticated, knowledgeable woman of the world."

Also, "She is a lovable fake, caught between identities, full of airs and pretentions, seeking to impress who and where she can, pushing her limits, a name-dropper. Her endearing qualities—a certain sweetness and courage—save her and keep her sympathetic even when her words or actions are outrageous. She is clearly a superb dancer."

So, she needs to be a great dancer, attractive, with the perfect Brooklyn accent that she is trying to lose. Hundreds of women were considered, and just weeks before production, the part still had not been cast. Badham found that most who auditioned played the tougher parts about Stephanie and forgot her thinly veiled sweetness.

Badham told me, "When you read her on the page, she is really negative and kind of ugly; not physically, but just the way she deals with people. And when women would come in to read, they would pick up on that dark side of her character. They would come in to be the most gorgeous women twenty, twenty-one years old. I just fell in love with them when they walked in the door.

"Right away, my little heart going, by the time they finish reading, I have had divorce and separation, estrangement, and yuck in there. Because I try to get them to find the nice parts of the character, you know, and the character likes to have fun with Travolta and tease him and poke at his weak side, which none of his friends will do because they're all in awe of him," he explains.

Karen Lynn Gorney was a thirty-something actor who grew up in show business. Her father, Jay Gorney, was a composer best known for "Brother, Can You Spare a Dime?" Her mother, Sondra Gorney, was an actor and dancer. Born in Beverly Hills, she had her first movie role in 1962's *David and Lisa* playing Josette—a patient inside a mental health clinic. In 1970, she originated the role of Tara Martin on daytime TV's *All My Children*.

If you watch as many documentaries as I have about *Saturday Night Fever*, you hear one particular story repeatedly. Gorney one day shares a cab on her way to Midtown when she and her new companion get to chatting. Ron Stigwood (the twenty-one-year-old newly hired assistant and nephew of Stigwood) tells her he is making a movie, and she replies, "Oh, am I in it?" (Ron confirms this.) She immediately auditions for Badham and Stigwood and gets the part.

According to Badham, "I think that one of the things that encouraged me, as far as casting her, was having seen *Rocky*. And the use of Talia Shire. Which just felt so totally right as opposed to somebody that was more traditionally glamorous." The casting choice caused some controversy before the filming even began. No one seemed to know Gorney or why she was chosen out of so many prospects.

McCormick told me internally they had their doubts. "We were all kind of stunned that that's the direction that Badham went on. Like, for whatever reason, he loved her. And you know, we did not. But in the end, she is fine. She couldn't dance. So that's a problem. And so, you had to compensate for that, but it did not matter. The point was she is somebody that is different than anybody he knows, and it ignites in him this desire to cross the bridge and look for a different life for himself."

Cali told me, "She had a relationship with [John] Badham, which was a little bit off-putting for the cast. You know? And down the line, it actually creates a little bit of tension with John [Travolta]."

The truth is, almost every single person I interviewed who was on set told me (unprompted) that Badham and Gorney had a relationship. For some, it was no big deal and for others, it made for a distraction. If they did not hide it while filming, it was known for sure when the movie premiered in December 1977. There are several images of them holding hands at press events.

In the January 9, 1978, issue of *People* magazine she insists she is really in love with John Travolta and that they "dream about each other—a lot!" Travolta denied it. The reporter notes that it appears as if Badham had moved into her Studio City home. She tells them that he not only pays half the rent but they also traveled together for cross-country promotional events. Then claims they are platonic: "He's a good a little number, but I'm not interested in him." Badham told *People* his divorce was a long time coming.

Of course, show business has a long history of on-set romances, when attractive people who had become intensely close for a period of time developed crushes if not outright physical relationships. Elizabeth Taylor and Richard Burton, Angelina Jolie and Brad Pitt, and Blake Lively and Ryan Reynolds are just a few examples of couples who met on movie sets.

Ron Stigwood explains, "Look, I am out of the film industry now. But when I came back to Australia, I worked on about twenty or thirty films, and there are always romances on films.

I mean, you put people together, and you work twelve, fourteen hours a day, six, seven days a week for three months. There's always gonna be some sort of interaction, and that does not necessarily mean that it is serious."

Badham's romance with the leading lady was just one of many obstacles the cast and crew had to manage during the three-month shoot. And the face of it all is a young TV star who is about to set the world on fire. If Badham can manage not to annoy him, it will go smoothly. (Travolta will often be annoyed by him.)

Most people I spoke with describe Travolta consistently as "generous," "patient," "hardworking," "lovely," "down-to-earth," and many variations of the word *beautiful*. The New Jersey native grew up in a family that respected art. His father, Salvatore "Sam" Travolta, was a former professional football player who owned a tire shop, and his mother, Helen, was an actor, acting coach, and director who was revered in local theater.

His sister Ann told me, "She was a local director in Bergen County. We lived in Englewood, New Jersey. She would direct musicals and plays in most of the schools. She is very well known in Englewood, for a lot of the different platforms that she would be part of."

Travolta is the youngest child with three sisters (Ann, Ellen, and Margaret) and brothers Joey and Sam. All would take up acting at some point in their lives, with the encouragement of both parents. His father, Sam, told *McCall's* magazine in 1978, "All my kids went out and got jobs as soon as they could. I had a tire shop; that don't bring in a lot of money."

When Travolta appeared on *Inside the Actors Studio* with host James Lipton in 2003, he talked about growing up in a theatrical family. His mother's way of conducting herself stood out the most for him. "You have to understand, in my household, everything was slightly affected. It was, 'Darling, do you really want another glass of orange juice?' It was that whole era of actors that we kind of resisted. And then I realized there's a lot of fun in behaving like that. And later on, I didn't mind being affected."

When his sisters would head into the city to audition, Travolta often tagged along, learning the ropes of how to get a job in musical theater. When he was sixteen, he worked in summer stock in a production of *Bye Bye Birdie*. When the gig was over, he called his father in tears, asking if he really had to go back to school. He was about to enter his junior year at Dwight Morrow High School, and the sensitive teenager felt like an outcast with his classmates. They were into rock and roll, while he memorized the *Gypsy* soundtrack.

His parents gave him one year to prove himself as an actor, and in 1971 the seventeen-year-old moved in with his older sister Ann in New York in a six-dollar-per-week tenement apartment. Within a year, he was supporting himself with musicals and dozens of commercials. By eighteen, he was in a touring production of *Grease*, playing Doody. It was there that he met one of his best friends (and sometime love interest), Marilu Henner.

Ann recalls, "He was eighteen, and I was twenty-three when we got the show of *Grease*. It was a national show. He was the baby. But, you know, he just went with it, and he had fun. We did an awful lot of theater, Ellen, Johnny, and I."

He also worked in Los Angeles for several TV guest spots on shows like *Emergency!* and *The Rookies* and a truly forgettable movie called *The Devil's Rain* before he landed the role of Vinnie Barbarino in 1975. To give some context on what America was like in the mid-1970s: the first season of the show was met with controversy. *Welcome Back, Kotter* was a show about a group of juvenile delinquents in a Bensonhurst high school who are helped by an alumni student as their new remedial education teacher.

At the same time in the mid-1970s, school busing programs

in cities like Boston were filled with racial strife. Thousands of people protested sending Black children to white school districts. Every evening, the nightly news showed parents holding racially charged protest signs and calling children racial slurs and telling them to "get out of our neighborhood."

The expression "Banned in Boston" was used in the film industry to indicate content that was considered vulgar in the largely Catholic city. When the ABC affiliate in Boston, WCVB-TV, learned about *Welcome Back, Kotter*, even before it aired, it pulled it from their schedule due to its potential to excite students.

In the pilot episode, the multiracial cast of "teenagers" had different gritty backgrounds, with Vinnie saying he dreams of being a mafia kingpin one day. It got so intense that school-teachers offered to coach the writers about their profession. Star Gabe Kaplan (who played the titular Kotter) wondered if junkyard owners hassled the cast of *Sanford and Son*. It took only a few episodes before they changed their mind as the sitcom leaned more toward the Marx Brothers than *The Blackboard Jungle*. All the "Sweathogs" were loved, but Barbarino was a huge source of attention. Travolta's feathered hair and dim-witted delivery made him a standout.

His parents, now retired but still living in their Englewood home, were besieged with Travolta fans who called, sent letters, and visited their home nonstop. Helen patiently tried to appease all with a stack of headshots of her son and promised he would respond when he could. Even when they peeled paint chips off the porch, Sam Travolta told *McCall's* he did not mind. "They meant no harm."

The producers offered Travolta his own show, but he declined. In his first break he filmed the soon-to-be horror classic *Carrie* and *The Boy in the Plastic Bubble*. He had a feeling his star was only starting to rise. Using his new earnings, he hired a publicist to get the word out that he was ready to move beyond playing teenagers.

Randal Kleiser, who directed Travolta in *The Boy in the Plastic Bubble*, told me he was impressed with the star's diligence. "He was very driven and obsessive about his work. He had insomnia, and so he often was up late thinking about what he was doing the next day or what he did that day. He would call me sometimes at night and ask which take I printed of a certain scene. He was really focused on his work."

To give an idea how busy John Travolta's 1976 was, in addition to his TV schedule, he released a self-titled debut album that led to a visit to *American Bandstand* to sing his hit "Let Her In." While not a great showcase for his voice, it did chart on the *Billboard* Hot 100. He was offered $25,000 per gig for a mall tour across the United States to support the record, but he chose to do *Bus Stop* with his sister for summer stock to continually hone his acting chops.

His forty-year-old costar, Diana Hyland, played his mother in *The Boy in the Plastic Bubble*. She was a willowy blonde who had acted opposite Paul Newman on Broadway and played Susan Winter in the popular nighttime soap *Peyton Place*. During filming, she and John felt a special connection, which flowered into a secret romance. He even became a father figure to her four-year-old son, Zachary, as her ex-husband had addiction issues and was unreliable. She told *People* magazine on November 29, 1976, "He is mature, sensitive, and giving, very easy to be with. John's the antithesis of Barbarino." Future castmate Paul Pape recalls seeing them together in New York before he even auditioned for *Saturday Night Fever* and was struck by what a good-looking couple they were.

In November 1976, *The Boy in the Plastic Bubble* and *Carrie* were released within ten days of each other. His date for the *Carrie* premiere was Hyland, which surprised Kleiser when he saw them. "I had no idea that they had formed a relationship when we were shooting the movie. It was kept very quiet."

Normally taking up covers of *Teen Beat, Dynamite,* and *16* magazines, he scored his first *People* magazine cover instead, talking openly about his romance with Diana Hyland, his love for her son, and how he was ready to leave the sitcom life behind. It was also a chance for him to promote his upcoming role in *Saturday Night* (as it was titled at the time), with a photo of John disco dancing with his instructor, Deney Terrio. It was the first step on a long journey toward becoming Tony Manero.

What Travolta did not tell *People* magazine was that despite his bravado about his prospects, he was, in fact, terrified to accept the part once the script was sent over. He had been playing a lovable dumbbell for so long he had a hard time deciding how to work with what on paper seemed like an awful character. Tony Manero was sexist, racist, and horrible to his family. How would he find vulnerability in this part?

Eighteen months later, in June 1978 and on the cusp of the release of *Grease*, Travolta told Tom Burke of *Rolling Stone* that Hyland had encouraged him to play Tony Manero because it had "all of the colors." When he hemmed and hawed over the shape of his body (he had gained weight enjoying too many long lunches with his fellow Sweathog Lawrence Hilton-Jacobs) and lack of dance skills, she replied, "Baby, you are going to learn!"

Inhabiting the character of Tony Manero became his new obsession, and Travolta got to work.

CHAPTER 4

"Getting into Character"

*Improvisation, Alexander's, Sal Mineo,
and Polyester*

Despite all the drama surrounding the firing of John Avildsen, the cast and crew of the movie pitched in to help where
they could as the filming was just weeks away. Kevin McCormick helped Lloyd Kaufman with his first time working as a
location manager. Though a lifelong New Yorker, Kaufman
had no relevant knowledge of the neighborhoods of Brooklyn
and did not realize the mob might be interested in a big movie
production in their region.

Later known as one of the key creators of B-movies with
Troma Entertainment and the 1984 camp classic *The Toxic
Avenger*, at the time Kaufman was just trying to find decent locations in Bay Ridge and Bensonhurst while working on a minus-
cule budget. He was also one of several who helped scout locations
for the disco scenes. His first choice was nixed by the head of production, Michael Hausman, as too challenging to film.

Hausman recalls, "We stop, and the location manager says,
'This is the location for the dance scene.' And so, we all got out,
went into the building, and got in a small elevator. And I said,
'Well, where is the location?' And they said, 'It's on the eighth
floor of this building.' 'So,' I said, 'how are you gonna get the
dolly and the equipment and the lights and everything up to the

eighth floor?' We got back in the car. There is no way that this is gonna be the location. Forget about it."

After checking out disco venues in all five boroughs, the 2001 Odessey location (where Nik Cohn had set his article) was the final choice, as it had several levels for filming, a bar with strippers, and, more important, the owner had a building across the street that could serve as a break room for actors and crew in between scenes.

John Badham is the kind of director who encourages his cast to take time to improvise and bond with each other before filming begins. One of those ways was having them head out to Bay Ridge and try to blend in with the crowd. Travolta had to be snuck in from a side door, as he was recognized instantly and stayed mostly to judge disco contests.

Movie newbie Donna Pescow was eager to find characters like Annette to observe. She and Paul Pape (Double J.) went together before 2001 Odyssey was renovated and updated for the movie. Pescow remembers, "It was like Disneyland. I mean, we had no idea what the heck was going on, you know? None of us had really gotten into a whole disco scene. So, we went there, and they just spotted us instantly as strangers, and they were not really thrilled that we were checking them out. It was not a friendly vibe at all." She thought it might have been her outfit choice—a denim skirt and matching jacket. Not exactly disco diva attire.

Pescow decided to hide out in the ladies' room, thinking, "I will pick up a lot of the conversation and how they kind of talk to one another and what they talk about. I spent so much time in that stall! Trying to disappear and listen to the women and the young girls at the mirrors. And I remember one girl was saying to her friend that she had not worn a bra, and it was hard for her to dance."

Pape had an easier time fitting in with the crowds, who

Paul Pape, John Travolta, and Donna Pescow at the
2001 Odyssey. *Collection Christophel/Alamy Stock Photo.*

teased him for playing a local. "The kids were great. We loved
hanging out with them, and there were a lot of them in the disco
scenes. They are all the local kids. We got them in the movie. So,
it was only a problem logistically at times, and I think one night
they stole our pickup. They stole the car, and it was found some-
where else. That's Brooklyn," he says.

Karen Lynn Gorney, who had earned a master of fine arts at
Carnegie Tech, told the *New York Times* on December 30, 1977,
that she fine-tuned her Bay Ridge accent based on her training.
"They taught us to write down accents phonetically. So, I did
that with all of Stephanie's lines—I wrote down the vowels and
the consonants. And I hung out with some kids from Brooklyn
and broke down their sounds methodically."

Badham, who is praised by most of the cast for collaborating well with actors, felt that every moment they were not
learning the script or the choreography should be spent bond-
ing. He told them to improvise at the rehearsal studio in Downtown Broadway. Pescow was treated like a bratty younger sister
by her much taller costars. "We would improvise the scenes

and get a sense of one another. We went out for lunch, and, of course, they treated me just horribly."

For example, when the group would go out for pizza, "They get in front of me. It was none of this 'ladies first' stuff. You know, there is none of that. I was like one of them, but it was great, because we had established this rapport with one another. So, by the time we started to film, it was so comfortable, and it was so genuine that it really translated on film, and it was really genius of John Badham to do that," she recalls.

Both Travolta and Barry Miller (Bobby C.) saw the similarities of their characters to the leads of the 1955 classic film *Rebel Without a Cause*. In the 2007 documentary *Saturday Night Fever: A 30-Year Legacy*, Miller recalls that he and Travolta played out a modern version of James Dean's and Sal Mineo's characters (Jim and Plato). According to Norman Wexler's script, among the Faces, the two are the closest friends. Miller, being so much smaller than Travolta, played up his hero worship of Tony Manero to make himself seem pathetic in comparison.

Travolta and Gorney rehearsed in a separate space, as Badham wanted her to feel like an outsider. It was enough work for the choreographer, Lester Wilson, and his assistant, Lorraine Fields, to produce the couple's routines and banter for the two to show their characters' growing attraction. Fields remembers, "It was so interesting. Just a whole new culture of people for me to know. John was a wonderful person to work with. I am talking about John Travolta. John Badham was very enthusiastic about making this film. He was all in."

Travolta talked to the Atlanta TV show *Cinema Landscape* in December 1977 to promote the film. He described his process for creating his character: "What I wanted to do is actually get some nuances and character coloration for my character. In other words, making him more authentic. Talking to young men and women around the club, seeing what their viewpoints were, what their values were, how they talked, how they even viewed me as John Travolta in their eyes a celebrity. You know how they would react to someone like me. So, I took all that into consideration and then developed the character."

Gorney stated in the 2010 documentary *Saturday Night Fever: The Inside Story* about Stephanie, "She was fighting against trying to be cool and create an act where she was sophisticated, and she could survive and rise in the world. So, she was sort of a symbol of what was really going on with women in 1977."

The main image people take away from *Saturday Night Fever* is Travolta's white suit. The journey to finding the right clothes for the cast was a monthlong challenge. All the actors and many of the crew joined the costumer, Patrizia von Brandenstein (and later an Academy Award winner for art direction on dozens of films, including *Amadeus*, *The Untouchables*, and *Limitless*), who was tasked with finding all the costumes for the cast off the rack. From Forty-Second Street in Midtown to the Leading Male in Midwood, Brooklyn, she would lead with her mission to buy as many bright polyester outfits as she could grab.

Beginning her career in costumes on and off Broadway, she was married to a man who was also a designer and who had once worked in a Cincinnati production of *Rain*, which starred the sixteen-year-old John Travolta. Von Brandenstein knew that Travolta, though young, was also dashing and elegant.

The higher-end fashion magazines looked down on this style—the kids at the clubs liked to peacock around in prints and tight pants. So, how was she going to dress this Tony Manero? After watching him in rehearsal, she remembers, "When we saw him, we were deeply impressed by this guy because he could dance ten hours a day. Did not matter to him. Because he was incredibly young, very strong. And so the question was, what is he going to wear?"

Von Brandenstein knew the importance of suit colors, with the disco being a dark space. She told me, "There were those who advocated for a black suit, and there were those who advocated for accommodation, like a dinner jacket. I wanted a white suit because heroes wear white, and he is the hero. He is the hero of the neighborhood, but he is also the hero of the picture." Travolta was a not an enthusiastic fan of the white suit at first. He thought Tony would prefer black, which he wears often in the film, but they convinced him that in the dark club with the lighted floor, the white would jump out more.

There were several suits made for Travolta that had to be torn apart and put back together to fit him impeccably. "So that was my aim. And it was communal, and we all agreed that he looked pretty swell. And I chose a heeled shoe because he did look very elegant and king-like, regal."

Last-minute shopping in Bay Ridge had its own challenges. Von Brandenstein clearly recalls, "We [Travolta and some of the cast] went with me. We arrive in Bay Ridge with limousines, and we go into the shop. And I think the school had just let out. After forty-five minutes or so, there was an excessively big crowd. And they called the police to escort us out. The kids were everywhere and were not a raucous nasty group. Nothing like that. But it was impressive. I began to think that maybe we have something here."

Syracuse-born jazz lover Paul Pape was not exactly on top of the disco fashion scene. But one of his first jobs in New York City was at a Midtown shoe store with an interesting clientele. He told me, "They catered mostly to mafia and pimps, and I sold shoes in the back. These were not your normal shoes. They were like lizard skin and suede embroidered. And we sold this patent leather opera pump with a goldfish in the heel. We had light goldfish in the back. You would drop the goldfish and plug it back up. They would buy them. And sometimes they had come back a day or two later saying, they did not like the shoes, but, you know, they had beaten the goldfish to death in the heel of the shoes."

The change in hairstyle also helped Pape find his character. "I had never had my hair blow-dried. I just kind of let it go. But when they did and I looked in the mirror, well, it was not me anymore. So, between what Patrizia did with our clothing and the hair and visiting these places, I think we all kind of caught on quick as to what we were."

One of the actors decidedly did not like the costume von Brandenstein had picked for them. Bruce Ornstein felt his character of Gus was underwritten, and he took his appearance seriously as to how it would make him stand out on film. "The woman who was the costume designer, we did not get along very well. I think she has since won an Academy Award. We had this dispute about what I wanted to wear. And I went up to [her] and I am creating this person, and you are not. And I appreciate your help, but, honestly, it is my decision. She said, 'No. It's not.' I said, 'Let's go talk to the director.'"

To Ornstein's surprise, Badham agreed with him and he was able to wear his own idea of muted colors and giving him a "twitch" to show how nervous he was. That Gus was not ready to join the Faces, full stop. "Like, he's enjoying the perks, but not ready to sort of commit himself," he adds.

Creating looks for Pescow and Gorney had its own challenges. According to von Brandenstein, "[Donna Pescow] was very petite. She wore platform chunky heels, but she was still short. And John is tall. So, that was important because, she looked up to him. Always. She follows him very closely."

She also recalls a jacket incident. "We gave her this appalling Afghan jacket. There were no buttons. It just sort of had sleeves.

But it looked a certain way, and we loved it. We thought it was perfect because a girl like that would have gone to Alexander's [a department store that went out of business in the early 1990s]."

The issue of it being unique was problematic when von Brandenstein remembers, "One morning, at about six o'clock, our producer, Kevin McCormick, called and said, 'The jacket is gone! You do not have doubles.' He sends a car to my humble loft, which was below Canal Street. We get in and we go to Alexander's."

She continues, "He bribes the night guard to get in. We call the supervisor on the floor. He comes and we hunt through ten thousand jackets. None of them is the right jacket. And we noticed a bin of those jackets—a heap. We dived into this big bin and we found a jacket. It is not exactly the same, but it is sort of the same. And that is the jacket photographed in the second half of this sequence. We went out to the disco that we had remodeled and put this jacket on Donna, who went on to fame and glory."

If you look at the movie poster, Gorney is wearing a red dress, in sharp contrast to Travolta's white suit. Many people have wondered why she does not wear it in the movie. Von Brandenstein explains that her character, "Stephanie, was someone who is much further along the path of growing up. And I wanted her to have a certain amount of sophistication. I have a drawing, a color drawing of that first dress, which we made. But we did not use it. Because they really felt that the red was too strong. One of the producers said, 'I think that dress looks like it should be on a bottle of Yago Sangria,' which was a supermarket brand of sangria."

Instead, in the movie, in the contest at the end, she wears a softer chiffon number. Von Brandenstein says, "I remembered I had seen a pretty chiffon dress that was worn over a cream-colored dress at a wedding. And we tried a couple of colors. We tried a cream chiffon dress over red. We tried it over blue. That was not the right way to go. Then we tried it over a rose-pink slip and added a satin belt. It is a very romantic-looking dress. And she wore it very nicely and danced beautifully in it. We created a very romantic dress for Stephanie to wear during the very romantic dance in the dance contest."

Keeping the outfits clean after three weeks of dancing at the club took a great deal of coordination. Von Brandenstein told me, "You have a hero, but you also have four principals and a whole crowd of kids who are dancing. You must be there [on set]. And I am amazed, but I had one assistant, Jennifer Nichols. She was excellent at wardrobe. We did a lot of the alterations ourselves and we recut that suit, extremely, carefully. We provided a wardrobe, but it was minimal because those [local] kids had the right look. And the camera is always on the principals anyway, but particularly the contestants we did up. And they were wonderful. Talented Broadway gypsies," she says with admiration.

According to von Brandenstein, "One of his [Stigwood's] personal assistants became part of the art department. Part of the wardrobe. We had Jenny Nichols, and we had him. And I can remember washing shirts and stuff in my washing machine before I went to work in the morning. I would wash them at night and dry them in the morning. Jenny and I, we would take turns. Jenny would take them home and I would. And because it was that kind of camaraderie. And it was easy to get this done."

Now with the wardrobe and motivations of the actors worked out, everyone noticed how great Travolta looked. This is how he got there.

CHAPTER 5

Building the Body Travolta

*The Lockers, Deney Terrio, Jimmy Gambina,
Lester Wilson, JoJo Smith Studio*

I t begins with the opening scene. The way John Travolta struts down the street in Bay Ridge to the Bee Gees' "Stayin' Alive" with the utmost confidence and assuredness. He is not being goofy or looking for laughs. As Tony Manero, he swings the paint can and surveys the neighborhood with a smirk. This man knows he is hot stuff, and you are lucky to see him at his peak.

As it is lovingly described in the April 3, 1978, issue of *Time* magazine, "When Travolta first appears in *Saturday Night Fever*, there's an instant charge—a shock of recognition, of excitement, of acceptance. He has the moves, the presence, the princely mystique. No one can fully define star quality, but you can find illustration enough. And in 1978, that walk is the best one around."

Travolta's transformation from a Sweathog to a lean dancing machine was striking to behold. His pose on the album soundtrack and movie posters in the tight white suit, platform shoes, and slim frame showcased a sex appeal never shown on the teen magazine covers from just the year before. His body was so chiseled that there were calls to have him film a nude scene. The black briefs he struts around in in front of his grandmother, yelling "Attica!", are the product of a negotiation between Travolta and director John Badham.

Don Campbell, founder of the Lockers dance troupe,
which hired choreographer Deney Terrio, in 1975. His work is an
early precursor of hip-hop dancing, and he is now considered a
legend in the art form. *Photo courtesy of his son, Dennis Danehy.*

On *Welcome Back, Kotter*, he was cute with tousled hair and
a shy demeanor, which for some people transmitted low energy.
Sure, he can do the "Barbarino dance," but what about a solo at
a New York City nightclub? Who will take this guy seriously?
Turns out it took a team of experts, along with the star's commit-
ment to his craft, that got him into Tony Manero shape.

After signing the deal, Travolta's manager, Bob LeMond, put
out a notice that he was looking for someone to teach his client
how to disco dance. A very eager twenty-six-year-old Deney Terrio showed up at his office with a stack of records and tapes, nervously trying to figure out his hi-fi stereo while explaining that
he literally made his living winning dance contests.

Born Denis George Mahan in 1950, Terrio was raised in
Massachusetts and Florida and taught himself how to dance as a

young man to impress his sister's friends. Privately he had dreams of movie stardom and thought he might be able to score a part in *Saturday Night* while teaching Travolta.

In 1973, Terrio appeared on the Roberta Flack variety show as a member of Don "Campbellock" Campbell's dance group, the Lockers. Of their talented former members, Toni Basil (of future "Mickey" fame) would have a long career as a choreographer, dancer, and singer, and Fred Berry who played Rerun in the mid-1970s sitcom *What's Happening!!* became a TV star. Their leaps, jumps, and splits made them a favorite act as they toured the country.

Don Campbell's son, Dennis Danehy, speaks for the Lockers, as his father passed away in 2020. "My father created the dance [Campbellock] in 1970 and was the only one really doing his dance for a year when he ended up getting on *Soul Train*. He became a star but noticed that the dancers weren't getting paid. So, he decided to picket the show and was kicked off. Within a couple months, Toni Basil was able to get a gig, for four dancers of my father's style on the Roberta Flack special put together by Dick Clark. And Deney Terrio was part of that. He was one of the few white dancers allowed in the Black clubs because he could dance. He was a friend of my father and got the call for the Roberta Flack specials," he adds.

In the August 28, 1975, issue of *Rolling Stone*, reporter Wayne Robins interviewed Basil, who described Campbell as "the Nureyev of Watts." Her choreography along with the talents of dancers (and future street dance legends) Shabba Doo, Slim the Robot, Fluky Luke, and Mr. Penguin made the Lockers' dancing (according to *Rolling Stone*) the "most elite cult."

For his big audition in LeMond's office, Terrio did an entire routine he had memorized to Kool & the Gang's "Jungle Boogie." The same choreography the Lockers had performed on

John Travolta and Deney Terrio train for *Saturday Night Fever*, 1976.
Reprinted with permission from the estate of
photographer Julian Wasser.

television for years, including on *The Midnight Special* in 1975.
(He admits this in the HBO documentary *Mr. Saturday Night*.)
Tall, slim, and handsome, in his tight satin pants and big smile,
he enchanted LeMond and got the gig. Although, technically, he
was not an instructor or choreographer, he would be the star's
mentor. At the time John G. Avildsen was still the director, and
Terrio hoped to be included in the New York crew for the filming.

For several weeks, Travolta and Terrio danced every evening
after *Kotter* rehearsals to get him to learn the moves. Even though
he had some dance training from working in musicals, he was
nervous about the movie solos. A perfectionist by nature, Travolta was completely focused on nailing the moves.

Either Travolta's publicist or the Paramount studios marketing department sent a photographer to watch them rehearse—the

revered Julian Wasser, who was famous for gorgeous portraits of famous people like Marilyn Monroe and Audrey Hepburn, and most of Joan Didion's author photos. The images and some grainy video of their initial rehearsals seemed to seal the deal for the media on who deserved credit for Travolta's amazing moves. Terrio also took the star to after-dark dance clubs in Los Angeles to build his confidence in drawing a crowd.

When performing in front of producer Robert Stigwood and Avildsen, they were pleased with the results. However, the director felt his star was still too heavy and appeared to be breathing too heavily due to lack of conditioning. It was decided it was time to get him into fighting shape. Enter *Rocky's* trainer—Jimmy Gambina.

Jimmy Gambina, a thirty-three-year-old Hollywood native and boxing expert, trained Sylvester Stallone to become the "Italian Stallion," and stars like Robert DeNiro and Robert Conrad depended on him to get them into proper condition for their roles. Jimmy not only taught boxing but was also an expert on stunt work, which the sparsely budgeted movie needed to protect the cast.

Gambina trained the actor for several months with a heavy emphasis on running and calisthenics, forbidding him from working with Terrio. He told me, "The point was, he was twenty-three years old when I started with him. I took thirty pounds off him, and I got him in great condition. Deney Terrio started to be his dance teacher, but he was getting him to do things that an actor can't do unless they're conditioned properly."

Leaning him up became the biggest dictate from Avildsen and Gambino. "[Travolta] had a big butt. He had a lot of hair and a kind of attitude that was just not conducive to playing this character, so I had to change everything about him," Gambino explains.

The trainer was mainly worried about what he perceived as his lack of stretching and proper calisthenics used during Travolta's time with Terrio. "Flexibility is the key to being a great athlete," he told me. "Because when you lift weights, you bind yourself. And as a fighter, the worst thing you could do is bind yourself."

According to Gambina, "Well, I got rid of him [Terrio] at the second week in the training. I said, 'John, I can't train you. This guy doesn't know what he's doing.' I didn't know Travolta that well, but I knew John Avildsen."

Despite being only five feet tall, Gambina presented himself as a man deserving of respect. Travolta's movie double, Jeff Zinn, recalls, "What I was struck by, just being on the set with him and watching him, was how Gambina carried himself. He moved through the world like he was ten feet tall."

Zinn adds, "I'm six feet tall and I moved through the world a little bit hunched over. He said something, and it really affected me. I started carrying myself in a different way because of what I learned from Jimmy. Because I thought if this little guy could present himself so strongly in the world, what's stopping me from doing that? Right? It was a cool lesson, he was lovely."

For Travolta's first visit to Gambina's boxing gym, he got a less than warm welcome from one of the biggest movie stars of all time. Gambina recalls, "Travolta would show up early while I was training Robert DeNiro [for *Raging Bull*]. And DeNiro says, 'You get this freaking kid out of here. I don't like this kid!' What the heck? He wants to be an actor and I'm helping him. And he kept saying this kid doesn't have a chance. I said, 'Bobby, if I do the picture, I'll make him bigger than all of you.'"

The workout routine was running six miles every day,

followed by calisthenics and a stretching routine before and after each session. He was told to get bed early and not spend time at the clubs "getting into character." By the time he was done, Travolta had shed extra weight and his cardio strength had greatly improved. Travolta was ready to work long days on the set and would be able to fit in his new, tight wardrobe.

"So, I got rid of Terrio and then everything started running smoothly. He was in great condition." Even though his friend Avildsen was fired, Gambina was brought to New York to continue their training.

In February 1977, Travolta headed east for the rehearsal. In addition to the readings of the script, Badham arranged for the thirty-three-year-old choreographer Lester Wilson to teach the cast as much dance as they needed for their individual parts, instruct "the Faces" movement for their characters, and arrange all the musical sequences used in the film.

Born in the Bronx and raised in Hollis, Queens, to a vibrant family, he had his first taste of show business in a talent show at Radio City Music Hall at the age of four, when he sang "Jesus Loves Me" and danced for the crowd to huge applause, said Wilson's sister Julie. Later at Jamaica High School, he was smart and popular, as part of the dance corps, the math club, and president of the student council. In his senior year he was voted Mr. Jamaica for his overall big personality. His magnetic charm and smile (as well as his tough rehearsals) are recalled by dozens of his friends.

His passion for dance began at the Bernice Johnson Dance Studio in Queens, along with future celebrated choreographer Michael Peters, who would work on several Michael Jackson videos and *Dreamgirls* on Broadway. Singer, actor, and dancer Ben Vereen, who won the Tony for Best Actor in 1973 for *Pippin,* was also a classmate and friend of Wilson. He told me, "He

Choreographer Lester Wilson (*right*) in Germany, 1971,
as the host of his own show, *Here Is Lester Wilson . . .*
Keystone Press/Alamy Stock Photo.

was an amazing teacher, and he loved his art. He loved the craft
of artists. We're creators."

Wilson received a scholarship to the Juilliard School of Music
and earned money by not only appearing in Bob Fosse's *Pal Joey*
but also, after each performance, running to the African Room
in Midtown for the after-hours shows in the chorus. None other
than Josephine Baker saw one of his performances and encouraged him to go to Paris and learn from the masters there.

Wilson bounced between Paris, Berlin, and the Nether-
lands, where his large afro and outrageous stage outfits made
him a regional pop star. When he returned to the States in the
early 1970s, celebrity variety shows were all the rage. His clients included Sammy Davis Jr., Ben Vereen, Dick Van Dyke,
Ann-Margret, Lola Falana, Red Foxx, and Liza Minelli.

In 1973, with Quincy Jones as a producer, Lester Wilson

wrote, directed, and choreographed the musical *$600 and a Mule* in Los Angeles. Based on the premise of former enslaved Americans being given those items after emancipation, it was bold and fresh and featured a large Black cast of dancers, which was rare for the time. His friend, director, costume designer, and choreographer Peter Menefee, told me, "He not only brought Black dancers to Hollywood, but he brought superb Black dancers who could cut it like nobody else, even better than most."

One of them was his longtime friend and assistant Lorraine Fields. Both had been hired to choreograph *The Wiz* but lost the job with Badham's firing. Fields, who had just recently embraced Buddhism, knew that better things were in store for them. She describes how they met. "He had a nightclub act in New York City, and he was teaching dance classes right down the street from the High School of Performing Arts. Back then, we only had ballet. They didn't teach us jazz.

"So, we would take his class and just get filled with jazz dancing. His style was infectious, and he was infectious as a person. And then that's how I got a chance to know him. Plus, he had done *Golden Boy* with Sammy Davis Jr. on Broadway. By that time, I had just graduated, and he asked me to audition. It was my first job with him, and that was in Chicago," she recalls.

Saturday Night Fever would be her first film, and she was excited about the opportunity. Badham was grateful for them. "He was that kind of funky person, and he and his dance captain, they were just perfect. He choreographed and staged all the dance numbers in there, and people really liked him, as well they should. Lorraine was a godsend, because she would keep him on the straight and narrow," Badham remembers.

Wilson had a habit of showing up late for gigs because he was out all night at the clubs. He would give all kinds of excuses, like he was double-booked and had to attend a fashion show or go work on a TV ad. But, according to Lorraine, "I don't think he double-booked himself as he partied. He enjoyed himself. That was the double-booking. He was just out because he was kind of a Pied Piper, and he was always around the latest and the greatest people, especially when he went to New York City. That was his spot. And he was part of that developing group of young, gifted Black artists."

When Travolta first met Wilson and Fields, he showed them all the moves he had learned from Terrio. Wilson told him they would incorporate as much as they could but also try some new ideas. They promised he would be supported, and prepared him for the task at hand. Filming dance scenes requires a different energy and incredible endurance, due to the need to make everything on film be in sequence. As Fields puts it, "When you choreograph something for a film, there's a sense of continuity. And so that's why you must do the same thing repeatedly, because it must match. You just can't make up something else."

On top of all his skills, Wilson was also an actor who appeared on several stage and TV productions, including a guest spot on *Good Times* in 1975 and in specials throughout Europe promoting his albums. Not only was the aesthetic important to him, but also that the movements rang true. He knew the meaning of connecting with the audience and that was by doing his research.

Wilson wanted Travolta to give attitude in every scene, whether he was dancing or not. It started in the opening scene, with Tony Manero swinging a paint can and walking to work. According to Fields, "The creation of the very first scene, Lester really wanted to give John Travolta this swag [swagger]. And the swag happened as soon as he got out of the bed and got in front of the mirror and combed his hair and how he walked down the street. This was all created by Lester."

She said that Lester also worked on the character's motivation. "Just taking moments. Find your moment in the mirror, find your moment when you get on the corner. Find your moment when you step off the curb. Just how you walk and how you look around. And just your whole attitude. That whole thing was just kind of created out of a narrative that was in the background of John's head, like, 'What am I doing? Why am I here?' Like, okay, yeah, I am all that and a bag of chips."

Fields told me how the creative process at the beginning of rehearsals helped shape the overall look of the movie. "Basically, the invention of it in the studio was when we had the most fun. We didn't think about if the movie was going to be great or not. We just wanted to do good work. But when we went to the opening night in Los Angeles and people actually stood up after almost every dance number, we were floored. We had no idea this was going to be that impactful. Kudos to the editor. Kudos to the music. Kudos to John Travolta, and just their vision."

There was a separate rehearsal space for choreographers JoJo Smith and his then wife, Sue Samuels (both in their midthirties), who ran the famous JoJo's Dance Factory. JoJo had been on Broadway for ten years before opening his own studio, one of the most popular in Manhattan. He was also first cousins with Lester Wilson, and there was a symmetry with their styles. They were hired to help Travolta and Karen Lynn Gorney form a connection on the dance floor.

Travolta was prepared for JoJo's funkier style, but Gorney was nervous. She told *Vanity Fair* in 2007 that she had had a motorcycle accident years before that was causing mobility issues. According to Samuels, "Karen Lynn Gorney needed help with her dance moves because she was basically not a dancer at all at that time. JoJo would send me in to work with Karen, move this way, move that way. She didn't have any moves. She didn't have use of her body. So, we worked on isolations and that kind of thing and so that she could move, at least looked like she's moving better, more relaxed. So, repetition and moving her body, it was just that."

Their son, Jason Samuels Smith (also a performer who starred in Broadway's *Bring in 'da Noise, Bring in 'da Funk*), told me, "At that time in New York, a lot of the studios that were independently owned by other dance teachers closed. JoJo's Dance Factory became kind of the refuge for all other dance teachers at the time to now come under this one roof, which became really one of the first mainstream studios that housed most every style."

Samuels was nine months pregnant at the time of these rehearsals, so the couple did not make it for any location filming. She remembers, "[Travolta and Gorney] were beautiful, friendly, excited. There were other dance movies, but in different genres, so this was different, the disco era. And it was very exciting. They're very nice people. They ended up using a lot of JoJo's dancers for the film in the famous nightclub scene where the floor lights up."

Jason talked about his father's style and the way he incorporated arm movements for Travolta. "I think he was street funk in his heart. The way he pulsed and all that, that came from the street. So that and his karate background made his arms move in ways which shot out. All his backgrounds came together to form that, and there was no term *disco* before that. That kind of launched the term *disco*."

Jason also feels that there is an undercurrent of Black culture featured in *Saturday Night Fever* that does not get discussed enough. He explained, "I would reiterate what is street. It's Black. It's Black culture. These are dances that folks in the Black community are doing at communal parties, at the club. So that's why I try to say all of it, even disco dance. Really, it's funk."

He continues, "In *Saturday Night Fever*, while it's not entirely appropriation, there is a bit of bringing some of this urban Black culture into the mainstream. Even though this has been happening in these communities around the country already. It was a window for the rest of the world to see it. Disco didn't last as a genre, but I do feel it transformed into what house music is."

With Travolta's physical appearance being taken care of, now was the time to prove he could inhabit the character. He showed up at 2001 Odessey in Bay Ridge and debuted his new look to the locals who showed their approval. While the women tried to flirt with him, the men scolded them to hold back. He was one of them now.

CHAPTER 6

March Madness, 1977

John Badham's First Month Filming

After the shocking number of fans who showed up on the first day of shooting, Badham knew that the actual filming of the movie would be much more complicated than what he had expected. In the early 1960s, there were no film schools to learn the ropes. After graduating from Yale Drama School, he flew out west to see if he could break into film and television. "And, of course, I couldn't get arrested. I finally got a job in the Universal mailroom, and I was thrilled to earn sixty dollars a week! I realized how hard it was to get in, and how many people were trying to become directors."

One of the biggest drawbacks for him was his lack of familiarity with Brooklyn. How each of its neighborhoods was unique in culture and attitude. Badham told me he might have been there one time before but he could not remember where or why. In the few weeks of pre-production available, he was often sleep deprived after visiting a slew of discos and nightclubs to witness the proverbial "tribal rites."

He quickly noticed that there were some clubs that were welcoming to newcomers—usually the ones that had a mostly gay crowd. Other places made it clear that they had a specific clientele to whom they were appealing. Especially in Bay Ridge,

John Travolta filming on location in 1977.
Paramount Pictures/RGR Collection/Alamy Stock Photo.

which had a large Italian population that would not appreciate "outsiders" coming in for the dance contests.

He remembers, "At this one contest, we're watching an African American couple. And I asked some people in the crowd, 'Would you be cheering for the two of them?' They said not only would they not be cheering, but they would just walk away.

"Just to start to understand that the level of racism and sexisms were all over the place. To kind of get through and have a sense of the neighborhood. The way that the people react. And that's reflected in the film, especially in the final dance contest, where they're booing this fabulous couple," Badham said.

As someone who had been raised in Birmingham, Alabama, he was aware of the location being the epicenter of the civil rights movement. He arrived there when he was five and told me, "I'd never seen an African American person in my life. So, it was a big surprise, but I immediately found them to be lovely people and bright and interesting and, you know, and why is everybody acting so ugly toward them?"

While he was at Yale, his family kept him up to date on the

local happenings "[Former Birmingham safety commissioner] Bull Connor using dogs, electric cattle prods, and the fire hoses. I mean, all that awful stuff in 1963. And the Selma March. It had to be done. It had to be."

The language in the film (both racially and sexually charged) was important to Norman Wexler and Robert Stigwood, who insisted it made the film gritty. The actors were all very attached to it as well, and resisted when Badham brought up that he would be filming two different takes—an R-rated version and a more TV-friendly version. Some of the actors bristled against this and tried to work on even more cursing in the rehearsals.

Badham explained to them, "Here's the deal. We're gonna film it with all the language that's in there. In fact, it's probably what's in the movie that is way worse than what's in the script, because the actors, once they started realizing they could ad-lib *fuck you* and *shit*, all that stuff, it just sort of kept creeping in.

He continues, "But I said, you know, one day, you're gonna want to sell this to television, and I don't care how far in the future we're going, there's no way that a network is gonna allow this language. What I'll do is when we finish a take with the master, and we've done it with all the language, we'll just do one more without the language. The actors stiffened up and said no. 'This is ruining the purity of what we're doing.' And I said, let me tell you about purity here. Have you ever heard of a thing called residuals? 'No. What's that?' Every time they play this on TV, you get a check. If we don't take this stuff out, there's no playing it on TV and no check for you. Okay. Let's do that alternate version. They switched right away, but that was their first movie."

Badham feels that some of the curse-free takes are better than those in the scripted version because the actors were more natural and not trying so hard. "And what was funny is my editor said, 'I think a lot of the takes where they took the bad language out, their acting is better because they don't care anymore.' He said I'm often using those performances because they're just better acting."

Dealing with a young cast was exciting for the director, as most were theater trained and were eager to learn how to act on camera. Bruce Ornstein, who plays Gus, was worried about his lack of screen time. He approached Badham with his own idea for a scene with just him and Travolta.

He told me, "So, I wrote this little scene, because I write also. And it was just Travolta and I meeting outside of a deli. We just walk and talk and I throw him an apple or something." Ornstein was impressed that Badham allowed his actors to come up with their own takes on their characters and encouraged them to experiment.

Denny Dillon plays the part of Doreen, who just loves to watch Tony dance, and offers to wipe his forehead at the club. At the first cast table read she was awestruck by the talent. It was a combination of theater veterans and show-business newbies. "And then John Badham told me near the beginning that he wanted me to be in the line dance. Because my character wasn't necessarily included in the script, so getting that with the boys and John and Donna. It was an otherworldly experience."

One of the highlights for Dillon was dancing with Tony to the Rick Dees novelty hit "Disco Duck." She thought it was strange coverage at the time ("The music and dancing were so goofy"), but years later Travolta himself called to let her know it was a scene featured in the "clean TV version," assuring her residuals for decades to come.

After reading both of Badham's books (*John Badham on Directing* and *I'll Be in My Trailer*), you get the sense that *Saturday Night Fever* was a huge learning curve for the director in how to treat actors, working on location, keeping the stunts safe, and the importance of setting up fight scenes properly.

For Paul Pape (Double J.), this came about when filming a fight scene set up by Travolta's trainer (and boxing expert) Jimmy Gambina. A rival Puerto Rican gang of the Faces was called the Barracudas. The scene was filmed in an abandoned garage that would also be the setting for a hospital scene. Badham instructed them all that it must look like a fight, but it was not an actual skirmish. *No* landing of punches allowed.

Alberto Vasquez, who plays a gang member, said, "It was a fight scene, And I had to fight with Paul Pape. And it was funny, because Paul was into this method. And I had studied Strasberg, but he was, like, so into that. And he actually punched me in my face!"

He continues, "I remember Badham was upset. Everybody was upset, Travolta left the set. They wanted me to go to the emergency room. I said no. I'm not gonna go, and we brushed it off." In *On Directing*, Badham writes that Vasquez "was tougher than us Hollywood wimps." They decided to shoot from his other side and completed the scene.

Vasquez told me, "What's funny, I had moved to California in the nineties, and I got a call to audition. It was John Badham, and he was dressed like a millionaire! I mean, his outfit was like a ten-thousand-dollar outfit—the suit, the tie, everything. He didn't remember me at first."

The fight scene ended on a high for Pape, because he got to perform his favorite stunt. "I'm proudest when you see us back up the car and drive through the window of the garage. We had one shot at it. And the cameras were set. I had to back the car up, drive it forward, and drive right through that garage. That was so fun. I was twenty-four years old. It was fun to be able to do that," he says.

Badham learned there is no movie worth someone being injured. He knew they were going to be extra cautious about the scenes at Verrazzano-Narrows Bridge. Opened in 1964, the double-decker suspension bridge brings Brooklyn and Staten Island together. Before that, residents needed to ferry back and forth. When it was used as a location, the scenes had to be shot at night, with several lanes closed for hours at a time.

Filming in mid-March meant it would be cold and windy. For Badham, it was stressful to manage, "We're high up above the ground level. So, at ground level, if the wind was about four or five miles an hour, it was thirty miles an hour where we were. And we had those lanes blocked off for the night. We were able to do that for the two or maybe three nights that we were there. But freezing cold, and we're all dressed up."

The Faces enjoyed their time knowing that there was a safety platform to prevent them from falling into the water. Pape calls this "fool's courage" and a part of being young. They enjoyed pranking Donna Pescow (Annette) especially. For one take they pretended to fall over. Badham describes, "They went out there and they dicked around, you know, playing with all the stuff. Then somebody had the bright idea of, 'what if they pretend to fall off the bridge?'

"And it came because when we got out there, you could see that there was a bridge railing to prevent you from going any-where. About ten feet further out were all the big spotlights that light the bridge, and so there were beams there that you could walk out and get to if you had to work on the lights. But in that ten-foot gap, they put steel mesh there so if somebody did fall, God forbid, that they would be protected and fall there," he said.

Badham also remembers how the prank turned out. "We said, well, what if they just deliberately fell into that and they're just screwing with her. It's a great scene. She's wonderful."

Pescow, seeing that the actors were just joking, yells in character (or perhaps this was her real reaction), "You fuckers!"

Pescow found it challenging to maintain her energy in her first film because she felt she had to give her most in every take. She told me, "The thing about the emotional output when you film a scene, oftentimes, they will say, you don't have to go full out on this because you're not in the shot. You must save your energy. I had no clue about any of that. So, I just kept thinking, I better do from one to ten, I better be at ten each time or it is not gonna work."

Pape loved making up the action on the bridge. "That was guerrilla filmmaking. When we were up on the bridge. When we were out on the girders running around and I'm playing with the lights. They wanted to put a guy wire or something for safety because they didn't have CGI [computer-generated images] in those days. They couldn't wipe it out on a computer or whatever, do it on a green screen. And because I was an idiot in those days, they caught me on camera just jumping up on the cables and swinging around saying, 'Let's just do it!' Those scenes where I'm out there on the lights playing around. I'm literally three hundred feet above the water in March and April with no safety net," he said.

Joe Cali remembers feeling ill during the shoot and Travolta had an unusual response. "I think John, being a Scientologist and all that, he would do some funny things, like one night, I had a sore throat. He goes, 'You have a withhold.' I go, 'What the fuck do you mean I have a withhold?' And he's telling me if I figure out what secret I'm keeping, my sore throat is gonna go away," he recalls with a laugh. "He was great. But, yeah, the bridge was a trip," he adds.

What many didn't know was that Shawn Hausman (the son of Mike Hausman, who was the production manager and in his first PA gig) has his own memory of filming at the bridge. "It was a night shoot. You know? We did quite a few night shoots, and that's like an experience to do when you're young, and it's like you're up all night and everything. I remember for that night shoot; I smoked a joint with a couple a couple of PAs, and we got a little bit high. But there was angel dust In the weed, and we didn't know!"

He adds, "We were so fucked up. And we're up all night closing off the bridge." I asked him if he remembers how cold it was, and he claims he honestly cannot recall because he was so "out of it." I brought up this story with Cali, who told me "All-night shoots? Where the hair and makeup guys had cocaine. It was the seventies! I wouldn't go near anything if it was a lot of dialogue, and we were running around. Fuck that."

In *I'll Be in My Trailer*, Badham recalls a scene at the bridge where Barry Miller's character Bobby C. is contemplating suicide. He is nineteen with a pregnant girlfriend he must marry. He is out on a beam, weeping and out of sorts. In the story, Tony is walking out to bring him in. To achieve this, and they had only one night for it, the stunt double held a camera to shoot the scene wearing Tony's suit. At the end, he walks on his hands and knees to reach Bobby C., who slips and falls into the water.

When Travolta heard that the stuntman was crawling, he said to reshoot it with the stuntman walking upright to Bobby C., because Tony would *never* crawl. The actor was furious and went to his trailer. Eventually Travolta got his way and Badham learned that it is always better to work out a scene with the actor's participation.

Badham also had a lesson in reining in his temper when dealing with Pape. There were two separate times when Pape would stop a rehearsal to ask where his close-up was. The first time he took the actor aside and assured him he would be in the shot. The second time, he lost his temper and sarcastically said, "Gee, Paul, you're right. I guess we don't need you in this scene, after all. You can go home. I'll give your lines to the other guys."

Pape swallowed his anger and went ahead with the scene, in which he was given a close-up, as planned. Badham told me, "I mean, he did it a couple of times, and the first time, you know, I said, 'We'll get there. Don't worry. We have to do it, but we're starting over your shoulder. But we'll come around to you.' And I totally understood. This is a guy's first movie, and he's thinking that he's gonna get left out. And then the second time he did it was in the hospital.

"When Bruce Ornstein's in the hospital bed, and we're shooting over him. Again, we're gonna come around and get him, but he raised the same question, and it had a bit of an edge to it. And I had to say, 'Look, I know a lot of directors that would be very angry about this. Because I could leave you out, which I'm not gonna do,'" Badham said.

"Anyway, we laughed about it later. And every time I've acted in some of my own films, that stresses me out so much that I can almost hardly remember my name," he adds.

Pape responded with, "He was definitely tired by that point. And I think he misunderstood something that I was saying. I will always appreciate Johnny. He gave me my break, you know. So, we don't agree on the interpretation of what he wrote in the book. Although I think he was very deferential to me, because he said he learned something from it. I just don't remember it happening quite the way he said. I had a wonderful experience with Johnny. He was very good about letting us all do our thing and, find our characters, and just find our way, and he was very open to improv."

Wherever they shot, the movie attracted crowds, which the cast said added to the atmosphere. Sometimes they sounded aggressive, but they wanted to make sure their culture would not be mocked.

Pape talked about coming out of the trailer and seeing kids everywhere and putting the actors on notice. "'You're doing a movie about us here. You understand? You're gonna do us right. No fucking around.' They literally owned the picture before it was even out because they knew it was about them. They knew it was about the neighborhood," he says, laughing.

Ornstein felt a little more nervous about the outdoor shoots. "When we would shoot scenes on the street, there were a lot of people from Brooklyn. Young men who were very, I suppose, envious. And they would be catcalling out to us and cursing on the sidelines, and they had to get police barricades and all that other stuff. And we had to ignore that as we were shooting. So, it was kind of insane. I mean, John was a huge star. It was wild."

Karen Lynn Gorney felt the female fans helped bring a sexual energy to the set. She described it in *Vanity Fair* in 2007: "All the screaming and crying, because they're sitting on their gonads." When the crowds became too much and crashed through barricades, the PAs would lock arms to try to keep the crowd at bay.

Shawn Hausman remembers, "People were insane, like, obsessed. To get John out, they had his double or something. They dress up as John coming out to his camper. But I would sneak John out the back door. And he was so patient and great with all the crowds and giving autographs." His father, Mike Hausman, said, "We had so much fun with John. We would put him in the trunk of a car, and then we would have another guy with a raincoat go another way and people would be chasing that guy."

For the most part, the first month of filming was going surprisingly well, but looming over the production early on was the health of Travolta's girlfriend, Diana Hyland, who had developed breast cancer in 1975 and thought she had recovered when she and Travolta started their relationship. Her cancer had reoccurred even though she had had a mastectomy.

About Hyland, Travolta (a year after her passing) told *Time* magazine in the April 3, 1978, issue, "There was something about her—a quality I can't define even now—that I found so appealing. It exceeded anything physical. She had every color I imagine in a person."

At the time of the diagnosis, she was starring in ABC's *Eight Is Enough* playing wife to her close friend Dick Van Patten. She had told him about having some intense backaches but other than that, she was fine with work. It was in January 1977, and because most of the cast were young (her character was a mother of eight) she kept the news mostly to herself, wearing a wig to cover the hair loss from chemotherapy. Van Patten made sure to tell her how pretty she looked.

John left for New York in mid-February and would fly out to Los Angeles every weekend to take care of her. When he got the call on March 24 that she was going to pass soon, the star left production to be with her.

Van Patten told the *Shreveport Journal* in July 1977, "We were filming our fourth episode when she had to be taken to the hospital." She explained that her cancer was terminal, and that Travolta was by her side. The cast and crew had only a few days to process the news before she was sent home.

Van Patten and his wife came over after Sunday mass to see Travolta and Hyland's parents with her as she lay dying. Unsure what to do, Van Patten brought a priest to read her last rites, even though she wasn't Catholic. Diana passed away in John's arms on March 27, 1977, at the age of forty-one.

Travolta told *Time* in the same article that he would have

married her if they had the chance. At the time, he and his sister Ellen looked into adopting Hyland's son, Zachary, but he was sent to live with his mother's family.

Travolta's trainer, Gambina, also left for the West Coast that weekend. Not to accompany John, but to attend the Academy Awards. *Rocky* was nominated for five awards that year. It would go on to win Best Picture, Best Director (John G. Avildsen), and Best Film Editing. Avildsen complained about Sylvester Stallone not earning an award for his acting or writing. (It was the year of *Network*.) Avildsen told the *Boston Globe*, "Sylvester's whole life was in the movie. It was painful when he didn't go up there [for Best Script or Best Actor]."

The date of the awards was March 28, the same day as Hyland's private funeral. Gambina was invited but did not attend, as he was already committed to the *Rocky* crew, and he had never met Diana in person. He felt uncomfortable.

Travolta headed back to New York on March 29 on a flight filled with celebrities, including Andy Warhol. The artist noted in his diary (published posthumously in 1989 as *The Andy Warhol Diaries*) that Travolta "kept going to the bathroom, coming out with his eyes bright red, drinking orange juice and liquor in a paper cup, and he put his head on a pillow and started crying. . . . I asked the stewardess why he was crying, and she said, 'death in the family' so I thought it was a mother or father, until I picked up the paper at home and found out that it was Diana Hyland who'd died of cancer at forty-one, soap opera queen, his steady date."

The cast and crew had a tremendous amount of respect for Travolta, as he always remained focused and hardworking. His character was in almost every scene, and though he was completely heartbroken, he dived into work. One of his first visitors when he came back on the set was Ornstein, who shared a love of flying with him.

"John was in his trailer by himself, and nobody wanted to talk to him, because you don't really know what to say. But I knocked on his door, and I said, 'How are you?' And that sort of formed the basis of a friendship that we had for quite a while. He not only handled that whole experience, but also just carrying a movie on his shoulders at age twenty-three is an enormous responsibility. To handle it in such an amazingly professional manner that you would not know that anything was going on with him. And, you know, it's extraordinary to think back upon the things he was going through at that time and still be able to film a movie," he told me.

Pape remembers not knowing what to say, as he himself was so young and the cast had met one another only weeks before. Losing his parents a few years later gave him a more nuanced perspective on death and dying. "We know something horrible has happened, and we certainly respected his feelings. But you don't feel that at the depth you might feel today. I lost my mother early. I lost my father when I was in my late twenties. When they died, I remember thinking my last tie to any thoughts of immortality are gone."

Pescow recalls, "He was such a pro. You could see the emotional hit. We became very good friends, and I could kind of sense when things were a little tougher for him in that sense. But, man, he just tried to power through it. And if he couldn't, he would just excuse himself and sort of deal with it."

Shawn Hausman said the crew absolutely "adored John" and felt he was really the glue that kept the production together, despite everything he had to manage at such a young age. "We were really making the movie for him. He was just such a sweetheart."

Diana would go on to win a posthumous Emmy Award for her performance in *The Boy in the Plastic Bubble*. Travolta accepted it in her honor.

When the actor returned to the set of *Saturday Night Fever*, he had a new mission. He would give the performance of his lifetime in Diana's honor. His most demanding work (the family scenes and the dancing) would be his focus.

CHAPTER 7

2001: A Brooklyn Odyssey

Once Travolta was ready to shoot his dance sequences, two locations were used. The first was the dance studio (which sadly no longer exists) where Lester Wilson and Lorraine Fields oversaw the choreography for the main leads. Gorney was very nervous about her dancing ability, so it was decided that they would start in the studio without the full cast and just a small crew to catch their scenes.

Fields made it her mission to make her terrified starlet comfortable. "It was her nerves, because I think she just really felt, sort of, 'I'm an impostor, and this is really going to show me and my dancing.' John Travolta was flowing and Gorney just wasn't as good a dancer. She could move, and if she was in our company, she would be fine. But now it's going to be put on film, and I think she just freaked out, so I had to calm her down. And I said, you got this. Just look in his eyes," according to Fields.

Wilson worked with Gorney and Travolta for all their partner dances except for the one time he claimed to be attending a fashion show. This was for the "Tango Hustle" scene, which Gorney describes as incredibly challenging in the documentary *Saturday Night Fever: The Ultimate Disco Movie*, as the partners dance side by side with an unusual count and she had to lift her leg high in the air, with Travolta who was a foot taller than her. She intones, "I defy any of you watching that scene to say that is easy!"

Fields took over this setup when Wilson was a no-show.

Martin Shakar, John Travolta, and Fran Drescher (in her movie debut), filming at the 2001 Odyssey disco. Drescher says the classic line to Travolta, "Are you as good in bed as you are on the dance floor?" *TCD/Prod.DB/Alamy Stock Photo.*

"That didn't happen often. Most of the time he was just not awake. But I would have to understand very clearly what it was that he was seeking. And if I ever needed to take over, then I would. I wouldn't be happy about it because I wasn't getting paid for that. I was just getting paid to be his assistant. But I guess that comes with the territory."

Another scene shot at the studio was between Travolta and Gorney as they prepared for the upcoming dance competition. Travolta was a big fan of Boz Scaggs, and of the song "Lowdown" in particular. They filmed their scene with the song playing in the background. Later, Boz Scaggs's manager nixed their involvement in the movie, which meant they had to shoot it again weeks later with a Tavares song. From then on, Badham learned the importance of *not* having music playing while filming.

Outside the confines of the dance studio, the biggest test would be filming at the 2001 Odyssey in Bay Ridge. Located at 802 Sixty-Fourth Street, it was purchased by Charlie Rusinak in 1955, and by the time the movie crew showed up, he had seen it go through several iterations. His daughter Denise told me, "It's the kind of business you must change with the times. At first it was a nightclub, Club 802, and it was like a supper club. And they would have a full show with an orchestra and a singer, an emcee, and a comedian. It was dinner and dancing."

She then explains that when it was transformed into a disco in 1972, "we had all the disco groups; the Village People, Harold Melvin and the Blue Notes, the Trammps, and the Spinners." This was the kind of music not played on the radio at the time. The DJs at these clubs were scouted by record companies (including RSO Records) to find the latest trends.

Alex Marchak was a regular at 2001 Odyssey and an extra in the movie. He told me, "At the time, the Odyssey was the place where people went. You know? They had all the great bands."

Charlie Rusinak dealt directly with Stigwood's office to rent the club for the filming with the understanding the crew would be updating the appearance of the club. He had only negotiated the exact amount he would lose in that time. According to Denise, "They compensated him for the loss. It wasn't really anything above that, though, because we had no idea. It really was not a lot of money. It was enough for him to cover his expenses."

As soon as location fees were known, certain people wanted in on the action. "The guys that were in control of the neighborhood had come to my dad and said that they wanted some money for this happening in Bay Ridge. That they would provide security and make sure that nothing went wrong. Right. And my dad said, 'I don't have any money to give you. What they're giving me is just enough to cover my expenses.'"

The Rusinaks found out some people do not like to be told no and went to production to ask for more money, but were told this was a small production. There was no money left in the budget. Denise remembers, "One night, we're at home, and in the middle of the night, my dad gets a phone call from the fire department. Somebody had thrown a Molotov cocktail into the club and had set a fire." Charlie Rusinak gave them the whole fee he received from RSO Productions.

Later they made up for the loss of income, but Denise emphasizes they did not become wealthy by this association. "A lot of people had assumed that our family made so much money. That really didn't happen. We did make a profit after the movie came out, and it was a success. There was a line outside every night for about a year. We had tourist buses coming from Manhattan because we had the car that John Travolta and his friends used in the movie," she said. Eventually the business died down and the club was sold.

At the time, though, it did not seem like a guaranteed success. "It wasn't a tremendous deal at the time, having a 'Sweathog' in the club," Denise explains. "We had no idea that the movie was gonna be a hit and critically acclaimed. We just thought it was gonna be some teenage B-movie. But, you know, it was fun. It was a great experience."

Getting the look of the club was another month of work, because it was a dark, dingy space with several floors. To brighten it up, aluminum foil and Christmas lights were put on the walls, and the notorious disco floor was put in supposedly because Badham saw a similar one in his hometown of Birmingham. It cost $15,000 and would become the standard at discos for years to come.

For Michael Hausman, the lights on the floor were very tricky to work with, "You had to coordinate the lights with the music. As I recall, they just flashed on and off, and sometimes the red ones went on and the blue ones went on and the green one. So, we just had to make sure that every day, the right spot of the music was the right spot on the floor," he told me.

Donna Pescow was impressed with the little touches. "I remember them putting aluminum foil on the walls, and I thought, That's so interesting. Ralf D. Bode, who is no longer with us, was the director of photography, and he wanted some kind of glitzy bounce-back or however one would phrase it. Everything looked even bigger, better, and disco-ey," she said.

Director John Badham loved the look they created, "Oh, it was a gas. Absolutely. You could see all the lights, which was a delight for Bode. We had brought the floor in. We found a place in way downtown New York that would make these flooring units in, like, four-by-eight units. We said, we needed something that's twenty feet wide and forty feet long."

Hausman noted in the 2010 documentary *Saturday Night Fever: The Inside Story*, "I remember it being complicated and always having to work on a small budget. But Bode had the idea of crinkling up tinfoil and putting it all over the walls. I think it really made that place look special."

Marchak was impressed with the new floor. "Then they put that floor in, and it changed the whole look of the whole place." However, many people found the smoke effects to be overkill. According to Marchak, "They took tubs, like, washtubs people would wash clothes in. And put dry ice in there and just throw some water and you would see like it's smoking around."

The smoke effect upset screenwriter Norman Wexler, because he could not remember any club having this. Badham said, "And I was just arrogant enough to say, 'Norman, they will after this movie,' and they did."

Badham also pictured the scene where the entire cast dances along to "Night Fever" with a smoke effect. "At the beginning, just coming around their feet. By the end of the song, we would completely bury the entire dance company in dry ice, which was great. It happened nicely, but when we finished, we'd have to open the stage doors and get all that stuff out of there because you couldn't breathe otherwise," he told me.

Pescow recalls, "Someone said it was frankincense. But they were using it with some kind of pump, like a thing that a couple of guys would carry. The floor was plastic or whatever that would be on the floor, and this was damp. So once the smoke started to either dissipate or once they had a ton of it on there, the floor became incredibly slippery. Oh, my goodness. It looked like the Ice Capades out there!"

Bruce Ornstein recalls, "So, the disco is very crowded. God knows what they're using for smoke. I just know that everyone was short of breath, and they must have oxygen units outside for us to breathe. I'm surprised that I'm still alive and have clear lungs and don't have emphysema. It was not a great environment."

Paul Pape told me, "Yeah. I remember it was bad. They didn't tell us if it was unhealthy stuff that they were using. I'm still alive, so I guess I survived it, but I don't remember being told that it was toxic anywhere."

"So much of it," Lorraine Fields describes it. "It gets in your throat, and it feels like you're smoking a fake cigarette. It was just weird. And getting it right and matching it with the shot, it was crazy."

Frankie Verroca was an extra who managed to be at the club for the entire shoot (the crew would let people go if they were on camera too often). He enjoyed the gig but remembers it was tough work. "It was so hot. I remember that because they'd closed the doors, and we'd be in there all day from early morning till seemed like six in the evening. And we would be doing all the scenes."

Marchak remembers, "It was hot as hell in there, because the air conditioning made too much noise. So, they couldn't have it on while they were filming these dance scenes, they had to shut them off. And it would get hot, as you can imagine."

Occasionally, the crew needed to open the doors to clear out the disco. Ornstein thinks he might complain under the same circumstances now, but he is sanguine about the movie's disco scenes. "It was a kind of a disgusting environment. But, you know, it was fun!"

Actor Adrienne King, who would become a "scream queen" playing "Alice" in the first two *Friday the 13th* movies, was a background dancer who got the gig with a few of her friends. Every day for weeks they would take the subway out to Bay Ridge in their disco gear and dance from morning to night. The smog would cling to their skin so much, it was coated on their arms. She told me, "It was so thick by the end of the day, we could peel a layer of grime. I still have this visual of one of the dancers on the subway going home. 'So, look at this.' He's, like, sliding a layer off his arm!"

Badham explains how they really made the smoke effects happen. "We found our special-effects guy, on the floor, passed out. Because he had to be down on his hands and knees. The way we had to work with dry ice is you take a big wash bucket and you fill it with hot water and keep it hot. You put the dry ice in there, and it starts immediately melting and pumping out smoke, then blow it around. As crude as it could be, but totally effective. And our prop guy, there's Jimmy Mazzola, passed out on the ground."

Keeping the crowd going between takes and featured in the film is Monti Rock III, who plays the DJ and was a friend of RSO president Freddie Gershon, who told me, "For the purpose of being behind a DJ's booth. You don't even have to write a script to him and just keep talking nonstop. I was his lawyer.

Well, he made the role, and it became a bigger role in the in the later stage version."

Ron Stigwood used to hang out with DJ Monti Rock III, as Rock was worried he would be assaulted if some of the locals found out he was gay. Ron told me, "Monti was a friend of Freddie Gershon's, and we became very good friends. He was very flamboyantly gay, and being where he was in Brooklyn at the time we were filming, he was a little bit nervous. I'm Australian. I hang out with anybody and talk to anybody. It doesn't bother me. And Monti was just a fun guy."

Lester Wilson and Lorraine Fields choreographed not only the cast but also the extras who were used in the film. Fields remembers, "There was so much dancing interspersed into everything. Lester had to get the background dancing together to kind of get them moving a certain kind of away at certain parts in the film because so much of it took place in the club."

Denny Dillon, who plays shy Doreen, who just wants to pat Tony's forehead with a tissue, thrived under Wilson's cues for doing the hustle. "Lester had names for everything. You know, 'You reach for the money, like you are on the bus, and you are putting it in the change thing.' He had a visual image for every single thing you did. And it was so beautiful. It was fun. So that brought us all together. It was like, there weren't lines in that scene, but we were learning the dance," she said.

According to Lorraine, "Yeah, he gave them reason to move beyond. Sometimes you give someone a dance move, they're like, 'Oh, I don't really think I can dance here.' But you can walk up the step, you can walk down the step. You can turn around when you hear your name, and you can shrug your shoulder when you don't want anyone to touch you. I mean, he just used the language that they understood to create the movement in their body. And it was wonderful to work with them. They were open to it. They were really into it."

For her big scene with Travolta, Dillon credits her acting coach for giving her a backstory for her character. "Mary Tarcai, my beautiful acting teacher, had coached me on that scene. I think that's why it's so good. And when we're in the middle of that plaintive, vulnerable sweet moment, Travolta blew some cigarette smoke in my face. He was so fabulous. I couldn't ask for more," she recalls.

She was also impressed with how professional he was during his first starring role. "I was knocked out, first of all, by what a mature actor he was. He handled the tragedy of Diana Hyland's death. He went to LA, went to the funeral, and I believed they were very much in love. Then he came back. No moods. I was knocked out by his maturity."

Denise was only sixteen at the time but had been dancing since she "could stand on my two feet." Though upset that she was not cast as the door check girl (that would go to Wexler's teenage daughter Erica), it was exciting for her to watch the different segments created by Wilson and Fields. Asked about Wilson, she said, "He was very fun. Very nice guy. Very high energy, enthusiastic, positive. A lot of the extras really were not dancers. So, to just try to get people to look like they knew what they were doing must have been a challenge."

Donna Pescow agrees that Wilson had a gift for helping dance newbies feel comfortable. "The guy was a genius. And a beautiful soul. Just an incredible man. I mean, he took a bunch of us who had no clue and felt like we were gonna just make complete asses of ourselves and made us confident. And made us good dancers."

Adrienne King remembers the grueling process of having to learn the steps quickly and be perfect for every take, but that

Wilson made it a fun experience. "When you have someone who's that high about creating something and knowing that all the elements of the perfect storm were around you. You could tell this man was ready to take off, the same way John was."

She compared being in *Saturday Night Fever* with filming the first *Friday the 13th* movie. "There's a different feeling sometimes when you get on a set and think, 'Wow, this is special. This is something extraordinary,' you know? It was his energy that was just pulsating. The fact that you saw John Travolta, who you knew from *Welcome Back, Kotter*. And I think that's all I knew him from at that point."

She adds, "You knew he was charming. But did you know he could dance? That he has this kind of talent? So, I think we all felt that we were together as a unit. Even though we were background dancers, we were part of the entire picture."

Pape remembers that in rehearsal, the actors toyed with the idea of having a scene where just the Faces danced in a scene, but it was quickly dropped. He felt that by the time the club scenes were shot, the cast had jelled so well together that their chemistry was caught on camera. He said, "We were completely into our characters by that point. What started out as somewhat foreign to us over time became more familiar."

Pescow affirms this. "The last part to be filmed, I'd say it was the dance. And we were in rehearsal up to that point. So, we really were given a lot of time to make it work well."

Joe Cali explains why he was wearing sunglasses in the dance scene. "When we shot that, the fight scene was the night before, and John punched me in the face. I tell him, 'You thought I was too much competition.' He laughed. So, he poked my eye, and I ended up wearing sunglasses in all the dance scenes because of the smoke and the light, I couldn't keep my eyes open."

Ornstein had his own ideas on how his character would

dance. "We worked on dancing for a couple of weeks, and I don't like the live dancing. I just couldn't get it, but I also felt that Gus was not among the best dancers who were there. So, it all worked. Convenient choice, but yeah."

For everyone present, it was a chance to listen to the Bee Gees' music in its earliest form. During breaks, the music was played on a cassette to have the actors and extras get to know the beats of each song. Fields was especially fond of "You Should Be Dancing." She says, "That's disco. And that's what took off. That's what everyone started doing. They had this backbeat—it was like a whole new song playing in the background against the vibrato in the foreground."

Martin Shakar played Tony's brother Frank Jr., who is leaving the priesthood. He felt somewhat out of place in the club scenes, as he was older than most of the cast and a family man. He remembers he was not hip to the disco music scene. "I'm too much of a square, I guess." But he was impressed with the spectacle. "It was great. I enjoyed listening to the Bee Gees and watching the dancing in the club. I was more of an audience, really."

Frank Jr. is experiencing freedom hanging out with the Faces as a relief from being in the stifling house with his disappointed family. He wears a sweater and looks more middle-of-the-road than his table cohorts. King was placed near Shakar as he walked into the club, which gave them the opportunity to chat during the multiple takes. "We talked quite a bit. He was so sweet. In one scene, he comes in and he stops and he talks to me. My big screen moment," she recalls with a smile.

Barry Miller's character is struggling with his personal life. His girlfriend is pregnant, is Catholic, and wants to get married right away. He tells Frank Jr. at one point, "My girlfriend, she loves the taste of communion wafers." The now ex-priest informs him he cannot give him permission for an abortion, and the mood changes as Fran Drescher approaches their table.

In her 1996 autobiography *Enter Whining*, Drescher, who plays Connie and says the immortal line "Are you as good in bed as you are on the dance floor?" describes being on set and watching Travolta slumped in a corner in between takes. It had been only a few weeks since his girlfriend's death, and sometimes he felt exposed and depressed in the environment.

King noticed that sometimes the actor seemed distant but never unfriendly. "I now know he was going through a lot. I did see him sitting off to the side, but actors do that, you know, when they want to get into their 'therapy center.' But I felt from him an incredible amount of energy and charisma."

After watching a few people approach him with words of encouragement and him waving them off, Drescher boldly walked over and said, "Whatever happened to 'let's go on with the show'? So what if *you're* tired? So what if you're run down? Maybe they *will* have to check you in to a hospital for exhaustion in the end, but right now I expect you to act like the star that you are, and finish the scene, then we can all go home!"

These were the words he needed to get into the mood for presenting his big solo. This was the culmination for him to show he could dance. That he deserved this part and could carry a picture. Now was the moment after all those dance lessons, calisthenics, rehearsals, all the miles run, and giving up junk food for five months. He had been through so much and he was ready to shine.

Lorraine Fields had the job of helping him stay on beat by pointing out the steps out of camera. "My most exciting time was when John Travolta did his solo and I had to choreograph the dolly. The guy that was on the dolly, I had to let him know when to go in, and then I had to give him counts of when to come out. So that we moved with John as he went upstage, we moved the crane, the dolly, into the dance floor, and as he was coming from the back of the stage to the front of the stage, I would have to count them down," she recalls.

Travolta having to act in every scene and be the best dancer in the room meant reserving his energy for the camera. Fields helped him. "He said, 'If you just do it in front of me for continuity, so I can remember.' And sometimes I would just point, okay, now you go that way. And then he would remember. And he could do it without thinking about it. You wouldn't see, 'What's in my brain? What's the next step?' As opposed to just doing it like he's freestyling. Yeah, it was fun."

Lorraine also gives credit to Wilson for some of the magical moments from the solo. "It is totally iconic. Totally. There are steps that people still use today. That whole pointing up to the ceiling and pointing across your hip, which was definitely Lester's creation. And the stopping in the middle and then picking it back up, that whole thing, that was totally Lester."

Travolta was obsessed with getting every move perfect, and the crowd loved it. King described him as a "racehorse ready to go." Cali, a lover of dance himself, told me what he observed while they filmed his solo. "Just the shape that he was in and the ability to do that was amazing, and I saw it when we first went into the rehearsal hall. I thought I could dance. Not even close!"

The star was so excited about his performance, he was eager to check out the footage in the edit bay. This was when he discovered that his entire solo was shot in closeups. No shots of his feet or legs. The jumps and splits—nowhere to be seen. Travolta was livid.

Erica Wexler was hanging out in the room when Travolta bolted. "I think it wasn't just editing. He just didn't he like the footage and felt it was from a bad angle."

Travolta demanded that Badham reshoot the sequence and was told there was no budget for this. That he had to accept this was the version of the solo people will see. Jimmy Gambina told the star, who was seething in his trailer, to get in his car right away. They were leaving for parts unknown until his solo was shot correctly.

Gambina told me, "So, I kidnapped Travolta (it was on a Friday), and we went out to the Montauk Yacht Club, at the end of the island. I called the office and said, 'Okay. You're gonna do the dance solo?' And they are yelling at me, 'Where are you?' I said, 'Are you gonna do the dance solo?' No. Bam. I hung up the phone. That was on a Saturday. And then Sunday, I called the office again. 'Are you gonna do the dance solo?' No." He called every few hours for the entire weekend, demanding on Travolta's behalf, but the production office would not budge.

Gambina was just as angry that they did not seem to appreciate how much work went into getting the actor in top shape. "We trained for months and rehearsed with Lester Wilson and his assistant. And Lester Wilson appreciated me having the guy in such great condition that he was able to do things that he ordinarily can't do with most actors. And I told John Badham you're just messing with him as an actor."

They were not alone on Montauk. Gambina told me, "I got this girl that he knew from Broadway. She played the bartender in the movie [actor Ellen March] who was a friend of John's since his Broadway days. The other girl I knew was Liza Minnelli's backup singer. We had fun!"

By Monday, Badham capitulated and told them they could have as many days as they needed. "We chartered a plane. He flew into Manhattan, and everything went smoothly. Everybody went to dailies the next five days, and the girls were going,

'Man, this guy's hot!' And everybody went crazy for the dance sequence," he remembers.

With that scene sorted out, there was an even bigger issue with filming Gorney at 2001 Odessey with a crowd of the cast and crew. In the dance studio, she felt she was in a safe space, but now that she had a big audience, she was so overcome with nerves she broke out in hives.

Lorraine Fields recalls, "By the day of filming, when she had to do her duet, her nerves got the better part of her, and she broke out in fever blisters. I told her, 'Act like you're in the rehearsal hall and let it flow.' But it just really got to her. But the more we did that [the more we talked to her], the more she stopped being so stiff and so nervous. We just kept talking her through it, and she got through it, right?"

Denise Rusinak, who runs her own dance company, bluntly states, "Did you know she had a dance double? Because we were all clapping and watching those dance scenes. The couples, all of us were on the sides, you know, up on the stage, up in the balcony, whooping and popping for them. We were there for the whole thing. She had a double with the same dress on, same hair."

Frankie Verroca observed, "She was a terrible dancer. I mean, I hate to say it, when I was there watching it, I was like, 'Oh, my God.' Her body was so stiff, period." Michael Hausman was impressed with Travolta's work, but of Gorney's, he said, "She was Badham's girlfriend at the time. And I won't say she couldn't dance, but I will say she had two left feet."

Cali noticed the difference in ability between Gorney and the double. "Karen came in, and she had a relationship with Badham. And it was very weird. They had to bring in this French girl who was amazing. I forgot her name. She was the dance double. Oh, my God. Was she fucking good! She was incredible."

Denise affirms, "I mean, obviously, the way they film it, they had her do it and the double do it. So, any of the fancy stuff in the legs and the twirling, they don't show her face. I mean, she looked like her enough, by the way they edited it. But, yeah, that wasn't her. She couldn't do that. She can never do that."

Marchak observed, "You know, because if you see them, when they're practicing. Right? He's the one that really has the moves. She looked just like a mannequin, really. Maybe just moving around a little bit."

Fields says that Badham tried to be as encouraging as possible for Gorney. "I think he just was her cheerleader and said, 'You can do it!' And it was a great opportunity for her as an actress. I think her acting was spot-on, but it was hard for it to translate the same way with her dancing."

The first time Tony sees Stephanie on the dance floor, she is moving to a salsa beat, and if one views 2017's director's cut in 4K, it is glaring how there is a double to cover for Gorney. So, it was decided for the big competition scene, which occurs at the end of the movie, that they would use a slower, more romantic piece to demonstrate how close the characters had become.

Badham told me how they came to that decision. "We picked something slow and romantic that we knew they could pull off beautifully. And then, when they get announced as the winners, it's clearly a fixed job. You know, it's a rigged election. He's just gonna give it to the Hispanic couple because he thinks they're the best. So that was a, you know, good twist."

Fields lived in Brooklyn at the time but not in Bay Ridge. She could feel the lack of diversity in the crowd and how unwelcome "outsiders" were. "It was like a foreign country to me, right? Everyone is talking with this accent, and John Travolta came out, they would call him the name from *Welcome Back, Kotter*. Barbarino!"

Fields remembers the disco contests that happened around New York, and even though many places were unofficially segregated, "African Americans went into that neighborhood because there is a dance contest, and it doesn't matter where the dance contest is. Great dancers are coming for the money to win." The prize in the movie is $500, which, adjusted for inflation, equals $2,500 in 2025. In the film we see a Black and Hispanic couple compete against Tony and Stephanie. Denise was impressed with their skills. "I mean, the other couples who danced in the contest against Travolta, they were clearly way better. They were phenomenal. I mean, as a dancer, I was like, these people are killing it!"

Badham described the competition between the dancers, "In shaping the script, I've got Travolta watching these people dancing, and then he and Karen come on. And there was no way that we were gonna have them dance the same kind of high-energy athletic thing, because they were gonna look terrible compared to these other two couples."

The Black couple in the competition were friends of Wilson and Fields. Geneva Vivino (whose professional name was Karen Burke) and Winston DeWitt Hemsley were Broadway veterans. Hemsley appeared in *A Chorus Line* and Vivino was in *Raisin* and *Chicago*. She remembers her first thoughts entering the club. "The floor had those stupid lights that lit up underneath you. It's a weird place. And it was dark in there. Not really much light."

Wilson choreographed all the couples who competed in the contest and kept his trickier moves for the "competition." According to Vivino, "Winston and I also were the same height. He had a long torso, and I had a short torso, which means my legs went over his head. So, it was difficult for us, but it was fun, because then we just did it."

The Hispanic couple shown in the film, Adrienne Framet (who is actually French) and Joseph Pugliese (born in San Juan), was also part of the friend community of Wilson, Vivino, and

Hemsley. Though each was offered the opportunity to hang around for other scenes, all declined. None were interested in being background extras but they enjoyed the experience.

Across the street, Charlie Rusinak owned a warehouse, where the actors hung out between takes. Denise loved this part of the experience. "They had rented out the warehouse for all the actors and the extras to hang out until we went onto set. So, we were basically back and forth all day long."

She continues, "We had breakfast there. We had lunch there, sometimes dinner. And we would just basically sit, hang out. There were tables and chairs. We would play cards, and the Faces were with us. The only ones that didn't hang out were Travolta and Gorney."

Drescher impressed everyone with her down-to-earth manner. Denise told me, "Fran Drescher was with us all the time. She was a hoot. She was so much fun. Nice, vivacious, friendly, and funny, exactly like the person she plays."

Cali enjoyed this hang time as well. "Oh, Fran Drescher was grand. Denny Dillon was really funny, too. Oh, my God. She was great. I loved her."

King remembers the incredible amounts of food available. "I'm surprised we did not gain weight because they must have known that we've got to let them sit down and feed them something. So, I do remember there was a ton of food on the set. Of course, it was downtime. So, what do you do during the downtime? You eat."

After the movie came out, the club was successful until the proliferation of disco madness ended. Charlie Rusinak passed away in 1983 and his family sold 2001 Odyssey in 1985. In 1987, under the new leadership by Jay Rizzo, the building was turned into a gay nightclub called Spectrum, but it never quite took off.

Former bouncer Vito Bruno noticed that the original floor

Lester Wilson, photographed in Germany, 1969. *United Archives GmbH/Alamy Stock Photo.*

Five-foot-tall Jimmy Gambina between Carl Weathers and Sylvester Stallone in 1976's *Rocky*. *TCD/Prod.DB/Alamy Stock Photo.*

Didi Conn and David Shire in London, 2019. Conn co-starred with Travolta in *Grease*, and Shire wrote the score for *Saturday Night Fever*.
Stills Press/Alamy Stock Photo.

Harper Lee, the author of *To Kill a Mockingbird*, and child actress Mary Badham (younger sister of director John Badham) on the set of the movie in 1962. *Everett Collection Historical/ Alamy Stock Photo.*

The Bee Gees on the set of *Sgt. Pepper's Lonely Hearts Club Band* in 1978. The film would tank at the box office. A rare loss for producer Robert Stigwood in the late 1970s. *Moviestore Collection Ltd./ Alamy Stock Photo.*

John Badham and
Karen Lynn Gorney in 1978.
ZUMA Press Inc./Alamy Stock Photo.

John Travolta warming up
at the 2001 Odyssey disco
during filming in 1977.
*Photo courtesy of dancer
Alex Marchak.*

Barry Diller, the chairman and CEO of Paramount Pictures from 1974 to 1984. This photo was taken at the Metropolitan Opera in New York City in 2009. *David Shankbone/Creative Commons Collection.*

John Travolta with his *Welcome Back, Kotter* costars at the 2011 TV Land Awards. From left: Ellen Travolta (John's older sister), Gabe Kaplan, Marcia Strassman, Travolta, Robert Hegyes, and Lawrence Hilton-Jacobs. *Zuma Press, Inc./ Alamy Stock Photo.*

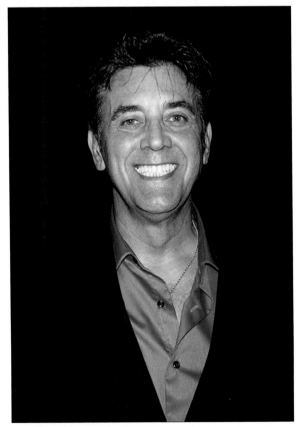

Deney Terrio from *Dance Fever* has been an active ambassador of the disco movement for fifty years. *WENN Rights Ltd./ Alamy Stock Photo.*

Five Teddy Boys Between Dances, June 1956. Not many people know that the author Nik Cohn was inspired by the teddy boys of his youth in Dublin for the Faces in the movie. *Smith Archive/Alamy Stock Photo.*

Pamela Marchant and Nik Cohn, 1968. Marchant (known as "Arfur") was actually from Montreal and was asked by Cohn to pretend she was mute in order to hide her accent.
The Who wrote "Pinball Wizard" based on her skill at the game. *Edwin Sampson/ANL/Shutterstock.*

The Who in 1975's *Tommy*. The main character (played by singer Roger Daltrey) is a deaf, mute, and blind pinball champion and was inspired by Arfur. *Pictorial Press Ltd./Alamy Stock Photo.*

Robert Stigwood in 1972. *Allen Waren/Creative Commons Attribution.*

JoJo Smith Studio business card, circa 1977. Smith began his Broadway career in a revival of *West Side Story* in 1964. His family continues performing and teaching dance to this day.

TRAMMPS

The Trammps, 1976. The band was uncertain how the song "Disco Inferno" would perform on a pop soundtrack. They played at the real 2001 Odyssey disco several times before the movie was filmed there.
Records/Alamy Stock Photo.

John Travolta and Karen Lynn Gorney in his famous pose and her infamous red dress.
AF Archive/Alamy Stock Photo.

Don Campbell of the Lockers in 1975.
Reprinted with permission from his son,
Dennis Danehy.

Adrienne King, a dancer at the
2001 Odyssey disco and star of the first
Friday the 13th movie, models her own
Saturday Night (the original title of the movie) T-shirt.
Photo courtesy of Adrienne King.

Freddie Gershon, lawyer and former president of the Robert Stigwood Group, at the Tony Eve Cocktail Party in 2012. *WENN Rights Ltd./Alamy Stock Photo.*

David Bowie in 1973 as Ziggy Stardust, a character partly inspired by writer Nik Cohn's lead character in his first novel, 1967's *I Am Still the Greatest Says Johnny Angelo*.
Roger Bamber/Alamy Stock Photo.

Lenny's Pizzeria in Bay Ridge, the site of the opening credits, 2021. It closed in 2024.
Author photo.

The home used for the Manero family scenes, 2021. *Author photo.*

Zack Reed and his partner, Lester Wilson, in 1986, when Wilson worked as the choreographer for singer Luther Vandross's world tour. *Photo courtesy of Zack Reed.*

Singer Yvonne Elliman, who worked with Robert Stigwood on *Jesus Christ Superstar* and had a hit with "If I Can't Have You" on the *Saturday Night Fever* soundtrack. *Photo courtesy of Alan Mercer.*

was up for auction. This was in 2005, and the event was sparsely attended. The twenty-four-by-sixteen-foot piece of Hollywood history went for $4,000, which began a legal battle. Rizzo claimed that Bruno had no right to purchase the floor and it belonged to him. In the end, Bruno won the right to keep the floor and waited over ten years before putting it up for auction at Profiles in History, an auction house based in California. In 2012, the floor was featured in a disco-themed episode of the television show *Glee*.

With great fanfare, in 2017 the floor was sold for $1.2 million to an anonymous buyer who some claim was Travolta himself. (He denies this.) In 2024, Julien's Auctions and TCM held an auction for the same floor, which went for $325,000 to yet another anonymous buyer.

Outside the club, the film had several dramatic scenes that tested all the actors and crew. In the next chapter, we delve into one of the most controversial scenes from the film and how conflict was managed during production.

CHAPTER 8

Annette

Who among us doesn't know an Annette? Or has been Annette in a romantic situation? Her very presence exudes neediness and insecurity. When Donna Pescow first auditioned for the part, Avildsen was still the director. Her agent, Gloria Dolan, worrying she would freeze under the pressure trying out for any part bigger than a cameo, told her it was for a small part.

After several auditions, and still not having a full script in her possession by the time she found she had gotten the part, Donna had just a few days before the movie started production. Her new costar, Karen Lynn Gorney (who had a full script), said she had a substantial role that the audience would root for—as the woman forever mooning over Tony Manero and his complete indifference. If you have ever had an unrequited crush, her performance feels extra real.

There are two powerful scenes for Pescow's character of Annette in *Saturday Night Fever*. Okay, two powerful scenes and one that was genuinely funny. First the funny. She and Tony (John Travolta) are at the stripper bar included in the 2001 Odyssey nightclub. Annette is warm for his form, but he ignores her every chance he can. Director John Badham encouraged Pescow's improvisation. Travolta first refuses to light her cigarette. Then, as she tries to talk to him, he watches a stripper.

Donna Pescow as Annette on location in 1977. She graduated from
the American Academy of Dramatic Arts in 1975, and *Saturday Night
Fever* was her first film. *TCD/Prod.DB/Alamy Stock Photo.*

Pescow recalls to me, "She really did dance in that bar—I
think. I am not 100 percent, but I am pretty sure that was a real
gig. Then there is a scene, there is a moment, where he leaves,
and I look down at my dress to say, 'Yeah. I got the goods.' You
know that kind of deal. And it was one of the first things we
filmed, and I was kind of nervous about suggesting it, but he
[Badham] said, 'No. Go for it!'"

About Badham, she told me, "When a director trusts an
actor that way, it is kind of like this incredibly great permission to
really take a chance and do something. And if it does not work, it
does not. But if it does, it just adds that whatever, you know, little
additional sense of reality. I loved working with John."

The second is when Tony meets Annette at the dance studio to tell her he is not going to enter the disco contest with
her. That, in fact, he is picking someone else (Stephanie) to be
his partner. The look of devastation on her face, with her glit-
tery makeup and doe eyes, is enough to make anyone ache in
empathy.

The most difficult scene to watch is when Donna Pescow's
character Annette is raped by two of her "friends"—Joey and

Double J. After being rejected by Tony Manero, the only man she is attracted to in Bay Ridge, she loses her sense of self and takes drugs to cope. The pills that Joey gives her leave her basically incapacitated and she is sexually assaulted in the back of the Faces' car. Though she screams no, there is no way to stop this violence.

Tony does not participate, though he is attempted to do the same to Stephanie after the disco contest went awry. He provides Annette no comfort and instead calls her a "pig." It is gut-wrenching chiefly because due to Pescow's incredible performance, the audience genuinely likes her. She is in love with a selfish man who will never appreciate her.

At one point he asks her (in the PG version) if she "wants to be a good girl or a pig?" She replies, "I don't know. Both?" But in this world, she is stuck. If she doesn't get married and have babies soon, she will be looked upon as an old maid. A horrible fate for nice Catholic girls. She believes she is aiming high with Tony because of his good looks, completely ignoring that the man (and his friends) are misogynistic creeps who barely see women (even family members) as people.

The original Cohn *New York* article featured a section where the Faces are chasing around Bay Ridge to find a man they suspect tried to rape Vincent's younger sister. Maybe this is why Wexler included these scenes in the movie?

The use of rape as a plot point, one of the most awful ways to put a woman in danger, was common in movies and films for decades but not shown due to the Hays Code. The Motion Picture Production Code ran from 1936 to the 1960s and was created to appease moralistic church communities that worried movies were a danger to the decorum of the American audience. Sexual assault in films may be implied on camera but never shown graphically until the mores of the late 1960s and 1970s made a dramatic change. As cursing and nudity became more commonplace in R-rated films, violence became more graphic.

In the 1980s, it seemed the most common way to put an actress's character in danger was to have her stalked, raped, or given a breast cancer diagnosis. When CBS TV's *Lonesome Dove* in 1989 was criticized on a panel for its violence and sexual assault scenes, CBS Entertainment president Kim LeMasters quickly joked, "Well, they were tasteful rapes!" (He immediately apologized.)

Annette's assault is not shown in the PG version, which was released a few months after the premiere, or in any of the versions shown on TV for decades. For folks raised on the PG version, it comes as a horrific shock. The character is clearly saying no as the Faces take turns abusing her. No one helps her, and she is left to ride off in the car with her tormentors to the next scene, on the Verrazzano-Narrows Bridge (where Barry Miller's character dies by suicide).

Some pages between the rape and Tony's reaction are omitted from the original script. Is the lesson here that you cannot trust anyone? That drugs are bad? Ladies—all men are predators? With Pescow's expressive eyes expressing shock, we feel her pain and regret. All she wanted was for Tony to treat her with some kindness. To see her as a potential mate.

I asked several cast members about the scene, and reactions vary from "That's how it really was then" to "She was willing to do anything to have sex with Tony." All who work with Pescow speak to her intelligence, professionalism, and bravery.

When I mentioned the use of intimacy coordinators in films to Badham, he said, "I do not need that to know how to be sensitive to people's feelings. It is overkill, but you sit down and you talk about it with the actors involved. What are we gonna see, how can we do this, and how can we do this in respect,

Donna? We were not gonna see any nudity here, which is probably the first big relief on her mind." This being Pescow's first movie must have been a dicey place for her and what she feels she can and cannot consent to on set.

For the blocking, Badham asked Pescow, "Would it be okay if Double J. (Paul Pape) puts his hand on your covered breast?" According to Badham, she told him, "John, would you do it instead of Double J.? I think of you as more like my dad." Which the director did, though he thought it was a weird analogy.

Donna told me playing Annette was a challenge because of the desperation that came from her home life. "She wanted to get married and stay in the neighborhood and live close to her parents and have holidays and, you know, someday she would work at a bakery. I don't think she had any career goals. Her goal was to get married and have a family. And I think this was sort of how she saw Tony. This was the guy she wanted and all of that. And it just spun out of control."

The filming was a closed set at an abandoned garage. According to Pescow, "I must thank John Badham for this. You know, it was a closed set. Only people that had to be there were there. And I was obviously very nervous about the whole thing. And being friendly with Paul [Pape] and Joe [Cali] was great, because I was able to express how nervous I was. Sure. And that I was also going to, you know, use all my method-acting training, and really dive in."

"I do not really think you see anything physically; I think you see it all emotionally. Yes. And, you know, no. I think that's part of why that is so powerful, because it is raw, but it is emotionally raw, not as much as it is physically," she adds while also debating Badham on set whether her character was a virgin before this takes place. (Pescow thinks not.)

Badham did not want to film the scene but claims Stigwood

would not budge on the issue. He told me, "I was just not happy about having to do it that way. But Robert really wanted to get the feeling that that this girl had been abused, and I said, 'Okay. I am gonna do ninety-nine percent of it sort of from Travolta's point of view. Him looking in the rearview mirror and not concentrate on what is happening to her.' Just the sound of her crying is plenty."

He had filmed other sexual assault scenes in his career, but Badham had a policy. "You just have to sit and talk with the actors and find out what they're comfortable with, and if they're not comfortable with it, then you stay away from it."

Joe Cali's recollection differs from Badham's on one key thing—him placing his hand on Pescow's breast. His character wore fingerless gloves and for whatever reason, he was not on the set when Badham filmed this part of the scene.

Cali told me, "I get the word that Badham had a call out and they wanted my gloves. And I go, what does he want my fucking gloves for? The prop guy had my gloves, you know, the cutoff gloves that I was wearing. And he went into the garage, and he reshot the scene where he got on top of Donna, and he is doing that thing with her face. That is not me. Those are not my hands."

He continues, "Which made me furious. I became very close to Ralf D. Bode [the director of photography] because I wanted to be a filmmaker. And the cameraman and then Dave Rawlings, the editor, we became really close. And they kind of thought that was bullshit, too, that he should have just brought me in when he shot the scene."

I asked him why he thinks Badham did that. "Because he is a fucking asshole as far as I am concerned. I mean, you do not take an actor's part, and if you are the director and play him, however, whatever. It is just to me, it is . . . there is no integrity in that, you know."

Paul Pape remembers how much fun the Faces had in teasing Annette, and found the filming of the rape scene traumatic. "It was hard to do, because we all really loved her. That was a shot near the end, too. It was hard to disassociate from the scene because you really care about her, and call us what you will. Call us actors or not. It is still a lot to take on and to be there. And I thought she was extraordinary in that scene. She did great. That is why she was so well received."

Jeff Zinn, who played Travolta's double, found it uncomfortable to lean in through the window during the scene, and praises her "emotional availability."

Pescow has nothing but praise for both the cast and crew for their sensitivity. "It was tough on everybody, because these are not the kind of guys that are like that. You know? And so, they had to sort of throw themselves emotionally into that place as well. And they [the characters] were not really interested in making Annette feel happy and good and what it was, you know, that was just basically guys getting off on what was going on. And they had to go into that mindset. And I think the thing that you deal with when you act in any way is you have to forget about who it is that you are playing opposite that you know and just really go to who they are playing, you know? So, you can work at that level."

I told Donna Pescow how much my heart breaks for her character, a phrase she often hears connected to the movie. "You know the thing about Annette that when I read the script and when I went to the club and, you know, I think everybody knows someone like her. And if we all look at our high school days and we think of who Annette is in that movie. I think the thing about that character for me was that wanting to be accepted, wanting to get what your goal was and going to whatever length, and then it all gets out of control," she tells me.

"And I think that is very common to young girls, you know, who are eighteen years old, who are just starting to sort of realize who they are. But at that time in the seventies, you know, there was still this stereotypical class system, whatever you want to call it, where girls were not generally respected the way, I would like to hope they are now, especially young girls," she recalls.

Pescow also has nothing but praise for Badham. "He has a great sense of each actor individually, where they like to go and whether they like to kind of stick solely with the script or go off the script and maybe try other things. And he is very collaborative, which is such a gift. Because many directors, you know, have an idea in their head of what the scene should be. And it is not disrespectful. It is just that that is what they want. You know? Where John [Badham] was very much into collaborating and improvising, which for me personally really brought that character to life."

In the end, her biggest worry was about the reaction to the scene from one person: her grandfather, Jack Goldress, who had worked for over fifty years at the RKO Albee movie theater in Brooklyn. She told the *New York Times* in 1978 that he was more of a father to her than her own father (her parents were divorced) and he encouraged her love of movies. Up in the projectionist booth she memorized the "Who's on First" comedy bit by Abbott and Costello, and her desire to be an actor was set.

Goldress was her date to the movie's premiere. "I was nervous because I am sitting between him and my mom, and it was very weird. At one point, I looked at him and he had tears in his eyes, and I said, 'Are you upset?' He looked at me and said, 'I have been running movies for fifty years. You think I believe they are real now?' And it was just such a gift. You know? And it was because he was okay with it. I am sure there was a part of him that was like, oh, wow."

In 1977, Donna Pescow was nominated for the New York City Film Critics Circle Award for Best Supporting Actress for that year.

CHAPTER 9

A la Famiglia

At Home with the Maneros

In the mid-1970s, working-class Bay Ridge was going through a crisis, like much of the country. The economy was struggling. The unemployment rate was rising, along with the cost of living. Unions were losing their popularity, and men like Frank Manero (Tony's father) found themselves middle-aged and unemployed. The civil rights movement was counter to their clannish loyalty to "their kind." Then there were second-wave feminism and the gay rights communities fighting to be heard.

The world Nik Cohn sought to uncover and understand was filled with people who were angry about the state of the world and unsure what the future would bring. New York City was on the verge of going broke and several worker strikes made city life miserable. This was the opposite of the pretty, glittering world the discos offered.

Norman Wexler prowled the streets and clubs in the Italian-centric neighborhoods of Bay Ridge, Sheepshead Bay, and Bensonhurst, to make sure the dialogue in the film sounded authentic. He was obsessed with realism and capturing the Catholic church's hold over the community. The scenes of Tony with his family clue in the audience to what motivates him to seek pleasure and escape.

The cast brought in to play the Manero family included Julie

Julie Bovasso, Val Bisoglio, and John Travolta filming on location in 1977. *United Artists GmbH/Alamy Stock Photo.*

Bovasso as Flo, the forty-seven-year-old stage actor and coach for several young actors, including Alberto Vasquez and Bruce Ornstein, whom she helped find roles in the film. Ornstein was in awe of her talent, "She was also a wonderful playwright. She won one of the first Obie Awards that were ever given out. When she was nineteen, she had her own theater company in New York. I mean, she was a real trailblazer."

Denny Dillon remembers her first table read with the cast. "I was of course struck with Travolta, who was so charismatic with the boys and Donna, but Julie Bovasso just took my breath away. She was so real and wonderful. She was Bruce's acting instructor, Bruce Ornstein. He took lessons from her."

Val Bisoglio, as Frank Sr., fifty in 1977, was the son of Italian immigrants who began his career on the New York stage. During the 1970s he spent a great deal of time as a guest star on detective shows like *Quincy* and *Starsky and Hutch*. He enjoyed the improvisation that John Badham allowed on set, including yelling "One pork chop!" during the family meal.

Twelve-year-old Lisa Peluso had shared a Broadway stage with Angela Lansbury in *Gypsy,* so she was not exactly a starstruck child actor. However, if there was one person she wanted to meet, it was John Travolta. She never missed an episode of *Welcome Back, Kotter* and was thrilled when she won the part of Tony's little sister, Linda. Because of Travolta's emergency with Diana Hyland, her first scenes with the family were shot without the star.

When he did show up, she bolted over to him and, not realizing then how intensely he had been feeling lately, begged him to the "Barbarino dance," which he did right away with a smile. Somehow, he was even more handsome in person and was incredibly sweet and patient with his young costar. She recalls one moment when he leaned in to pick up a loose eyelash from her cheek and all she could think was, "Why can't I be older when this moment would be so perfect?"

Rounding out the cast for these scenes were Nina Hansen, as the grandmother, and Martin Shakar, as Father Frank Jr., the beloved, favorite son who shows up to tell his heartbroken family he is leaving the priesthood. Shakar was immediately drawn in by the Norman Wexler script and had a lengthy speech about his conflict with organized religion as his audition piece that sadly did not make the final print.

"There was a scene in the bedroom that was quite long. It was a long speech. And I guess it needed to be cut. That was shot in a bedroom on location. They cut it down and made a removable wall so there would be room for the cameras and lighting and stuff," he explains.

Shakar auditioned with the aforementioned speech, in which he explained to Tony why he was leaving the priesthood. This was important to Wexler, and he was saddened when it was cut due to time constraints. Here it is from the original script:

> For a young priest, the life can be very limited—sick calls; boring, trivial errands for the pastor—it doesn't match your ideal serving of God by serving man. Hardly

spiritual. Then you think of the church's political activism, intrusions, its positions on birth control, sex, freedom of expression. But, most important, one day you look at the statue of the Madonna and Child and it doesn't have that mystic glow about it. Or you look at the crucifixion and all you see is a man dying on the cross, not God, not the son of God—a man. And you know your faith, the rocklike edifice of your faith, has more than a small fissure.

A friend of Shakar's was actor Sam Coppola, who plays Travolta's boss, Mr. Fusco, and called him to talk about the filming at the store just a few weeks before. "He told me about the area back then, they hardly could move. They had to make special arrangements with the neighbors. I'm not sure what special arrangements meant exactly, but finally they got things shuttled down and there apparently were hundreds of fans."

It wasn't as intense fans-wise when the cast filmed at the homes in Bay Ridge. There are some photos you can find in Facebook groups of locals taking pictures of Travolta's trailer, but it doesn't look as chaotic as in other locations.

Shakar appreciated how hard Travolta worked, including his improvisation of "He hits it. He hit my hair" at the family meal. Also, the fact they were shooting on location, which added to the realism of the scenes.

The house was filmed in two homes standing side by side. The shots of Travolta entering and exiting a front door were on the left and have been updated by homeowners who specifically bought the place due to its connection to the film.

The movie interiors are the home next door with the same owners for over thirty years who have kept the same structure all these years later. It's truly like standing in the Manero household when its owner Shanta Kumari graciously showed me around.

The neighborhood itself (the homes are called "the bookends") was built in the 1890s, and she bought the place with her parents knowing the movie origins in its walls.

"The house is pretty much in its original condition, since it was built with all the woodwork that you see in the movie. The wood paneling, all that, it's still there in its original state, including the stairs, the windows. We love the house because of the woodwork."

In 2017, the documentary *Saturday Night Fever: The Ultimate Disco Movie*, hosted by Bruno Tonioli (*Dancing with the Stars*) and cohosted by Kevin McCormick, was filmed at her home, and she gets requests all the time from fans around the world who want to see the Manero home in person.

"It was called the bookend because this house and the one next to it were the same, followed by three brownstones. [It's] one of the first structures on Seventy-Ninth Street. And this was the main thoroughfare. Went right down to the park, which at that time was mostly farmland, but it had a dock there. And there was no Belt Parkway, so it would have a beach. It's still the main entrance to the Belt Parkway Park or whatever you want to call it, which is really nice if you live here."

Yelena Sionova and her husband, Michael Grazidei, purchased the "Manero house" just before the pandemic because he was not only a Bay Ridge native but also a big lover of the movie. "He was a big fan, and this house was on sale for a while. As soon as I walked in the house, the little details I found were so charming. And I really fell in love. So, we just lightened things up and fixed it up to modernize it a little bit to our taste, but it was really all done by the previous owners. So, it was very easy and move-in ready," she told me on a personal tour of her home.

In the end, the Manero family is in a state of flux. Frank Jr. is moving out, having left the priesthood, which is devastating to his mother. The tension we feel inside their house, with its dark interiors and all the family shouting, lets the audience know that the Maneros are scared as their institutions are failing them— their jobs, the Catholic church, and New York City itself. How long will they be able to afford to live there?

This general fear of the future and the defensiveness of residents who worried the movie would make fun of their culture make sense, considering how often cast members felt the energy from the streets. People proud to be from Bay Ridge, Catholic, and Italian, holding on to a last grasp of the world they knew and fearing any kind of change.

Tony makes it clear by the end of the film that he needs to leave Brooklyn and find his future in Manhattan with few skills but a desire to take the risk. He is ready to leave everything (including his friends and family) behind.

Lisa Peluso was too young to view the film (or go to the Radio City Music Hall premiere) at the time. We chatted about the deserved R-rating for the original film (versus the PG version released to theaters later). "I don't even know why they haven't canceled it, because it had date rape. It had homophobia. It had racism. It had the f-word every five seconds," she told me while agreeing it is still a classic, despite its controversial tone.

Ten years later, in 1987, at the first reunion, Peluso was invited to meet the Bee Gees backstage. She was shocked that the band were big fans of hers, as she was by then a big soap star (*Loving* and *One Life to Live*). She recalls, "They knew about my character! I came to find out that a lot of musicians watched daytime TV because I dated a few. They watched because they would stay up late and sleep in. Then they would turn the TV on for the soaps."

These days, Bay Ridge has a large vibrant Chinese community where the 2001 Odyssey once stood, and the homes on the street where the Maneros lived sell for millions, as Brooklyn continues to be changed by gentrification. Homes in south Brooklyn that sold for an average of $55,000 in 1975 now regularly sell for over $1 million.

Bovasso, a Brooklyn native, would go on to appear in the movie's sequel as well as *The Verdict*, *My Blue Heaven*, and *Betsy's Wedding*. She passed away in 1991, at the age of sixty-one, due to cancer. Bisoglio would go on to work in television and film, concluding his career playing "Murf" in *The Sopranos* in 2002. He passed away in 2021 at the age of ninety-five. Nina Hansen, for whom there is little information since her last film credit in 1990 for *The Exorcist III*, improvised her performance, as she had no lines in the original script. She will forever be known for yelling "Basta! Mangia!" at the Manero family table.

While the movie is being shot in Brooklyn, Stigwood has his twenty-four-year-old music supervisor putting together his first movie soundtrack.

CHAPTER 10

Panic about the Disco

The Soundtrack That Took Over the World

Before the soundtrack album of *Saturday Night Fever* went on to sell over forty million copies—the largest sales figure until the 1983 release of Michael Jackson's juggernaut, *Thriller*—two things were said about the music in this film and were repeated as objective truth in most documentaries and think pieces:

1. The Bee Gees were "over" before its release.
2. Disco, as a style of music, was just a fad and was on its way out.

Were there low expectations by Paramount executives? Sure. Was there a lack of coverage in music magazines like *Rolling Stone* and *Creem*? Absolutely. Did scores of angry white males have an aversion to a form of music they thought was for other races, girls, and "sissies"? Yup.

However, the actual truth is that the number of dance clubs was growing even before the Nik Cohn magazine piece was written (he was reporting on a trend, see?). There were two features in the *New York Times* in 1977 alone, *Forbes* magazine estimated in 1976 that the ten thousand discos opening that year (up from fifteen hundred just two years before) would gross $4 billion, *Time* magazine in 1976 discussed the growing number of disco bands touring the country, and even *Rolling Stone* featured the

The double album jacket of the *Saturday Night Fever* soundtrack from
RSO Records. It would go on to sell more than forty million copies
and would change how movies promoted their soundtracks.
Antonio Siwiak/Alamy Stock Photo.

Bee Gees on its cover months before the release of the *Saturday
Night Fever* soundtrack and also released their own book about
the dance music craze titled *Dance Madness*.

Across the United States, towns big and small had trend
pieces talking about local dance clubs being filled with a mixture of people enjoying the music. Cities like Wichita, Kansas;
Fond du Lac, Wisconsin; Minneapolis, Minnesota; Myrtle
Beach, South Carolina; and Salt Lake City, Utah. The *Daily
Utah Chronicle* (published January 17, 1977) interviewed a popular DJ named Otis "Disco Daddy" Lee, with a loyal following
on the local college station and his nights at the popular gay
club the Sun Tavern.

One place that was filled with locals looking for the disco
beat was Salt Lake City, a deeply religious town. At that time,
Black people were not allowed to be members of the Church of
Jesus Christ of Latter-Day Saints. Nor was it gay-friendly. The
fact that this music and style could find a home there, however,

is an indication that dance music was gaining in popularity and was not just a passing phase.

Lee expressed worry about disco eventually reaching critical mass. "Eventually the constant beat found in disco music will get boring." For him, the key was to mix ballads and softer sounds between hard-charging songs. Dennis Hunt in the *Los Angeles Times* on February 8, 1976, wrote about the state of disco music and its most successful artists, such as Donna Summer, the Average White Band, Gloria Gaynor, and the Temptations, and worried that "a problem that disco music faces is that, as it becomes more and more popular, it will attract lots of inferior artists who are merely trying to cash in on a trend."

Discos came to the US as rock clubs in the early 1970s, such as Rodney Bingenheimer's English Disco in Los Angeles, which was filled every night with stars like Led Zeppelin and John Lennon. In 1974, *Billboard* magazine started listing Disco/Dance charts to make up for the rise of this kind of music starting to dominate radio with artists as varied as Rose Royce ("Car Wash"), Elton John ("Philadelphia Freedom"), the Bee Gees ("Nights on Broadway"), George McCrae ("Rock Your Baby"), Frankie Valli and the Four Seasons ("Who Loves You").

Whether you want to call the music R&B, soul, funk, or just plain dance music, the beat was infectious and catching in popularity. In 1976, David Bowie played "Fame" on *Soul Train*. The same year, *Time* magazine wrote a lengthy piece about the Trammps and their hit "Disco Inferno" (while also saying how annoying disco usually was). And in the summer of 1977, the *Star Wars* soundtrack featured a hit single, "Star Wars Theme/Cantina" by Meco.

Ed Cermanski, an R&B musician active since the 1960s, who joined the Trammps in 1975, remembers, "It was around 1973, when 'Rock the Boat' (by the Hues Corporation) came out, disco started to become more prominent. I noticed the difference was that people began to dress up and began to touch-dance, which was not what was going on a few years before. It would go from one song to another, and people would be on the dance floor for hours."

Joe Cali loved Manhattan nightlife and went to several discos in downtown Manhattan in the mid-1970s. "I remember going to Finaldi, which was the bar on my corner. We also used to hang out at Milady's on Thompson Street. There were all these after-hours clubs that you'd get home at noon. Dancing all night. And it was very transsexual in that area back then."

I asked him how he felt about disco, as a white, straight man, back when he was filming the movie. "Disco was a big part of my life. I love disco. You know? Donna Summer's a queen. The best."

The Bee Gees are too often presented as has-beens who found a resurgence with the soundtrack. The facts do not support this. For over three years prior, they were gaining in popularity with their new, funkier sound, which featured Barry Gibb's falsetto and tight musicianship. Their 1975 album *Main Course*, recorded in Miami's Criteria Studios (where Eric Clapton found success with *461 Ocean Boulevard*) included future classics "Jive Talkin'" and "Nights on Broadway." After that, their 1976 release *Children of the World* produced hits such as "Love So Right," "Boogie Child," and "You Should Be Dancing." All were massive hits around the world, and they were filling arenas with their tight sound. Far from being forgotten by the music world, they were thriving.

Another 1976 disco hit was "Disco Duck," by Rick Dees and His Cast of Idiots, which Kevin McCormick told me was "an RSO production and was the first hit on RSO Records. Which they were incredibly ashamed about afterward. So, disco was around, but it wasn't ubiquitous. But I knew about dancing, and I know I loved the music."

In the 2007 documentary *One Night Only*, Barry Gibb said, "I think in 1973 or '74, we were pretty much done for. I mean, any group that was popular in the sixties, nobody really wanted to know about in the seventies. So that was happening to us, and I think everyone had grown a little tired of my real voice or Robin's. I think the sound was just people wanted to change."

Barry also recalls the difficulty for the band to get back together and be each other's champions rather than have endless squabbling. He told Timothy White in the May 17, 1979, *Rolling Stone*, "We knew it would take us five or six years to become anything like we were before we started on the drugs, and before we got fame and huge egos. And six years is what it took. We had to become brothers again and forget those little things that aggravated us about each other. It was an awful lot to get rid of."

Barry then went on to explain the popularity of his newly discovered falsetto. "I go into the studio and sing some ad libs over 'Nights on Broadway' and we discovered that that there was this falsetto voice hiding back there. And it just became something new for us, and it was something that everybody wanted."

In the same interview, Robin Gibb said, "*The Saturday Night Fever* soundtrack had a very sort of complex beginning because we were coming off two major hit albums. Not only on the white charts, but on the Black charts as well. So, we were in a pretty good position going into a new album at the Château d'Hérouville in France where we decided to follow up these two albums. We weren't even thinking of soundtracks, although we weren't against doing one."

In early 1977 to avoid the English tax system, they chose to produce a live album at the Chateau d'Hérouville, where Elton John had previously recorded his album *Honky Château*, and where the Grateful Dead had once pulled off a free festival for the locals, at which Jerry Garcia reportedly said, "Everybody just had a hell of a time—got drunk, fell in the pool. It was great."

The Brothers Gibb found the place to be cold, drafty, and a miserable choice after spending the previous two years encamped in South Florida. As they were deciding which performances to mix for the record, Robert Stigwood sent them Norman Wexler's script for them to read before giving him the hits he required to sell the movie.

Stigwood's plan was to release a double album filled with disco hits and with David Shire's score, complete with photos from the movie set so that anyone who couldn't see the film could experience it on their own.

In *Rolling Stone*, on July 14, 1977, Robin Gibb told reporter Frank Rose that although the band had had several hits recently, the media did not appreciate the fact that they were world-class songwriters. "They don't know their business. They don't *make* it their business to know how many records the Bee Gees have written. I call it just—musical ignorance!"

In the same interview, Barry Gibb described how Stigwood approached them for the soundtrack: "Give me eight minutes—eight minutes, three moods. I want frenzy at the beginning. Then I want some passion. And then I want w-i-i-i-l-d frenzy!" The reporter noted they wrote "Stayin' Alive" in less than two hours. The band also credited the instincts of Stigwood with their music, to which he replied, "I can't make any contribution to their songwriting. I wish I could. I'd be taking their royalties, I assure you."

Bill Oakes, the head of RSO Records, arrived with Stigwood at the château and realized the band had no interest in reading the script. Barry said in the HBO documentary *The Bee Gees: How Can You Mend a Broken Heart* that the band decided they didn't need to, as they had five songs ready. They would be "Night Fever," "Stayin' Alive," "How Deep Is Your Love," "More Than a Woman," and "If I Can't Have You." They also gave their hit "You Should Be Dancing."

Oakes was a young, handsome executive for RSO who felt a bit overwhelmed but hopeful with his first soundtrack. He told his boss after hearing rough first versions on a cassette tape that they had several hits on their hands already. In the 2022 *Billboard* magazine for the forty-fifth anniversary of the film, he said, "We've got the score. We got it."

The next step was going to Oakes's new office (the size of a janitor's closet) at Paramount, where the executives derided his project as "the little disco picture." He heard from the cast and crew recommendations for bands to fill out the already strong first side. Charles Rusinak Jr., who DJ'd for his father's club, 2001 Odyssey, told Stigwood that the Trammps were one of their top bands and had a huge following. His sister, Denise, recalls him also telling Stigwood about Tavares and Kool & the Gang.

At the time, Oakes was married to Yvonne Elliman, who was working with Eric Clapton after touring with *Jesus Christ Superstar*. She told me how she wound up on the soundtrack, via an email interview. "I sang a song handed to me from Stiggy and my ex-husband, Bill Oakes, recorded it, and that was it. I was in the Eric Clapton band, and after leaving that wonderful situation, had to front a band of my own, which was on a completely different level of 'rock n roll majesty.' During that readjustment, I was told to lose my guitar in any photo shoots for eight-by-ten headshots, put red satin pants on to replace my jeans, and to sing songs leaning toward disco."

When I asked Yvonne how she felt about this change, she said, "I was of two minds about listening to that advice. I recorded a couple more albums, choosing songs that definitely did not embrace the disco sound, and because of sales being disappointing, was dropped from RSO. Much to [record producer] Al Coury's reluctance in doing so."

She told me about the rising resentment of disco by rock fans. "So the whole disco vs. rock disturbance that was brewing in the country (mainly dispatched by DJ's who were smashing disco records at football games and at radio stations) put me in a confused state. I knew my heart really belonged to rock—the genre that moved and inspired me. That doesn't mean I resented having a number one record on the *Billboard* charts—that was exciting. Today, I still get asked to perform that song in variety-type shows featuring other artists who also benefited from the disco movement."

Robert Upchurch is a member of the Trammps who sang on the original recording of "Disco Inferno." He explained to me how the group came to be on the soundtrack. "The song was written by Ron Kersey and Leroy Green. Kersey was a former member of the Trammps, and he became part of the production team that produced it. It was recorded in Philadelphia at Sigma Sound Studios, which should be a historical institution."

When I asked him about how prevalent disco was in 1976, he replied, "I mean, by that time, disco had been well established throughout the world. Anytime you think of disco, you think of the flashing lights, the crowds, the driving disco beats, and everybody dancing. You know, everybody seemed a lot happier during those times."

We discussed whether the Trammps had embraced a disco sound before. "You know, we really didn't even like the song originally. I mean, there's sometimes you could tell when you have a hit and then sometimes, they sneak up on you. And that was the case for 'Disco Inferno.' It was a new beginning, and it was different from anything else we'd ever done at that point."

The band won a Grammy as being part of the Album of the Year award in 1978 (the only disco record to ever win it). "I mean, just knowing that you were nominated, first of all, is an honor. But then to win was another great moment for the group. So, we were excited about that as well."

When asked about hearing it for the first time in *Saturday Night Fever*, he said, "Oh, it was good. It was fantastic hearing yourself sitting in the theater, that was fantastic!" And about the fans who still come see the group all these years later? "Even today, we get that same response from different audiences. We were just in England for a big festival and it's amazing. Their dedication from even the early years, you know, all the way up until today, you know, it's unbelievable. And we appreciate the fact that so many people still like and relate to our music. So, thank you."

David Shire, a well-known composer whose work includes soundtracks for *All the President's Men*, *Zodiac*, and *The Conversation*, went to Yale with the movie's director. "John Badham was the stage manager of my first college, and we've been friends ever since. When I started working at Universal, he was already a director there. I had just done a movie with him and then another television movie when he asked me to take on this film."

He remembers how ambivalent Paramount was about his work. "John told me they didn't give it [the movie] much attention. They didn't treat it like they were going to release a bombshell. I remember one incident when they used a record for a dance sequence instead of a machine that gave a steady beat. We just had some ridiculous setups with major features like that."

Shire is married to Didi Conn, who played Frenchy in *Grease* and was one of the first people to see the film in the summer of 1977. She told her husband, "John did an advance screening of the movie for the cast. And afterward, he said, 'Do you like it? Do you think it's anything?' She said, 'John, you're crazy. It's gonna be a smash.' But he was nervous about it. He didn't know what was gonna happen."

When Shire took the job, he saw a rough cut of the film. "All the disco numbers were hidden, they had temporary ones. So, I was able to write four pieces. "Manhattan Skyline," "Salsation," and "Night on Disco Mountain." The fourth one didn't make the cut."

When asked about what he thought of disco music at the time, Shire said, "Well, I was very aware of disco before I worked in the movie. I might have written some source music for another movie that sounded like it. But it was a new experience for me to do it and I enjoyed it tremendously. I'm very proud of the work. 'Manhattan Skyline' was used by CBS football for a while. That was, please, I'm deceased!"

When Bill Oakes delivered his final product to Stigwood in person, he was following a truck on the way to the airport with a rather garish bumper sticker—"Death to Disco"—which filled him with dread. He told *Billboard* in 2022, "We didn't create disco, we created a real, global across-the-board demand for it."

The biggest argument I can make for disco not being on the decline as the movie was being made is the opening of Studio 54, which happened on April 26, 1977. Steve Rubell and Ian Schrager picked one of the largest buildings to house it, the former CBS television studios at 254 West Fifty-Fourth Street. It was cavernous, compared with other clubs, with a large balcony area. The two native New Yorkers brought on a third partner for the $400,000 needed to update the building and build a sound system to rival that of any Broadway theater.

Schrager said in Rizzoli's *Studio 54* that they picked April as the launch date, as their funds were low and were hoping to make some money before people left the city for the summer. It was an immediate hit and was filled with celebrities as varied as Mick

Jagger, Mayor Ed Koch, Andy Warhol, and Alice Cooper. They invented the "velvet rope" to keep out most of the eager visitors. It felt special to be included and the club's name was on the gossip sheets around the world. New York was cool again and the disco was loved by a diverse audience.

Stigwood's plan was to release the album a full month before the movie hit the theaters. This was his marketing plan. The suits at Paramount were not enthused about this film to the point that they were avoiding publicity. Long-lead publications (magazines) need three to four months for their journalists and editors to see the movie, write a review, set up interviews with the stars, request artwork, and make room for the film. The movie came out on December 16, 1977, and the only press it received was from dailies and weeklies.

RSO knew that its best shot at getting screens and attracting an audience was to have hit records climbing the charts to build anticipation. The official release date for the soundtrack was November 15, 1977, but a single doled out on September 15, 1977, "How Deep Is Your Love," quickly went to number one on *Billboard* and was followed by the Bee Gees' version of "More Than a Woman."

By the time of the movie's premiere, "Stayin' Alive" was played so often that Michael Eisner recalled in the HBO documentary about Robert Stigwood, *Mr. Saturday Night*, that he went on a ski vacation hearing the song in the parking lot, then at the lift station, and then up in the lodge. He told Barry Diller to buckle up because they might just have a hit on their hands.

Stigwood knew this would happen and used the music as a bargaining tool for getting more screens and a bigger percentage of the profits. Freddie Gershon told me it went back to his ability to take care of musicians, "He understood music, and he understood musicians. He had the patience at that time and willingness to give of himself and become paternalistic to all of them."

The success of the soundtrack is hard to fathom in today's world of billions of streams and artists no longer being able to make a living on sales alone. If you wanted the music, you had to go to a store and pick it up. People would wait in line for hours for a new release.

The *Saturday Night Fever* soundtrack numbers are astonishing by any standard. According to *The Bee Gees: The Biography*, by David N. Meyer, "Twenty-five million copies sold between 1977 and 1980, at the time the most copies of any sound recording sold since the advent of sound recording. To date, over forty million copies have been sold."

The double album spent eight full months, between January and August 1978, at number one. While most records at the time (the biggest being Fleetwood Mac's *Rumors* and Peter Frampton's *Frampton Comes Alive)* sold for $8, the soundtrack was $12, which, according to Meyer, made it the "top-grossing album of all time when it hit eight million units (because of its higher price)."

Reporter John Milward, in the *Chicago Daily News*, on February 13, 1978, notes, "What is most significant about the success of *Saturday Night Fever,* though, is the merchandising savvy displayed by Robert Stigwood, the producer of the film and the Bee Gees' manager. Stigwood's move into the movies is a natural calculation—he realizes that the broad-based audience for a hit movie will let the Bee Gees cross over into an even wider audience than their recent black-white mix."

Gershon told me that Paramount had no clue that they were sitting on a gold mine. "Neither business affairs, the legal department of Barry Diller and his executives' team ever asked to participate at all in the album. I'm sorry. Assholes. No vision. I'm telling you, no vision. Robert confronted him long afterward and said, why? He said, 'Well, we don't have a record company. We're a movie studio.' No."

Ron Stigwood claims about his uncle, "I think Robert made over one billion on the soundtrack and the movie. You know, that was the sort of money that was flying around."

Donna Pescow told me she constantly meets fans of the soundtrack. "It's the music. The music is so extraordinary, and the music touched so many people. And a lot of memories and a lot of their connections with this film have to do with the music. Yeah. So, it's like a twofold kind of situation. And all of it's under the heading of personal, you know, how it hit them in a personal way."

The only movie soundtrack that has outperformed *Saturday Night Fever* is Whitney Houston's *The Bodyguard*, which has sold more than sixty-six million copies. After the success of this feat in 1977, movie studios started working more to make their films and soundtracks have some synergy, including big 1980s staples such as *Footloose*, *Flashdance*, *Purple Rain*, and *Top Gun*, to name just a few.

Oakes, interviewed by the *Atlanta Constitution*, on March 17, 1978, told them after their success with the 1975 soundtrack for *Tommy* (they knew they were on the right track), "It showed us there that kids would go to a movie house if the music was right, and loud enough and heard properly."

The album's cover features the Bee Gees in white outfits that show off their tanned skin. Francesco Scavullo, one of the most famous photographers of the 1970s, captured the band in their glory. With the new music playing in the background, he supposedly told the group they had a huge hit on their hands.

The center image on the cover is a shot of John Travolta, in his famous white suit, with his right hand pointed to the ceiling and his left pointed to the floor with his hip out. Susan Samuels tells me this pose was inspired by her ex-husband JoJo's choreography. "It was part of the way JoJo used his arms. When he slid out to that movement, and the hip went out that way, that's just JoJo using his arms in his dancing."

Jason Samuels Smith related a story about a time when his father was very ill and living with him. He visited a record shop in New Jersey. "I found this mirror which said *Saturday Night Fever* and had John Travolta in the epic pose. I went to the record store owner and told him my father choreographed this scene and this was his move. I asked how much for it, and the owner told me, if your father choreographed it, you could have it."

The one thing missing for Stigwood and the Bee Gees was Best Songs nominations for the 1978 Academy Awards. Though they mostly wrote the bestselling soundtrack from that year, for an incredible series of months the album charted at number one. But no disco songs made the list that year, with the winner being Debby Boone for the title song for the sappy romance movie *You Light Up My Life*.

It was not that they could not handle valid criticism and feedback, but they were hearing from reporters and editors wanting to tear them apart for simply existing. As Barry Gibb told *Rolling Stone* on May 17, 1979, "So we try and live like that, or at least live with it. But I've never gotten over harsh criticism. It's so painful. Pretty soon the bubble will burst anyway, and I would like for the Bee Gees to stop before we wane."

Stigwood used the same soundtrack release strategy for 1978's *Grease*, with the album dropping on April 14, 1978. The album included "Hopelessly Devoted to You" and "You're the One That I Want," and both appeared on the *Billboard* charts before the movie appeared on American movie screens on June 16, 1978. It went on to sell forty million copies.

The year 1978 is also when the Bee Gees' youngest brother,

Andy Gibb, twenty years old, became a pop sensation with "Love Is Thicker Than Water" and "Shadow Dancing." The top twenty songs of the that year, according to *Billboard*, include Barry Gibb and the Bee Gees with "More Than a Woman," "Grease," "Stayin' Alive," "Night Fever," "Emotion," "How Deep Is Your Love," and "If I Can't Have You." IN. ONE. YEAR.

One other lasting effect of the soundtrack is that the American Heart Association recommends that when giving CPR (cardiopulmonary resuscitation), the chest compressions must be 100 to 120 beats per minutes, and that "Stayin' Alive" specifically is the best song to hum to and maintain that beat.

The soundtrack is obviously important to the film's success. So, what about this movie still attracting new fans all these years after its premiere?

CHAPTER 11

What's It All About, Tony?

Saturday Night Fever is a movie often remembered as a light disco flick with John Travolta in the white suit and wall-to-wall Bee Gees music. The sanitized television version has been viewed so often that it can come as a surprise to people when they watch the R-rated director's cut.

Tony and the Faces are not good people. Racist, sexist, homophobic, cruel barbarians who are filled with rage and self-loathing. The women in the story are desperate for the men to appreciate them. Stephanie is the "modern girl" who is being used by a man from her workplace and twice her age, so he will not have to pay a large alimony to his ex. We hear racial and homophobic slurs, witness awful sexual encounters, watch Tony scream at his mother for being a "loser," and see a main character fall to his death because he cannot imagine marrying someone he impregnated.

This film is downright *ugly* at times, and yet ... it is so relatable. We are witnesses to a young man who was raised with little expectations and many grievances. He discovers he is good at dancing and realizes he may be able to rise above his circumstances.

In the basic plot, as mapped out by Norman Wexler, Tony Manero and his hoodlum friends, "the Faces," have boring daytime jobs. They are about nineteen years old, all live at home, and live for the weekend, when they can get dressed, go to 2001

John Travolta and Karen Lynn Gorney near the Verrazzano-Narrows Bridge in 1977. *TCD/Prod.DB/Alamy Stock Photo.*

Odyssey, get wasted, and (if they are lucky) have a quickie in the backseat of their dumpy car.

Tony's parents yell at him for not being as perfect as their other son—the priest. Annette is a local girl who dreams of a life with Tony, but he barely tolerates her. There is a big contest at their favorite club and Tony plans to have Annette as his partner until he notices Stephanie, a local girl who works in "the city" and doesn't fawn all over him.

When the Faces are bored, they drive around their neighborhood, high on pills and looking for action. Their biggest enemy is "the Barracudas"—a Puerto Rican gang that sometimes gets a little close to their "turf."

Stephanie notices Tony is a good dancer at their local studio and becomes his partner in the big contest, leaving behind a brokenhearted Annette, who can't imagine why he "hates her." Tony and Stephanie hang out, where she tells him she is on a self-improvement kick, trying to speak and behave in her new fancy PR agency job. Tony's friends hate her, but he doesn't care. He is smitten.

Tony and his friends like to spend their free nights hanging out at the Verrazzano-Narrows Bridge, which, at the time, was the longest suspension bridge in the world. They climb about the beams and scare Annette by pretending to fall over.

One of the Faces, Bobby C., is in a predicament—his girlfriend is pregnant, and he must marry her because she is Catholic. He would rather she get an abortion, but she refuses. He tries several times to have alone time with Tony to discuss it, but Tony always brushes him off.

Frank Jr., Tony's brother, comes home to tell the family he is leaving the priesthood. They are devastated by this news, but Tony (possibly feeling better now that his brother isn't so perfect) takes him to the club to show him his dance moves and prowess with women. Afterward, he has a fight with his family where he insults his mother.

Tony helps Stephanie move to her new apartment on the Upper West Side, where he meets the man she used to live with. He is much older and is very condescending. When Tony erupts at her for "sleeping around," she breaks down in tears and tells him how hard it is for her to fit into the NYC job world. This man was the only person who would help her, and in return she helped him hide money from his ex-wife.

Tony feels bad about their argument and takes her to the Verrazzano-Narrows Bridge to cheer her up. Turns out he has memorized all sorts of facts and trivia about it. Tony is thinking of leaving "home." Frank Jr. moves out and encourages Tony to stick with his dancing and follow his dreams.

The night of the contest at 2001 Odyssey arrives and Tony is wearing a white suit. There is a Black couple the goes first and they are amazing. Tony and Stephanie have a slow, sweet routine and are followed by a Puerto Rican couple who are clearly better than most people at the club. Tony and Stephanie win the grand prize, which angers him. He tells off his friends for "not being straight with him" and just feeding his ego. Tony drags Stephanie into the car and attempts to rape her. She knees him in the groin and runs away.

The Faces and Annette (two of them have just raped her) head back to the Verrazzano-Narrows Bridge. Tony shames Annette for allowing herself to get assaulted, while Double J. and Joey have a laugh. Bobby C., realizing now he must marry his pregnant girlfriend, hangs out on a beam and scolds Tony for not being a better friend to him. Then he "slips" as Tony tries to rescue him. Tony later tells the police, "There are ways of killing yourself without killing yourself."

Tony winds up at Stephanie's apartment the next morning and she reluctantly lets him in. He promises to "be good" and unloads how much he hates his life. He wants to move to the city like her. She asks him about his skills, and she tells him at least she could type. Tony is willing to do anything to make it in the city and promises they can be "just friends" in the future. End scene.

Not exactly a "feel-good" picture, but Tony's journey resonates with people to this day. I asked several cast and crew members why they feel that *Saturday Night Fever* keeps finding new fans and why, almost fifty years later, they think people stay enamored with it.

Donna Pescow told me, "People are very territorial about this film. And I think part of it is because of where they were in their lives at that time. The disco scene, the club scene, society was shifting at that point. Also, it's about people wanting to have goals that maybe were not as common to those who they grew up with. They are taking a little bit more of a leap to find their own way. I think also maybe for women to some extent, were saying,

'You know what? Maybe I do want to do something different.' They are thinking about getting out of the neighborhood."

For Paul Pape, he is not recognized as often these days, but when he is, people tell him how much the movie means to them. "That movie was so important to people. It is a certain point in their life, or it was a turning point. It was a touchpoint in their life. How much has it changed their life? What an important part of their youth that it was? You know, it usually comes back to something like that, they want to share the personal side of it, what it meant to them. There are a few movies like *Rebel Without a Cause* in each generation that speak to that generation. So, it's nice to be a part of one where to some people it really, it's personal to them. It's nice."

Joe Cali has aways advocated for the most amount of grittiness and realism involved in the story (and wishes it were even more so than what was put on the screen). "I have a strong feeling about Tony's desire to get out the neighborhood. That things are fucked up in that community, and he gets out in the end. That this woman Stephanie represents something."

Cameraman Tom Priestley said in the 2010 documentary *Saturday Night Fever: The Inside Story* that the movie hits people deeply because of its lack of artifice. "I've worked on a lot of big films. And this film, by all counts, is not a big film, but it has a soul to it."

For director John Badham, he wanted to shine a light on the uglier side of life in the 1970s. "You understand that the level of racism and sexism—all the isms, were all over the place. It gives a rough sense of the neighborhood and the way that the people react. And that's reflected in the film."

Executive producer Kevin McCormick gives credit to Stigwood for having his finger on the pulse of the culture. "This movie existed in the world, to his credit, in the way people really spoke. There is so much stuff that people would broom out of it nowadays, but it really caught the essence of what was happening at the time."

In the early 1970s, Norman Lear's *All in the Family* (based on *Till Death Us Do Part*, whose concept was imported from the UK by Robert Stigwood) featured a main character, the middle-aged Archie Bunker (played by Carroll O'Connor) from Queens, who complains about modern mores. His bigotry is stated loudly and proudly in front of a studio audience. His main antagonist is his son-in-law, Michael Stivic (Rob Reiner), who speaks the more liberal or progressive point of view.

By 1977, kids and young adults were paying attention to shows like *Happy Days* and *Welcome Back, Kotter* with a kinder voice and no political agenda. But the movies were getting edgier, with features such as like *Mean Streets, Dog Day Afternoon,* and *Taxi Driver.* Their characters are "antiheroes" who are angry about the state of the world.

Even in competition films, *Rocky* and *The Bad News Bears,* for example, despite all their hard work and drive, they wind up losing in the end. The point of Rocky Balboa and the Bears is that they tried, they did their best, and that helped them grow into better people.

The film felt fresh in 1977 for its current pop culture references, such as the ubiquitous Farrah Fawcett poster in a red bathing suit, along with the photos of Sylvester Stallone and Al Pacino. They were all sex symbols of their time, and it's natural that they were included in Tony's room. His dancing in his underwear yelling "Attica" to his scandalized grandmother (who sneaks a peek, anyway) is a big laugh in the film. Even the incredibly cheesy and annoying "Disco Duck" coming from the Faces' car speakers feels real to life.

The audience is so taken with Travolta's performance and

Tony's journey from living in a home filled with anger and feeling powerless—to being a person who wants to grow. The scene where he takes Stephanie to the Verrazzano-Narrows Bridge shows he can step away and put another person's concerns first. He even asks her at one point, "How come we don't talk about how we feel when we are dancing?"

Unlike the mensch version that was developed by the first director, Badham's Tony Manero is not a nice guy, but he is authentic and has respect for ethics, something that comes from Wexler's script. He gives away the big 2001 Odyssey prize because it's the right thing to do. The fact that he then uses racial slurs to make his point afterward is exactly how a Brooklyn punk raised on the streets like him would express himself.

This film speaks to the uncertainty of what was happening in the US with a new president after years of scandal. For people living in Bay Ridge at the time, the civil rights movement, or the gay rights movement are not considered important. Women were meant to be wives and mothers. The movie shows us how angry and regressive the Faces are and how ineffectual they feel about their lives and uncertain about the future.

When they happen upon a gay couple, they harass them. Women are treated as objects, and their racial politics are basically that anyone who is not white is not worthy of respect. They are angry white males who seek escapism in music but do not acknowledge the race or sexuality of the people providing that music. It's a white world in a city where diversity is supposedly encouraged. They are becoming relics of their own generation but have no idea how to change anything.

I often asked the actors what kind of lives their characters have and their future might be. For Pape, it started with his choice to have Double J. stare into his lighter's flame. "Well, the idea was that I wanted to burn these guys up. I was that mad. He's the kind of a guy who didn't necessarily start out that way, but he became a bit of a counterpoint to John, to John's leadership. Double J. was the kind of guy that wanted to lead the gang but was incapable of it because they had too much of a hair trigger."

He continues, "Like a Sonny Corleone, he wouldn't have been the perfect leader. He wouldn't have the discernibility, but, you know, he certainly had the ability to challenge on a physical level or on that module. So, then I came up with the lighter thing. There's a way of just showing how wired this guy is and how ready he was to go, when somebody pissed him off."

When I asked what he thinks happens to Double J. ultimately, "I'm guessing he would have spent time in jail at some point. He might be out now. Probably still not doing much and there's a filmmaker out here [Los Angeles] that is a fan of the movie, and if it ever comes off the ground, he wants me to come back as my character working in a bakery."

It would be similar to what Pescow sees for Annette. "I think she's living in the neighborhood and leading the same life that her sisters did. I think she's probably got a bunch of kids. Maybe when she hits forty, she will turn around and say, 'What did I do for me?' And she should be okay with it, but it sort of was getting on that same sort of assembly-line lifestyle as she saw and wanted with her own family."

When people recognize Cali, they often ask him about the scene at the White Castle in which his character literally barks like a dog, to the amusement of his friends and to the horror of the other customers. It was improvised on the spot by Cali, who was a huge dog lover, when he noticed Stigwood on the set looking grumpy.

He was just going for a laugh. "What happened, I thought there was a lot of tension going on, and Badham was flipping out. I can't remember the details, but Stigwood came to the set. We're in the White Castle shooting the scene, and Paul Pape hits me the line. 'Hey, Joey. Your mother likes dog biscuits.' And I just jumped up on the table. And because it's handheld, they went with it. I started barking like a dog, and they shot the camera up. Stigwood fucking loved it!"

For Bruce Ornstein, "I feel kind of bad for Gus. I hope that he will have had kind of a normal life, got a job of some sort, and learned how to deal with some of his insecurities. I just feel like a lot of those guys didn't really have a lot of potential. You know? The boys and I toyed with the idea of 'Where are they now?' You know, I think that would be, that would be an interesting movie to make, 'Who's alive, who isn't.' I thought about trying to write something about these guys getting together at the, you know, fiftieth anniversary of Bobby C.'s death."

Pescow sees and hears more positive feedback from people who tell her why they care about this film as much as they do. "John [Travolta] and I were discussing about when people talk about *Saturday Night Fever*. It's not just, 'Hey, I loved your movie.' It's also 'Oh, man. I was in high school,' or, 'I met my wife at the time.' It's always some personal story that somehow is connected to this film or when they saw this film. Where they were in their own life. And it's just amazing how deep it is for some people because it became personal. Not the story as much as the time and when they saw it."

Because of the complicated nature of a picture that is equal parts fun, sad, joyful, and scary—Paramount had *no* idea what they had on their hands. This worked best for Stigwood, who negotiated a deal of a lifetime for the soon-to-be classic film.

CHAPTER 12

RSO vs. the Suits

The Business of Saturday Night Fever

When Barry Diller and Michael Eisner accepted the deal to produce *Saturday Night Fever*, their expectations were about as low as could be. They had no faith in the script, the music, or the drawing power of Travolta. They merely saw it as a quick $3 million investment that, if slightly successful, would help negate the terrible performance of 1977's slate, including *Islands in the Stream* and *Sorcerer*.

The upside to this was there was little interference in the day-to-day running of the set. Kevin McCormick recalls, "It was great. I mean, they saw dailies, never came to the set, or maybe came to the set one day, but it was very arm's length."

According to Badham, Diller has quite a reputation for being a demanding boss and leader. The director grew used to saying, "No, Mr. Diller. This is right. This is the right number." And he told me, "It was terrifying. Barry Diller, when he gets angry, is terrifying."

The part of the film that most upset the suits at Paramount was the cursing. It was graphic and there were occasional tirades from Diller about the language. Especially when the film had a couple of not-so-great screenings in the fall of 1977, according to McCormick. "Michael Eisner does not remember it, but we had tested the movie in Memphis and in Atlanta, just to sort of see,

Michael Eisner in 1977 as the president of Paramount Pictures. *Source: Wikimedia Commons.*

'Does it have any life here?' And we were recruiting based only on a photograph, we have no idea whether John had any resonance as a movie star at all. We got an audience to see how they would react to the language and the urbaneness of it. And the big event that night in Memphis was the Campus Crusade for Christ, which had sixty thousand people present."

The Atlanta screening got a warmer reception, "But out of it, Eisner said we should soften the language. And Stigwood said no or he said to compromise, 'I will take two "fucks" out to get more points,'" remembers McCormick.

Director Badham recalls, "Barry was the chairperson, and Michael was the president of Paramount, and they were both nervous as they could be about it because of the vulgarities. And Robert had final cut, and his instructions to me were do not cut a word. And Michael Eisner is going, 'Can you get some of this stuff out of there?' And I produced a strategy, which I thought would help, which is in a particular scene and now you could count up the number of hells, damns, fucks, and shits and so on. And I said, let us just say, for example, in a particular scene, there are twenty-five of these. Who would know if there were suddenly, I got rid of five fucks, there's now twenty?"

Badham continues, "So, I could call up Mike Eisner and say, I got twenty-five percent of the 'shits and damns' out of there. 'Oh, great, John.' Thank you, I said, but the whole thing was, Robert did not tell Barry what we were doing. Because I do not think he would notice it. If he noticed, I am in deep trouble."

Badham recalls Stigwood's skills. "He was used to handling difficult artists like Elton John, Peter Frampton, and the Bee Gees, I mean, these are not easy guys. You know? They are difficult to manage, but he was, in addition to being tough, he was incredibly supportive. I mean, he was willing to break shit. As the computer guys say. Let us get in here and break some stuff here."

Badham continues, "We're gonna have this language. We are gonna have this sexuality, and what we are gonna be doing is a musical, but nobody knows it is a musical."

Later, as McCormick remembers, "When the new cut comes in, there are only two 'fucks' missing. I do not know why Michael was confused and thought more was happening, but I am in the airport in New York on my way back to LA, where the movie's being cut. And I am paged, which has never happened before in my life, And I pick up the phone and the woman says hold for Michael Eisner, and he got on the phone and started screaming. 'Who do you think you are? This is hideous.' And Stigwood just thought it was the funniest thing in the world."

Stigwood was known to lose his temper from time to time, so he was not offended by Eisner's rant. McCormick says, "Yeah. It is a game. Like, what is he gonna do? He knew I did not have to change it because he wants me to."

Stigwood made his bones by thumbing his nose at convention, which Paramount found out about soon enough. According to Freddie Gershon, "The sense of what Robert is, is a throwback to the Warner Brothers, to Louis B. Mayer. He is a throwback to the guys who ran these empires, who can build these empires. The essence of who he is as a person is a visionary who is willing to take risks, but he is not an administrator of a company. That was my job, but he was a great partner in doing that. We played chess games with people."

Gershon talks about Stigwood's investment strategy: "There's so many ways Robert was different from everyone else. I do not think the town understood where the wealth came from. Why would Robert Stigwood take the risk? I do not know. When I said everything went bad with Paramount, it went bad. They did not believe in the movie after we started. This movie was not gonna be made by them."

"We were several weeks at the principal photography. There was a man named Gordon Weaver. The guy who did all the marketing buys and arranged for the teaser trailers to be made and bought the print ads. And he suddenly was not buying. He was not doing it," Gershon tells me. "Now, the person who noticed this was Kevin McCormick. He tells me and he tells Robert. Robert does not see anything bad about it. I see some bad signs on the horizon. I do not know how to explain it, but they are all, Sammy Glick from *What Makes Sammy Run?*" (a novel written by Budd Schulberg about his father, who was a narcissistic Hollywood mogul).

"They're all ambitious people. And they all want to be David Geffen, you know? They want to go to the mail room at five thirty in the morning and read all the mail. That is who they all are. And so, he claims during our shooting that he has a focus group. He claims the focus group came back and told them, meaning the higher muckamucks, meaning Barry Diller, said that [the movie title sounds like] 'it's a venereal disease you'll pick up on a Saturday night,'" according to Gershon. He then tells me, "In one of my warehouses, I have that from him. But that is exactly what he the bottom line is, and we all have to reconsider what we are doing here."

Gershon explains that this is the moment the movie "went from becoming a net film under an ordinary deal and not very expensive by my standards or anyone's standards. It was maybe three million with some of the advertising being five thousand. It was not a lot of money. And the big thing I will tell you that no one knows is that the net deal became a gross deal. Robert Stigwood, me, and the empire of RSO was born with the wealth of what happened for *Saturday Night Fever*."

He continues, "We renegotiated the deal because Barry Diller was relieved to find out that we would entertain an idea where if he just wanted to distribute the movie, but not pick up the cost or the risk of paying for a negative. We had sufficient funds to do that, and we had lunch together with Robert, me, and Barry Diller, and Barry was happy. It was, like, I could go back to my people and say, 'Okay, we will still get the movie, but we're not taking any risks.'"

He tells me the details of this new deal: "We'll advertise it. We will promote it. We will distribute, and he [Barry] felt he had gone through with a great deal, and that the studio was not happy with the movie. And he asked Robert, how can you afford to do that? And Robert said, 'Because I'm rich.'"

The most important component for Stigwood was in the Norman Wexler script, which he just about worshipped. Gershon was impressed with his loyalty. "Robert's willingness to go to bat for him all the way, he never gave up on that script. It is really something that you do not see in Hollywood anymore."

Stigwood would not loosen the language, even though

Paramount was worried about attracting a teen audience with a film that had an R rating, at a time when parents were more vigilant about these things. Gershon told me, "Someone from Paramount said, 'Well, we are gonna lose the entire junior market because they are not gonna be able to get into the film. And there will be stories about how you cannot bring your kids to see the movie.' And they only know John Travolta from *Welcome Back, Kotter*. And Robert was, 'You fool!'"

Gershon was most impressed by Stigwood's trust of his instincts. "But he only played it with his gut. And I said, 'Robert, how do you know someone is right at this point?' He said, 'Darling, while you're sleeping at the Plaza, I'm out gallivanting, trying out all the discotheques in Paris.' He said, 'It is gonna be the hottest thing in America.' And he was right."

Though he was correct in his prediction and the movie made heaps of money for Paramount, Gershon felt resentment from the C-level staff there. "They never forgave him for being successful in it. They could not forgive him. They never would for him being right."

Ron Stigwood learned about how motion picture studios negotiate the number of screens a movie gets. "They [Paramount] only wanted to release it on a few screens both on the East and West Coast. It was Robert that went back to them and said, 'No. This is gonna be a multiscreen release.' At that time, it was ten thousand dollars just to make the film print. So, each film was ten thousand and, therefore, if you had twenty cinemas you are playing—that is two hundred thousand dollars. Which is why a lot of films were shown in one cinema, and then they were physically taken to another cinema (months later) at a time. Robert went back to Paramount said no."

Robert Stigwood always thought big, and he knew about the disco trend growing across America as well as around the world.

Ron Stigwood explained to me that his uncle told Paramount, "I want to do a big-screen release, and he would cover the cost. And that is how he managed to renegotiate the point distribution that he was getting, because Paramount said, 'Well, if you want to do that, you need to cover the cost.' Robert agreed and then they gave him more points toward it, not thinking that the film was gonna make any money."

Ron described those early negotiations. "When Paramount wanted to release this film, they had no idea. When they were seeing the rough cuts, the studio executives just kind of walked out and did not know. And they thought it was gonna be, you know, over in a week. They thought it would hit so many screens and it would just sort of disappear into the ether.

"He wanted to release in hundreds of cinemas, not just in New York and Los Angeles, but in mainstream America. And Paramount had never done that. I mean, they do a limited release and the word-of-mouth bills, and they do a bigger release. By the time it reaches middle America, it is probably six months old. When *Saturday Night Fever* was released, it was being released in small cities in middle America, pretty much at the same time, it was being released in New York and Los Angeles, and it just went through the roof," he adds.

Director John Badham recalls, "There was a phone number that you could call that collected all the box office receipts from all over the country. My friend, Ned Tanen, who was president of Universal at that time, was spending the weekend with Barry Diller. And he and Ned Tanen tell me that he can hear Barry Diller on the phone Sunday morning yelling at the guy, the poor fellow, who must read in the grosses, saying, 'That's wrong. There is too many, there is too many zeros.'"

Ron concludes, "The interesting thing is that the studios

have tried to emulate what was done, but they've never done it successfully."

In 1999, Stigwood told the *Wall Street Journal* that of the $228 million gross at the box office for the film, he made 45 percent in an unprecedented deal. He elaborated to Simon Fanshawe of the *Sunday Times* the same year, "I picked Paramount because it was doing badly at the time. They needed movies." When asked how he managed their reluctance to the crudeness of the language, he said, "It was a street movie, and I told them no kid going to see it would believe it is full of 'goddamns.' So, I said to Barry Diller . . . that I would 'consider' taking out five 'fucks' if they gave me another three percent. They said yes."

Stigwood finished his story with the *Sunday Times* by relating that, after this deal, the head of business affairs at Paramount said, "Never let Diller loose with Stigwood again." Fanshawe told me he was impressed with Stigwood's business acumen. "But that's Stigwood. That sort of business sense is incredible. I love that comment from somebody who says Barry Diller was never allowed to have breakfast alone with people again!"

Paramount's lack of interest in the picture extended to early screenings that did not include reporters, for fear of bad reviews. After one of them, with the Bee Gees and Travolta in the audience, the music was bedded so low that one could hear shoes scuffling on the floor during the dance sequences. According to the 2021 *Mr. Showbiz* documentary, Barry Gibb called Stigwood in a fury, telling him to "turn the damn music up!"

Bobby Zarem was hired by Stigwood for publicity, and faced constant pushback from the New York Paramount public relations department on getting artwork or access to any actors for interviews. The dictate from the LA office was to ignore his requests and to keep the powerful weeklies such as *Time*, *People*, and *Newsweek* away from the screenings.

Zarem was notorious for his handwritten pitches to journalists, his Southern accent, and his laserlike focus on his job. Whatever needed to be done to get the press interested in his clients, he would do it. Like a more rage-filled version of the Tony Curtis character (Sidney Falco) in *The Sweet Smell of Success*, Zarem was not afraid to throw office equipment at colleagues.

When Anthony Hayward of the *Independent* wrote about Zarem's death in 2021, he included the story of when told he could not have any publicity stills for *Saturday Night Fever*, Zarem forced his way into the Paramount marketing offices to get his hands on the color slides, which he sent to major publications like *Newsweek* and *Time*.

With the movie about to hit theaters and the soundtrack burning up the charts, no matter how little Paramount thought of the movie at the time, everyone involved would soon have their lives changed forever.

CHAPTER 13

Fever Rising

On Wednesday, December 14, 1977, ABC TV aired a special, *Disco Fever: A "Saturday Night Fever" Premiere Party*, which was as lavish and over-the-top as Stigwood insisted the movie deserved. Hollywood journalists like Army Archerd and Rona Barrett interviewed the stars as they arrived in Bentleys and limousines.

An array of celebrities, including John Ritter, Jim Brown, Suzanne Somers, Penny Marshall, Hugh Hefner, and Peter Frampton, joined Travolta (who brought Lily Tomlin as his date), the Bee Gees, Andy Gibb (the youngest Gibb brother, a recent addition to RSO Records, and a teen star on the rise), and Yvonne Elliman on the red carpet on what became a sixty-minute commercial for the movie that Stigwood got for free, as ABC used it to promote their own shows and stars.

When the movie opened that Friday, it became a sellout right away. Director Badham remembers, "I had been in New York for the opening and came back, got into Los Angeles on the night that it opened, and it is playing in Westwood at the Village Theatre, which was a great theater, still is. I asked the driver if he would swing through Westwood, and I could see what was going on at the theater. As we drive around the block of the theater, this is ten o'clock at night."

He also recalls, "They're in line for the midnight show, the line is going around, all the way around. And I go into the lobby, and all the Paramount executives are there. There's these forty-year-old adults, fifty-year-old adults jumping up and down like little kids."

Pescow says, "There was a theater on Broadway that had this cement kiosk thing in front of the box office. And they showed the previews of upcoming films. And I am walking past this theater, and there's a ton of people standing around this little thing. And I kind of snuck in there, and it was the trailer for *Saturday Night Fever*, which I had never seen. And I am standing there, looking at this, and I am completely oblivious to the fact that people are starting to look at me. One guy said, 'Aren't you that girl?' And I said, yeah. It was unbelievable."

Pape told me that Paramount's low opinion of the film extended to the West Coast premiere, which much of the cast was not invited to. However, he and Pescow were taken to a theater in Brooklyn to catch the audience's reaction. "We just wanted to see how the local kids reacted to it. So, they snuck us in and planned to get us out before the lights came on. As the movie was playing, all the kids in the audience were going berserk. They were throwing popcorn at the screen. They were talking to each other. I remember thinking, 'Wow, this is really striking a chord.' And then the lights came up before we got out of there and they figured out we were there and there was this crush. I had never had anything like that happen to me before."

He continues, "It was people rushing up to tell us that how well we've represented. We nailed it. It was the neighborhood exactly as it is. I do not think you could make a movie like that today with the language and all that. As far as they were concerned, it was as authentic as they could have possibly hoped for, and they wanted us to know that, and that it meant a lot to them that we did them right. It is amazing the ownership that the kids in Brooklyn took up with that."

Ornstein and Cali felt the effects of the rise in the film's popularity when they attended a Broadway show a few weeks after the opening. "Joe was filming a pilot and I was in a soap opera at that time, and we were deluged by autograph people. It was crazy with flashbulbs, and I am thinking, 'Wait. Is there someone here? Am I missing something? You know? Did I just commit a crime?' We were so freaked out, you know, because neither of us nor any of us were used to that sort of thing."

He told me they decided to leave early. "We stayed for about half the show and I said, 'Let's get out of here and get a glass of wine.' I did not realize at the time what kind of impact it was making on people and what kind of impact it had socially. So, when things like that would come up, I did not really know how to handle it. You know?"

He also made the mistake of leaving himself listed in the phone book. "I would get calls from all over the place. And then, on the street, now people do not do it as often because it has been so long. But when I go to signings and things like that, you know, people recognize me."

The only people who were assured of success were Stigwood and Travolta. Having just finished his starring turn in *Grease* and in the middle of filming his third season of *Welcome Back, Kotter*, he told the *Los Angeles Times* the day of the West Coast premiere he was looking forward to working on his next project with Lily Tomlin and her partner, Jane Wagner (which would become *Moment by Moment*). "I get so excited about it, I called at two thirty a.m., and woke Lily and Jane to talk about it. Basically, it is about a younger man falling in love with an older woman."

Stigwood knew the soundtrack and film would work together in unison to attract a wide audience, but no one could control the critical reaction. Cali reminded me that the movie opened to terrible reviews, and in my research, I found some doozies.

Variety titled its review "Teenage Rock Music Cheapie: The 'R' Stands for Raunchy." Calling out the R rating as a "self-induced handicap," the reporter calls the film "shrill" and "vulgar." The reporter goes on to describe the plot as an "ethnic horror story" and "lots of opportunity to boogie on the dance floor and make out in automobile back seats." Also, about Travolta's performance: "It won't win him any new fans."

Elston Brooks of the *Fort Worth Star-Telegram* describes the screenplay as "pornographic." Al Frank of the *Daily Record* states he finds the movie "fake" and cannot get over Gorney wearing a red dress in the poster and a white one in the film, and Clyde Gilmour in the *Toronto Star* writes "Frankly, I hated it and found the experience sitting through it a boring two-hour ordeal."

David Ansen of *Newsweek* offers praise for the performances and dancing but finds Wexler's script "hackneyed subplots borrowed from other movies." Janet Maslin of the *New York Times* also calls out the "gruesome tricks of the Norman Wexler's screenplay" while still enjoying the first part of the film.

One reviewer who would become a superfan was Gene Siskel of the *Chicago Tribune*. He saw it seventeen times in the theater and then bought the suit at an auction for $2,000 in 1978. His longtime cohost at the weekly syndicated movie review program *Siskel & Ebert*, Roger Ebert, respected his friend's inclusion of *Saturday Night Fever* as being his favorite movie because Siskel could relate to two of its biggest themes: the desire to leave home for a better life, and the trickiness of men and women being platonic friends.

In 1977, on the PBS weekly show *Sneak Previews* (which would evolve into the nationally syndicated *Siskel & Ebert*), Siskel stated in his review, "Oh, it is a very entertaining picture. And I think when I see a picture like this, I realize, 'Hey, it isn't that tough to make a good movie.' All it has to be is something that is real. That dinner table scene, it is a little broad with the hitting going around in the circle, but that kind of thing does happen. And the dancing, all they did was capture a world that we have not seen before. They go into this disco, and you find out that somebody really gets off on dancing. It is a very real kind of picture, and I like it just for that."

Ebert later describes being impressed with Travolta's performance, "a great, cocky affirmation" and while "vulnerable and mostly lovable; playing a kid of nineteen, he looks touchingly young." Ebert also acknowledges Tony's failings with the women in his life, including Stephanie, whom he "attempts to rape" and Annette, which would have been called "an energetic courtship at that time." (He wrote this in 1999.)

All was not bleak in the review department; other critics had a more nuanced appreciation of the film's message. Syndicated reporter Bernard Drew compared the movie favorably to *Rocky* and *Mean Streets*. He states he "likes virtually everything in this film and the music," and "it's the most ingratiating of the year." Joseph Gelmis of both the *Washington Post* and the *Los Angeles Times* said the film is "surprisingly good" and sells "both disco and Travolta well."

Dorothy Smiljanich of the *Tampa Bay Times* wishes that the producers had worked harder for a PG version of the film so it could reach a wider audience, which eventually happens. This is after making a fortune in its R-rated format and selling the TV rights for several million dollars.

The most important person as far as critical acclaim would go to Pauline Kael of the *New Yorker*. She was famous for being prickly, and in a 2010 *Slate* piece titled "Pauline Kael Reviews: The Ones She Got Wrong," she reportedly hated (in no particular order) *The Red Shoes*, *2001: A Space Odyssey*, *The Graduate*, *Dr. Strangelove*, and *Vertigo*. In her career, one of the most famous examples of movies she saved from oblivion was 1967's *Bonnie and Clyde*. Her rave of that masterpiece changed the box office strategy for it to a tremendous success.

Her review in the December 26, 1977, issue of the *New Yorker*, titled "Nirvana," was a love letter to everything from the writing, direction, acting, choreography, and cinematography. Travolta was so proud of the review; he had his assistant make sure every reporter who interviewed him had a copy of it. It was after this that Travolta wondered if he could possibly be nominated for an Academy Award for his performance.

Travolta told James Lipton in *Inside the Actors Studio* in 2003, that he was flying home from a Mexican vacation in February 1978 when he heard about the Academy Award nominations. He told Lipton, "I could not get anyone early enough to find out if I had been nominated, and I arrived at Los Angeles Airport. I thought if there was no one there, it would mean I did not get nominated. But if there was a group there, then I did. So, I ran across and all my friends are there, and they were cheering."

Though Travolta lost to Richard Dreyfuss for *The Goodbye Girl*, he was nominated for the Golden Globes as Best Actor and won the National Board of Review for Best Actor for his performance. He and Donna Pescow were nominated for the New York Film Critics Circle Awards, and Norman Wexler was nominated for his script by the Writers Guild of America. The Bee Gees, in addition to selling millions of records, won the Grammy Award for the Album of the Year.

Pape moved to Los Angeles for his career in 1978 and found that his role in a disco film got him into clubs more easily. When he would visit back home, he headed straight to Studio 54. "Here I was, a nobody, and suddenly they would sit me with Bianca Jagger, Grace Jones, and all these people. And I am just in the Twilight Zone, going, I have no idea what just happened in my life, but it is different."

He was also reminded sometimes that he was not as famous as Travolta. "One of my favorite stories. I am on the subway a couple of weeks after it opened, and I am standing there, and I hear this guy. He looks pretty much down on his luck. And he says to me, 'I know you. You are in that movie.' And then I am thinking to myself, Okay. I am starting to get recognized. He then says, 'You're in that movie. *Mr. Goodbar*, man. That is a really good movie!'

"He thought I was Tom Behringer. Yeah. So, any ego I had at that point just kind of went out the window. You know, I will never forget that moment," he tells me. Pape has been a successful voice artist for decades, but it came after years of trying to escape the notoriety of playing Double J.

"Donna and I kind of came out [West] together at the same time with the same agent out here. And I did not have a publicist. I just paid off any bills that I had. I did not know how to parlay this or how to take advantage of any of this. I was a deer caught in the headlights for a long time, and it was not just a hit movie. It is this whole phenomenon that would go on and on," he recalls.

Pape experienced typecasting and was looking for more acting work. "I would go out and audition, and people would go, 'Hey, would love to cast you, but you're so identified right now.' I heard a lot of that, and there are a million different things that come at you that you are expected to just somehow be ready for, I had never had any time to get up to speed on any of that. I do not regret any of it in hindsight, but for a guy that likes to think he is on top of it, I felt like I was behind the eight ball. I did not understand the business at all. And it is a business, ultimately."

When I ask Pescow about quotes from early interviews, she admits to me she was so stunned by the experience of doing media for her first movie role that she went blank when talking to the press. "When we would do these interviews, I would kind of gear myself up to just be who I am and remember I'm supposed to answer honestly or whatever, but somehow it worked because I didn't know how to do it.

"Right before this movie, I graduated, the American Academy of Dramatic Arts in 1975. And then I was doing theater, and then this happened. I did not know any famous people. I mean, John was the most famous person I had ever met. Unless I was in a play with people that were very, very well known, you know? But I had no experience with any of those things," she adds.

Ornstein and Cali connected after the shooting. "Joe Cali and I were, like, sort of best friends for many years and we produced a cable television talk show back in the day after we did *Saturday Night Fever*. He introduced me to my first wife. He was the understudy for a role at the Public Theater, and he left to do a TV series. He told me about the role and was helpful in my getting that part."

Saturday Night Fever was worshipped by its fans, but there was much rumbling and grumbling by the rock set and comedy world. *Rolling Stone* barely gave the film coverage or increased its reviews of disco records. *Crawdaddy* (founded in 1966 and is one of the earliest rock magazines) had Travolta on the cover, but as a cardboard cutout that Gilda Radner posed with as part of their "high school issue." Travolta gave an essay about his first girlfriend, but for the most part, rock publications stayed away from the movie and the Bee Gees.

Mad magazine and *Cracked* had their issues lampooning the film, which is looked at as an honor. *Saturday Night Live*, in their February 24, 1978, episode (with O. J. Simpson as the host) had its cast member John Belushi with his "samurai" character in a sketch titled "Samurai Night Fever." Belushi would dress up as a samurai in a white costume and a wig and use his sword to break things on the set. He would also mumble his words to mimic a Japanese accent. Simpson plays his brother, who instead of leaving the priesthood, wants to no longer be Black. "It was hipper in the sixties," Simpson says in character. When they later meet with their friends at the local bar, Dan Aykroyd (in character and with a broad "New Yawk" accent) announces how proud they are to be "young, stupid, and have no future at all. I love Brooklyn."

While the film was out for a few weeks, the *SNL* audience roared with approval and could understand all the movie's beats. There was no social media at the time and the film was available only in theaters, so it is remarkable how much the culture absorbed its themes.

The white suit became shorthand for disco and was shown either as an homage or a joke. TV shows were looking for their own disco series but, in the meantime, used the opportunity to add dance and club scenes as often as possible. Everything from *CHiPs* to *The Love Boat* to *Dallas* to *The Muppet Show* had a disco attached to it.

In future films, the white suit is part of the storyline for *The Jerk*, *Airplane*, and *Revenge of the Nerds*. Other "disco movies" that tried to repeat the success were *Thank God It's Friday*, *Xanadu*, *Roller Boogie*, and *Skatetown U.S.A.* with a young Patrick Swayze. Actor David Naughton had a hit with the 1979 disco song "Makin' It," which led to a short-lived TV series of the same name (co-starring Travolta's sister Ellen and Naughton) that year.

Karen Lynn Gorney made several appearances as a judge at discos after the film's release and appeared unsure as to what to do next. She told *People* magazine, in the January 9, 1978, issue that she wanted to focus on a music career, and she had fired her agent. Later she would tour with John Kenley's *Count Dracula* and told the *Akron Beacon Journal* in 1978 that she had known *Saturday Night Fever* would be a success because "only Stigwood could package a thing like that." She told Gannett News that she declined most parts offered to her, because "most scripts are trash."

Travolta spent most of 1978 being one of the most famous people in the world. In June of that year, his next Stigwood production was *Grease*. The $6 million budget had Travolta work the summer of 1977 with the same director of *The Boy in the Plastic Bubble*—Randal Kleiser.

The star only had a few weeks' break from filming in Brooklyn when Kleiser saw him on the West Coast set. He told me, "When he first arrived for *Grease*, he was exhausted from all that dancing. You know, the stuff he did at the disco where he slid down on his knees and up and down, that was incredible. So, I told Patricia Birch [*Grease's* choreographer], 'Oh, man. He is really tired.' She had to tone down some of the things she wanted him to do."

During the shoot, Travolta was extremely sensitive about Hyland's death and used work to escape his grief. His publicist often warned reporters not to bring the subject up and turned away any requests for a quote about it. While filming one of *Grease's* most energetic scenes, he found out *People* magazine, in its June 13, 1977, issue, had him on the cover sporting a huge grin, with a headline saying how he "tries to forget his lady's tragic death with a million dollar movie career."

"We were shooting 'Greased Lightning' when *People* magazine came out. They had told John that they were not gonna exploit that. And when it came out, he was very upset," said Kleiser.

A year later, Travolta was being interviewed for *Rolling Stone* with a cover photograph by Annie Leibovitz (both a *huge* deal) and writer Tom Burke seemed determined to knock his subject down a peg or two. Perhaps thinking his interviewee would arrive with a swelled head or would not be hip enough for their audience—the June 15, 1978, issue features such gems from Burke saying John's publicist is more "efficient than foxy" and wondering what Travolta would order for lunch, he asks his audience, "Why is it so inviting to mistrust him? Because he looks too good and made it too fast?"

Robert Stigwood's media profile exploded in 1978 with appearances with the Bee Gees on the major talk shows like Merv Griffin and the *Tonight Show*. *Newsweek* had a cover story for the "Impresario" on July 31 of that year. At that time, he had *Saturday Night Fever*, *Grease* (in theaters for just over a month at this time and already a smash success), and the opening of his biggest production—*Sgt. Pepper's Lonely Hearts Club Band*.

After being publicly insulted by Paul McCartney for managing the Bee Gees, Stigwood took the Beatles songbook and created a story starring the Gibb brothers, Peter Frampton, and George Burns. With double the budget of *Grease* and directed by Michael Schultz, the movie features an array of actors and musicians covering Beatles songs to varied levels of success. The Earth, Wind & Fire cover "Got to Get You into My Life" is especially strong.

It was a box office dud, but the double album soundtrack was yet another bestseller. McCormick was not involved in this production but he admires his former boss's imagination. "So I went to the premiere, but the irony of it all is when you know the history. Stigwood gets thrown out of Brian Epstein's company because the Beatles don't like him. And they take the Bee Gees and leave, and that's how RSO gets started. And [the Beatles] hated him. They really thought he was terrible, and they could not stand the Bee Gees. So, years later, he creates something where the Bee Gees star as the Beatles! Dude, it is both incredibly ballsy and so stupid," he says, laughing.

Ron Stigwood told me there was concern about plagiarism with this particular film. "The whole thing about *Sgt. Pepper's* is amazing. It is just that when you start putting the whole thing together, and you look at it, at its entirety, you think, where did this come from? And there was a big worry at the time when someone in production, I forget who, drew the comparison to *Yellow Submarine*."

The 1968 animated film starring the Fab Four was a minor hit at the time but is loved by die-hard Beatle fans. Ron explains, "When you start looking at *Sgt. Pepper's Lonely Hearts Club Band* and the Beatles' *Yellow Submarine*. Yes. The parallel becomes quite apparent. And so, there was a big concern at that point about plagiarism, but, basically, the fact that is, it was very, very close."

The *Newsweek* cover story touches on the major signposts of Stigwood's multiple successes but also includes his unnamed detractors, who accuse him of being just a "party thrower" and "It's all a fluke, a lucky streak." Publicist Bobby Zarem, from the time he essentially mugged a marketing associate to get some slides of *Saturday Night Fever* for press, had had a falling-out with Stigwood telling *Newsweek*, "He's a bastard and a lowlife. He uses people and screws them." Stigwood shrugged off these comments, saying Zarem "should live with his psychiatrist."

Meanwhile, around the world, dance schools were giving disco lessons to packed rooms, and restaurants created spaces for a dance floor. Beauty and fashion brands embraced the "new look of the '70s" that was full of shine and glitter. The hippie look was over, and with a new decade around the corner, the media decided that everything surrounding *Saturday Night*

Fever was a harbinger of the shiny 1980s that was sure to come after this terrible decade was over.

Something else that happened at this time—a fight over the credit for Travolta's dancing. Who turned Barbarino into Tony? That would be a most contested issue that would take decades to solve.

CHAPTER 14

"I Wonder Why He's the Greatest Dancer"

There are two big controversies I wanted to resolve in writing this book: John Travolta had a double for some parts of the opening scene, and Deney Terrio "taught John Travolta how to dance" and therefore deserves credit for being the film's choreographer. After interviewing dozens of people and spending a mind-numbing number of hours doing research, I have cracked them both.

Let Us Start with the Opening Sequence

The movie starts with a shot of New York City as the camera pans down to Brooklyn and an elevated N train passing through the neighborhood of Bay Ridge at Eighty-Sixth Street. With the Bee Gees' "Stayin' Alive" as the soundtrack, John Travolta struts his way to work carrying a paint can. It's captivating to watch Travolta own his sexiness.

Director Badham told *Yahoo! Entertainment* in 2022, "I knew the first thing we should see were Tony's feet in those very special purple shoes." He continued, "You can tell that his mind is not on his work; it's on dancing, looking cool, and being a stud out on the street. It puts the focus right away on who the main character is and what is on his mind. It just happened to come together beautifully like that."

John Travolta, 1977. *Alamy Stock Photo.*

Tony Manero is not wearing headphones or carrying a radio. He hears the beat wherever he goes. As Pauline Kael describes it in her 1977 review in the *New Yorker*, "It's his pent-up physicality—his needing to dance, his becoming himself only when he dances—that draws us into the pop rapture of this film."

For the opening sequence, it was first used as coverage when Travolta was in Los Angeles taking care of Diana Hyland. Jeff Zinn was his double (and would be for a few more movies in the 1980s) and felt the pressure of getting the walk correct. He knew Travolta would want to do it all, but there were certain shots Badham needed and he did not want to have the street overwhelmed with fans.

Zinn told me, "He [Travolta] had to go to California overnight. What can we shoot? Let us put Jeff into the wardrobe and shoot the opening sequence, which is basically how it came about. So, I started rehearsing that walk into the camera. And we did many takes of it, and it was pretty cool. They're blasting, 'Stayin' Alive' over a portable sound system speaker. And I am just trying to feel the beat and feel the music and there was a woman on the set who kind of inserted herself. She told me that she was a dancer, and tried to give me notes on my walk, which I politely heard and then did my own thing, because I felt like I had a rather good feeling for it. It is not really a walking tempo. So, to stay in the rhythm was a challenge, but the results speak for themselves," he recalls.

Apparently, Travolta was not happy with how it came out and insisted he shoot the scene with only his footage, as he was the only one who understood how Tony really walked. He had practiced with Lester Wilson and had his own ideas from his research at the clubs.

A few years later, Zinn had a 365-day calendar full of movie trivia. One day he pulls a page, and he recalls to me, "It said, 'Did you know that the walk at the beginning of *Saturday Night Fever* was not John Travolta? It was Jeff Zinn, who was his stand-in photo double.' And so, I have always called this my stupid claim to fame. Right? It is this sort of iconic moment in film history."

Travolta was not amused, as he had spent months perfecting every element of his performance and he famously told Badham that he wanted to be the only "Tony" in that sequence. The debated shot is when Tony is lifting his platform shoes toward the camera. I checked with Badham and his final verdict, that he sent via email to me:

"I believe Jeff is correct that it is his feet and shoes that are featured in the opening walk of *SNF*. John Travolta was in California for the funeral of his close friend, and this shot was one of the few we could shoot that day. Jeff was the logical choice to double the walk. When John returned to work, we went back to the same location and shot full-figure shots of him walking down the street.

"In both cases we used the playback of 'Stayin' Alive' to keep everything on the right beat. The trick was in making the edit from Jeff's feet to John's feet as the camera rises from the feet to show John's upper body. The editor, David Rawlins, cleverly masked the edit with one of the credits (it might be Music by David Shire) that distracts our eye, so we do not notice that we have cut from shot A of Jeff's feet to an identical shot of John's feet. (Sorry to nerd out on this bit of trivia.)"

Zinn was relieved by this news, but he wanted to make sure that people know that he realizes its 99 percent John Travolta in the opening. "Absolutely. He goes up to the window at the pizza parlor, and that is his sister serving him. And there is the scene where the pretty woman walks by, and he turns around. Of course, that is all him."

Controversy 2

"Every dance move that John Travolta did in *Saturday Night Fever* came from me. The finger point, the splits, knee drops . . . I invented all of it." Deney Terrio, *Financial Times*, June 29, 2012.

The above statement by Mr. Terrio is utter nonsense.

In the HBO documentary *Mr. Saturday Night,* he admits to learning all of those moves from the Lockers in 1973 for the Roberta Flack TV special. The fact that every documentary about *Saturday Night Fever* interviews him makes sense, because there are photos of him and Travolta dancing. They had dance sessions for a few weeks in 1976, but that is his total involvement in the movie.

In the opening credits, the choreographer is presented as "Musical Numbers Staged and Choreographed by Lester Wilson." Deney Terrio never spent one day on the set. None of the actors other than Travolta know him from the shooting of the film because he was not the choreographer for the movie. So why does he still claim to be the dance inspiration for disco fifty years later? Because the media let him.

Wilson's name was mentioned in a few of the movie reviews (including the *New Yorker*'s), but most of the publicity was focused on Travolta, the Bee Gees, and Stigwood. When Travolta is interviewed about the pre-film training, he focuses on his running and his visit to dance clubs. He sees all the prep in total to create a character rather than solely focusing on certain aspects of it.

Travolta's *Rolling Stone* cover feature in 1978 (which was syndicated in newspapers across the country) mentions him taking lessons "with a member of the Dancin' Machine, a top disco group, and he began physical workouts with the trainer Sylvester Stallone used for *Rocky*." Neither Gambina, Terrio, nor Wilson is name-checked.

When asked by host James Lipton in *Inside the Actors Studio* in 2003, Travolta gives credit to both Wilson and Terrio. "It was Lester Wilson that did the actual putting together of all these wonderful steps and added some of his own. But it was Deney Terrio that trained me for that six-month period before the movie. So, it was really two people."

He also states in the same interview that the famous "finger point" pose that is used for the poster of the movie and on the soundtrack was his own idea. "It was an afterthought. [After] a fourteen- or fifteen-hour day, the photographer said, 'Do you have anything else in you?' And I said, 'Oh, jeez. Okay. How about this?' I can't believe they picked that shot. I didn't know it would create the iconic figure that it ultimately It became."

Lester's assistant, Lorraine Fields, recalls Wilson being disappointed with his credit from the beginning. "I think the thing that Lester regretted the most was that his name was so small on that marquee. It is like we could hardly find it. And mostly that he was disappointed that he did not sell himself more. Like, 'My name should be right underneath the director's name, because I am creating the aesthetic, I am creating the style, the movement.' The movement, the swag, and the attitude were a lot of the movie. It was not the whole movie, but it was the parts that really allowed people to stand up and clap."

It should be noted that there is no chorographer's union, so getting credited in film and television is never guaranteed. Artists like Bob Fosse and Debbie Allen turned to directing to have more control over their art and get their proper credit. Wilson at this point had been working for more than ten years around the world with his dancing, music, acting, and, most important—his choreography. His troupe, called the Lester Wilson Dancers, were featured in most of the top variety TV shows of the 1970s and 1980s. He produced his own musicals and was constantly "booked and busy."

Ben Vereen told me he can always spot Lester's work on sight. "The dancing in the movie, its Lester. Look at the movement. You will see it yourself. That is all Lester. The extensions, the arm movements, the couples dancing. He thought out everything that he did to make his work perfect."

Vereen met Wilson at a dance studio in Queens in the 1960s. He told me, "Lester was an amazing teacher, and he loved the craft of artists. We are creators. I met Lester at the Bernice Johnson Dance Studio with Michael Peters, Lorraine Fields, and Michelle Simmons. We became like a little troupe for Bernice Johnson. Ben Vereen also said Lester was one of the best choreographers to work with not only because "he was unique, like nobody else. You floated on the air."

This is not to take away from Terrio's work with Travolta leading up to the filming, but there is a massive difference between training one-on-one and putting together multiple routines for duos, solos, and the background characters who were also in the scenes at the disco. Wilson and Fields were on the set and collaborated with the director, the lighting crew, the production office, the camera crew, wardrobe, and the actors. There is not one single scene with dancing that is not connected with them.

The smart thing Terrio did was to package himself as the "Man Who Taught Travolta How to Dance" which is technically true. This does not make him a choreographer. But his resemblance to Travolta, coupled with his friendship with Merv Griffin, made him catnip for the talk show circuit of the 1970s.

Griffin, born 1925 in San Mateo, California, was many things in his life—singer, actor, talk show host, and television giant who not only hosted a successful afternoon chat show (*The Merv Griffin Show*) but also created *Jeopardy!* and *Wheel of Fortune*. He would become a billionaire in the 1980s but at the time of *Saturday Night Fever* he wanted to capitalize the public's new fascination with dancing.

Dance Fever was his idea for a syndicated thirty-minute competition show with dancers from across America being judged by celebrity guests. He pictured the handsome and eager Terrio as the host and wanted to capitalize on his connection to Travolta. He just needed America to get to know this new dancing star.

With Griffin's connections, Terrio appeared on not only his eponymous program but also *Dinah!*, *The Mike Douglas Show*, and local talk shows across the country. Terrio would dance and then offer his favorite stories about teaching Travolta and how he would have been the choreographer, but "my director was fired." The host would notice his resemblance to his star pupil, and he would give a big grin in return. At one of these appearances, none other than Fred Astaire complimented his abilities.

Throughout 1978, Terrio promoted his *Dance Fever* and continued the narrative that he was responsible for the dancing in *Saturday Night Fever*. He appeared in the March 7, 1978, *Orlando Sentinel* as "Titusville Dance Expert Put Travolta on Steps to Oscar." In the interview, he claims that Travolta sought him out for his expertise and that, together, they created the choreography for the movie. He discusses his deal with Griffin and a ninety-minute disco TV special to serve as the pilot for *Dance Fever*.

In the *Daily Oklahoman*, August 13, 1978, Terrio described Travolta as "not a great dancer. He's a good one but not great." The two spent months rehearsing at a dance studio before hanging out at clubs across Los Angeles to get him into character. He claims he was offered a role as assistant dance director after Avildsen was fired and Badham was brought on but "I didn't want that." Executive producer Kevin McCormick disputes this claim.

Meanwhile, Lester Wilson was approached by the Brookville Marketing Company for a home learning system called *Dance, Dance, Dance*. The book includes photos of dances from the Latin Hustle to the Bus Stop, featuring a variety of dancers, including Wilson and Fields and cost only $4.95 with a mail-in coupon. For $9.95, you get "Magic Footprints," which you place on the floor in order of the steps and a "disco album" to get into the beat. Wilson starred in TV commercials for the product, and at the time of this writing you can order copies of the book (sans the footprints or record) from eBay for $65 to $200. It was a very 1970s item to sell to the public, but it was not like hosting your own TV show.

Terrio made notice of this to the *Miami News* on September 27, 1978, with the headline "Mirror, Mirror, Disco Deceiver . . . Who Taught Travolta to Dance in 'Fever'?" Talking to reporter Jon Marlowe, Terrio said he was fired a week before the filming and that John Badham had him replaced with Lester Wilson. Also, he was "frozen out of everything. Lester still goes around telling people he taught Travolta to dance. See, you gotta understand that competition in the dance world is the most vicious in the whole world."

In December 1978, the writer Albert Goldman, whose biographies of John Lennon and Elvis Presley would cause huge controversies in the 1980s for their salacious nature, took on the trend of disco. Simply titled *Disco*, Goldman's review of *Saturday Night Fever* included slagging Wexler's script, making sexist comments about Pescow and Gorney, and mentioning the controversy about the credit for the choreography. He belittled Wilson's TV commercials and cited an interview with Terrio in the *SoHo News*, dubbing him "a smart-sounding young fellow" and therefore deserves all the credit.

Wilson was not interviewed about his work and he didn't think to hire a publicist to get the word out. He kept booking gigs and becoming better as a choreographer with major engagements on Broadway, in films, and on TV specials with Ann-Margret, Lola Falana, Olivia Newton-John, and Liza Minelli.

Maybe it was because Wilson was Black, gay, and unapologetically himself.

On today's social media, artists can produce content of their work and tag their colleagues. Online platforms offer a chance to reach an international audience, something that simply did not exist in the 1970s. His family tried reaching out to the media whenever they noticed a mention of him, but it was barely a whisper compared to the media titan that Griffin was.

Everyone associated with the movie had moved on to their next adventures, and eventually *Dance Fever* entered the TV universe in January 1979. It became a juggernaut that lasted far longer than the trend of disco (the final episode was in 1987). Wisely focusing on a variety of dance styles, the show attracted millions of viewers and Terrio's version of his "work" on *Saturday Night Fever* became gospel.

On August 26, 1979, after *Dance Fever* became a certified hit, the *Los Angeles Times* interviewed Terrio, who said he helped

Travolta with his acting and discussed locations with him, even though the film was going to shoot in Brooklyn. He also mentioned that the solo routine that Travolta danced at 2001 Odyssey was his creation and took six years to perfect. The exact routine he did with the Lockers on the Roberta Flack TV special that Don Campbell and Toni Basil had choreographed.

Terrio became the spokesperson for a disco dance instruction album called *Night Moves*, which included his own commercial and was sold in record stores.

In August 1979, Terrio talked about Wilson in an interview with *Rona Barrett's Gossip* magazine. He described him as a "jazz choreographer" and that "John did not go with him; he did all my stuff. Which was very smart of him. But, as you can see, Lester is selling footprints and I have my own television show." In the same interview he boldly claims he spent hours with Norman Wexler, giving him ideas for his script. That his personal stories inspired major scenes in the movie. (Kevin McCormick dismisses this, as Wexler did not conduct research at L.A. clubs.)

Finally, when asked if he choreographed all the dancing, he replied, "Yes, I choreographed his whole solo dancing and most of his couple dancing. By the time he went to Lester, the movie had already started filming, and NO dancer works on a film during production. The dancing had to already have been implanted in his head by the time he was filming."

Diane Day Crump-Richmond was one half of the duo Motion, which danced with Deney Terrio on *Dance Fever*. As a friend of Wilson and one of his favorite dancers, she was conflicted about taking the gig, considering the bad blood between him and Terrio. "When I did *Dance Fever*, Lester was a little upset, but he knew unless you can keep somebody working all the time, that dancers do other things. With *Dance Fever*, we did that fast and I had to be available within six weeks. And I made that syndication money, which is great money."

She told me she knows Wilson's choreography so well that she could tell on sight his work on *Saturday Night Fever*. "Lester knows Deney Terrio did work with John Travolta to get a certain kind of style. But Lester would put that into a choreography-based dance. Deney did not choreograph that."

When working on press for the show, it was challenging for Crump-Richmond to listen to Terrio give interviews. "It was really hard working with Deney because he was always bringing *Saturday Night Fever* up, and we sat there and had to be in on his interviews. So, we had to listen to him blow smoke up his own butt."

She continues, "I grew to like him. It is just that I knew he [Terrio] had problems, ego problems and drug problems." Terrio has admitted to having addiction issues, which caused him problems on his show. Crump-Richmond says, "We had good choreographers come in, and, you know, we just could not work with him."

Terrio's personal issues made it hard for him to keep in shape for the long day shoots. "Deney would come in from eleven a.m. to two p.m., and he would be exhausted. We were doing long numbers, really fast numbers. We had a lot of them to do, and he just, you know, he just was not in shape."

When I mention the influence of Don Campbell on Deney's moves, she told me, "Deney takes all that stuff from the Lockers. He did not originate anything. He was a club rat; he went from club to club. That is probably why it affected his Hollywood career. He just would not go home. He would stay out all night going to those clubs and going to those after-hours places."

Crump-Richmond also makes sure to credit JoJo Smith and Sue Samuels for their work with Travolta and Gorney. "He

[Lester] loved JoJo's work, and JoJo loved his work. Lester knew that Karen was taking classes, and that they were fine-tuning some stuff. They just blend it all together, the whole direction of the choreography, to make the picture come to life."

Part of my confusion about the lack of coverage for Wilson was how interesting he was. According to Noel Hankin, author of *After Dark: Birth of the Disco Dance Party*, "Wilson was good friends with Josephine Baker, who encouraged him to go to Paris. While there, Wilson started an extraordinarily successful show called *The Young Americans*, with Liza Minelli and Johnny Halliday. He also performed at the 1968 Olympic Arts Festival in Munich, where he was the first American to receive the German equivalent of an Emmy Award."

Perhaps no one (including PR guru Bobby Zarem) had any idea of Wilson's résumé, but he left an impression on people. Travolta told *Vanity Fair* in 2007 about Lester Wilson, "Such an interesting guy. He taught me what he called his 'hang time.' He would smoke a cigarette to greet the day, and he infused my dancing with an African-American rhythm. ... Lester would put on some music and he would say, 'Move with me, mother-fucker—move with me!'"

In the same interview, Paul Pape said, "I don't think Lester got nearly the credit that he deserved. That movie was Lester."

Nevertheless, Lester's family has felt his absence in the coverage the movie gets on its several anniversaries. Lester's sister Julie told me, "I remember one time, Donna Pescow told Phil Donahue on his show that Lester choreographed *Saturday Night Fever*. I jumped and yelled. Show business is tough."

Terrio has served as an unofficial brand ambassador for disco for almost fifty years and he is exceptionally good at it. He travels the world hosting tours that include Tavares, the Trammps, and Yvonne Elliman. Past *Saturday Night Fever* cast members have been his special guests at his shows, and though he cannot do as many splits as in his youth, he looks amazing and knows how to work an audience.

While the soundtrack was taking over the culture, the unavoidable backlash was rising. It would explode in one of the oddest places to see a disco bashing: on a hot summer evening in Chicago at a ball game.

CHAPTER 15

Demolition Men

The Demise of Disco

By the summer of 1979, there was a critical mass of people who not only hated disco music but were enraged by it. Hundreds of rock stations across the country (including WKTU in New York City and WDAI in Chicago) switched to a disco format, with huge ratings lifts. One of those DJs left without a station was Steve Dahl, who was fired on Christmas Eve in 1978 and picked up a morning slot at the album-oriented rock station WLUP ("the Loop") with a huge chip on his shoulder.

From his first day on the air, Dahl attacked his sworn enemy. "WDAI is now Disco Die!" with thousands of fans who followed him wherever he made personal appearances. They called themselves "Coho Lips" (after a breed of salmon introduced in the Great Lakes waters that nearly destroyed the fish population—in other words, a parasite) who were out to destroy disco records every chance they had. Dahl was their leader, and throughout the year their grievances were amplified in the culture.

WKRP in Cincinnati was a popular sitcom in the late 1970s about a rock station fighting for ratings. The morning DJ, Dr. Johnny Fever (played to perfection by the late Howard Hesseman), often railed against dance music and wore a T-shirt that said Death Before Disco. The disco craze was often mocked on *Saturday Night Live*, and when *Rolling Stone* featured the Village

Disco Demolition Night, July 12, 1979, in Chicago at Comiskey Park,
home to the Chicago White Sox. *Album/Alamy Stock Photo.*

People on their April 19, 1979, cover, their editors were flooded
with hate mail.

The Rolling Stones released a disco single, "Miss You," and
Rod Stewart followed with "Da Ya Think I'm Sexy?" The Muppets had a disco record as did Ethel Merman (who performed it
on *Dance Fever*). Even Kiss, the rockiest rock band of the 1970s,
caved in to the trend with one of their biggest hits, "I Was Made
for Lovin' You."

Noel Hankin, the co-owner of Midtown's popular Leviticus club, told me, "The white males back then, many of them
did not want to get dressed up. Women didn't mind getting
dressed up. Black folks back then didn't mind getting dressed
up, but the white guys, they didn't want to get dressed up. They
didn't want to pay admission price to get in, and they didn't
want to have to learn to dance to get the girl."

Comiskey Park (home to the Chicago White Sox) tried
different promotions to attract younger fans to the stadium.

With some Chicagoans unhappy about their favorite stations changing formats, the idea of having a "Death to Disco" night, blowing up some records in a dumpster in center field, seemed like a fun idea. Even if you did not hate disco, there was fatigue setting in for some who felt it was played too much, too often—that there was no escape from it.

It is important to know that at that time, there was only terrestrial radio. No satellite stations or listening online. The radio picked up the stations with a strong enough signal to reach you. Also, most people did not wear headphones, which were bulky and inconvenient to carry. You could hear music everywhere over speakers in elevators, in malls, at stores, at the dentist's office, and even in parking lots, as well as from people carrying "boomboxes." A popular song could become a part of your universe without your being able to tune it out.

According to Hankin, "Another major factor in my opinion is the over-commercialization of the use of the word *disco*. They attached, slapped it on poor products, bad music, bad films, and the word *disco* just went downhill real fast."

The year 1979 was a rough one for disco, as its growing takeover of the culture was creating resentment from non-fans of the genre. Mostly rock fans who not only hated the music but were angry about their favorite rock stations changing formats overnight. This would lead to one of the ugliest aspects of the hatred of music and culture.

Michael Veeck oversaw promotions for the Chicago White Sox, and it was his job to try and fill the fifty-thousand-seat ballpark with a losing team. They were lucky to see twenty thousand in the stands, and the owners were pressured to produce big ideas. Back in his father's day, Bill Veeck (a World War II veteran who lost a leg serving his country) would give away pigs, arrange weddings at home base, and even concocted a scoreboard that lit up and "exploded" with smoke.

"Teen Night" meant charging $0.98 and a disco album to "burn" as the way of entry. With Dahl promoting the hell out of it on his show, over seventy thousand showed up, ready for a riot. The proud DJ showed up in a military uniform and thanked his "disco army" for showing up.

It was a doubleheader that night, meaning two games were being played. In between the first and the second, the "Disco Demolition Night" blew up a stack of records while the lights on the scoreboard imitated an explosion. This is when thousands of fans flooded the ballfield. With the drinking age being nineteen at the time, the crowd was fully loaded. (Supposedly, actor Michael Clarke Duncan was among those who took to the field.)

There were signs and T-shirts that said Disco Sucks, which was also the mantra of Dahl and his fans. On YouTube, it looks and sounds like pure mayhem.

Dave Hoekstra, the coauthor with Steve Dahl of the book *Disco Demolition: The Night Disco Died*, writes, "When the records blew up, the audience flooded the field. Fans tore out seats. Bonfires were lit with pocket lighters. Chicago police arrived at White Sox Park on horseback."

In the Bee Gees HBO documentary, *How Can You Mend a Broken Heart*, music producer Vince Lawrence talked about being an usher at Comiskey Park when he was just fifteen years old. He told the *Undone* podcast (from Gimlet Media) in 2016, "I said to my boss: 'Hey, a lot of these records they are bringing in aren't disco—they're R&B, they are funk. Should I make them go home and get a real disco record?' He said no: if they brought a record, take it, they get a ticket." He laughs. "I want to say maybe the person bringing the record just made a mistake. But given the number of mistakes I witnessed, why weren't there any Air

Supply or Carpenters records—they weren't rock'n'roll, right? It was just disco records and Black records in the dumpster." To him it resembled a "book burning."

Lawrence remembers the staff having to go through the locker room to exit the stadium. Even though he was wearing a T-shirt for Dahl's station—he said he heard racial slurs thrown in his direction.

Soon after the incident, Lawrence was chased by a white teenager in a pickup in the blue-collar neighborhood Bridgeport, which is close to Comiskey Park. To drop charges, he was offered $5,000, which he used to buy two synthesizers. Lawrence would go on to become one of the innovators of house music in Chicago. He feels that the event did not cause the "death of disco" but ironically took it in a new direction, to one of the most popular genres of music around the globe.

Hankin sees the similarities in the (largely) white male anger in 1979, and what is happening with today's "culture wars." That inclusivity was the reason disco was not special and therefore deserved the hatred. He explains, "I would say my argument when people say disco sucks, that whole 'white male, you need a guitar, and blah, blah, blah.' Disco was welcome to anybody. You could be tall, short, fat, skinny, beautiful, not beautiful, white, gay, bi, straight. Everyone belonged."

Dahl's anger against the Bee Gees for embracing a new style is the kind of entitlement a rock DJ could have at the time. He made fun of them for their looks (especially Barry, who is beyond handsome, while Dahl has a great face for radio) and he used a phony falsetto voice to play corny satire songs from the band. The fact that the band embraced this trend without apology or irony was insulting to rock snobs.

The Bee Gees were known as a pop/rock group for several years, but it was not until they leaned into a funkier sound that they reached worldwide fame. They wore white suits, opened their shirts to show off their tanned skin, went on chat shows with their manager, and were basically comfortable with being famous. For some reason, it was cool for Led Zeppelin to seek fame and fortune, but not the Bee Gees.

The 1970s were a wild amalgam of so many things; some people think the Vietnam War happened only in the 1960s, but in fact did not end until April 30, 1975, with the fall of Saigon. Despite all the claims of progress with the civil rights movement, race remained a lightning rod issue with school busing in major cities.

Stigwood's client Eric Clapton went on a racist rant onstage in Birmingham, England, in 1976, decrying against "foreigners," saying, "Stop Britain from becoming a Black colony. . . . England is for white people, man." Rock Against Racism was formed in the UK to combat rising incidents of racial harassment.

Second-wave feminism was thought to bring equality to women, but the Equal Rights Amendment (as of this printing) still has not been passed. Anita Bryant used her middle-of-the-road fame to attack gay people. It is still legal to discriminate against the LGBTQ community in much of the United States.

It is hard to conceive that a sound that is so relentlessly joyful could cause so much drama. I recall listening to the Village People with no idea about gay culture at all. That the members were dressing in stereotypes of men from "the Village" went completely over my head. But the fact that *Rolling Stone*—the bastion of white, hetero rock supremacy—gave them a cover made people angry.

Comedians and comedy writers were using words like *disco*, *the Bee Gees*, and *the Village People* as punch lines to strike back against effete men and a music they find annoying.

Meanwhile, Travolta decided to strike out in a new direction.

After completing his trio of films with Stigwood (1978's silly *Moment by Moment*, a romance with Lily Tomlin released just six months after *Grease*, which sent his career downward for a bit), the star was lucky enough to catch on to the next "big thing" that happened in music—country music and 1980's *Urban Cowboy*, which led to a rise in cowboy-styled bars with bull-riding machines taking over many former discos.

In 1980, the Bee Gees filed a lawsuit against Stigwood, claiming he was taking a disproportionate share of the profits and exerting too much control over their artistic direction. Stigwood told the *Daily Telegraph* in 1998, "I was so incensed. By the time the accountant had finished going over everything, it turned out I overpaid them. They had to write out a check to me!"

Eventually, all parties made up and the Bee Gees even contributed to the sequel to *Saturday Night Fever*—1983's *Staying Alive*.

CHAPTER 16

Far from Over

Staying Alive was Robert Stigwood's last chance to bring Tony Manero on screen, and in the early 1980s he hired Norman Wexler to write the script. The idea for this version of Tony Manero was that he was still struggling to find himself and missed home. He heads back to Bay Ridge to visit Annette and Joey, who are now married with kids. It would have the same flavor as the original, but Travolta would not join in on anything that did not show Tony improving himself.

After seeing *Rocky III*, a film written, directed, and starring Sylvester Stallone, Travolta wanted to see Tony achieve his professional goals. He asked Stallone to direct and collaborate with Norman on the script. Wexler's daughter Erica told me it nearly destroyed his sanity. "That, for Norman, was a horrible event. He wrote the sequel after Travolta had a dip in his career.

"Norman wrote a good script with the same tone and grittiness. He did not have him become a dancer. He had him struggling with lots of odd jobs and all this. And it still had the same kind of attitude and truthfulness. What would become of this gentleman if he really came to Manhattan? How hard it would be for him," Erica remembers.

Joe Cali regrets this version was never filmed. "I'm sure the guys [the other actors who played the Faces] all told you, but getting the script, being in it and married to Donna, working in a garage, John coming back from the city and just seeing what

John Travolta returning to the role of Tony Manero in 1983's *Staying Alive*, directed by Sylvester Stallone. It began as an original screenplay by Norman Wexler. *United Archives GmbH/Alamy Stock Photo.*

our life is like, you know, so great. And then fucking Stallone takes the script and just said, 'No. We do not want anything from the other movie. It would have been great to see a me with a pot belly and a little bit older with kids screaming and, you know, just perfect."

He continues, "Sly took that out, which is too bad, because he would have done great with it. Anyway, I saw the movie, and I did not love it because it was too far off from what the original was. You know, you need that balance for his character [Tony]."

Part of what inspired Wexler's script, according to Erica, was that he hated the velvet ropes at popular nightclubs and its implied elitism. "Studio 54 was a massive thing then, and Norman hated all that kind of pretension and snobbery about getting into clubs and you are special, and you are a star. You are not a star. It is the degradation of other human beings," she explains.

Erica told me the script had Tony Manero take revenge against the world-famous nightclub in the script. "So, the thing climaxes where he breaks through the line at Studio 54 and there is a riot. Again, all the resentment of all the people who are not allowed in because you are just plebes and you are common, low-class, and not Bianca Jagger or whatever nonsense."

If there was anything Stallone was okay with, it was elitism and celebrity. This was the 1980s and people wanted to see winners on the screen. According to Erica, "And then he [Stallone] rewrote the whole movie, and it was just tawdry."

The story takes Tony from Bay Ridge to Times Square in the mid-1980s, when he struggles with several odd jobs, lives in a cheap hotel (the pre-gentrified era of New York City), and has a girlfriend, Jackie (played by Cynthia Rhodes), whom he cheats on frequently, and is often flirting with other women right in front of her.

He is warm for Laura, played by Finola Hughes, who was in *Cats* on the London stage before this gig. Laura is a rich, successful, and gorgeous stage star with killer hair who sleeps with Tony and then quickly dumps him, so that we as an audience are supposed to hate her. Tony winds up in the chorus line for her Broadway show, while Kurtwood Smith plays the mean choreographer.

The story and dialogue are laughably bad when it is not just being filler for the last production number wherein Tony steals the lead solo while onstage in front of his mother, who is in the audience. The show (within the movie) is called *Satan's Alley,* and its plot is indecipherable. We should be rooting for him, but this Tony is a narcissist and a creep.

Speaking to the *New York Times* on July 10, 1983, Travolta discussed whether being a sex symbol was demeaning to his talent. He replies, "I like sex and I feel sexual, so if that's coming across, then I don't want to deny people's perception." He also stated he did not like Wexler's script for the sequel because it was "an anti-dance piece, very cynical."

Stallone put Travolta under his uber-athletic wing with a calisthenics program that leaned him up while also building his muscles. Cameos from Donna Pescow (Annette) and Val Bisoglio (Tony's father) were filmed, but for some reason they were not included in the final cut. Tony's mother (Julie Bovasso) returns to give him sage wisdom and a slice of pie. (What is more wholesome and American than Mom and apple pie?)

Norman Wexler tried to have his name removed from the credits, but he shares it with Stallone. Erica told me, "That's what happened to Norman. He took the money, but he hated the whole thing. It is a shame." I have been told off the record that the movie studio spent weeks trying to find Norman during the early press events. As was his wont, Norman made himself disappear from the shame of the association.

Herb Michelson of the *Sacramento Bee* wrote in his column on August 4, 1983, that he felt *Staying Alive* was a "silly" movie and, according to his sources, Norman Wexler was "incensed" about the movie and said, "I know it's the sour grapes of a rewritten writer after the fact" and that the film is "vacuous, impoverished, and crude."

To promote the film in the August 18, 1983, *Rolling Stone*, Travolta poses in a loincloth on the cover—tanned and oiled up within an inch of his life. The results are startling. Richard Avedon took the photos, and in the age of Chippendales dancers and MTV, he is smoking hot and has come a long distance from the earnest young actor who wanted to be taken seriously in 1977. This Travolta is open for attention and *horny.*

Nancy Collins ran the interview and expressed shock at how honest and candid he was with nary a publicist in sight. Travolta explains that in the six years since the original film, his character had grown up and that he was going through similar issues with women in real life.

Since the death of Diana Hyland, he had not been romantically linked to anyone long-term. Travolta explains about having an on/off relationship with actor Marilu Henner and a few other women "on the line." And as for Tony Manero's reasons for his behavior toward women in his late twenties, "He is never willing to commit to one woman. He sleeps with one girl and, as soon as he is finished, calls the other to make sure she is not sleeping with anyone."

When Collins asked Travolta for his personal definition of love, he said, "I do not mean to sound whimsical or neurotic, but I have discovered that my life is malleable. I have the ability to feel like I am in love with a few people at the same time. It is not as if I am a farmer. If I were, I would have no problem being with one person, committing to that lifestyle. But I am in a business where I find it very hard, at this point, to be monogamous."

Also, at the time when this interview took place, he was not as involved in Scientology, saying to Collins, "I have not had any auditing for about a year and a half." And "I try to separate the material and the organization, because I don't agree with the way the organization is being run." (This was three years before the leader L. Ron Hubbard passed away.)

After the sex talk (wherein he admits to having fantasies about Jane Fonda and Lesley Ann Warren and denies he is gay), Travolta explains he wanted *Staying Alive* to be more about show business than what Norman Wexler had put in his screenplay.

Stallone and Travolta wanted Tony to be a dance teacher who finally gets his big break in a big, splashy production.

Travolta trained for months under Stallone's guidance, and the experience was the opposite of what boxer-trainer Jimmy Gambina used to get the star in shape for *Saturday Night Fever.* For months, the *Rocky* star made him lift weights for hours every day on top of cardio.

There is not any real talk about character development in this piece or in any interview I can find from this time that stands out. The story as told to multiple outlets was that Travolta (as Tony) was back and sexier than ever. And that was about it.

Travolta's sister Ann told me he worked extremely hard to get his body in shape for the film. "I remember going up to his house in Santa Barbara, and there was a big tent that they had made up. It was like a big, huge dance place. For *Staying Alive.* I remember seeing him at a theater in LA doing all the dance routines. What he did to his body? Oh, my God!"

What many people do not remember (or know) about *Staying Alive* is that it was a big hit in 1983. With a budget of $20 million, it made $64 million at the box office and is the eighth most successful film that year ahead of *Risky Business* and *National Lampoon's Vacation.*

The soundtrack, which in addition to the Bee Gees also included Stallone's brother, Frank Stallone, sold over 3.5 million copies. Frank's song "Far from Over" was a top ten hit on the *Billboard* charts (and is catchy as hell, if you ask me). The critics hated the movie, but people showed up in droves and more than twenty million tickets were sold in America alone. It also played for years on cable TV to high ratings.

Travolta admitted the film's weird history when his costar Hughes showed up in the audience for his interview with James Lipton's *Inside the Actors Studio* in 2003. He told the crowd obviously delighted to recognize her, "Everyone secretly loves *Staying Alive*, because they know all her lines. They do not remember mine, but they know all hers."

Celebrity sightings in *Staying Alive*: Richie Sambora, formerly of Bon Jovi, as a member of Frank Stallone's band; Patrick Swayze is featured as a dancer for *Satan's Alley*; and Stallone himself makes a cameo, wearing an enormous fur coat and bumping into our lead character. (The director later admitted he should have made the movie darker and grittier.)

For die-hard *Saturday Night Fever* fans, saying the sequel is a disappointment is an understatement. It is like saying ice cream should not be heated like soup. The film is not even so bad that it is fun. This movie takes itself very seriously while forgetting to include any of the magic of Tony's character from the original. The dance sequences are filmed at baffling angles, and nothing about *Satan's Alley* segment makes any sense. It currently sits at 0 percent on Rotten Tomatoes.

Pauline Kael of the *New Yorker* felt the publicity for *Staying Alive* hurt Travolta's career trajectory for a while. "Suddenly, everyone was making fun of him for posing on magazine covers. They were reviewing his body instead of his movies. The ridicule got out of hand."

Stallone and Travolta promoted the movie on the *Tonight Show* on July 8, 1983, when it was hosted by Joan Rivers. After showing off Travolta's physique to the appreciative "woots" from the audience, they discussed their working relationship.

According to Stallone, "It was interesting because I never thought that I would end up working with someone who is so close to me in a sense. We are both of Italian descent and about the same age or whatever. When the idea was presented at first, I said, 'I do not think I can do it.' But when I met him in the challenge, in the dance, I thought it might work."

Stallone went on to say, "I was a little worried about it because I did not know that much about dance. But I said, maybe if I approach it from a very athletic point of view and knowing how dedicated John is, we could do something that is so much different than disco, because this has nothing to do with disco."

After the release of the sequel, no one thought to touch the original film or continue the story in a new direction. During the mid-1990s, TV and movie properties were being adapted into Broadway musicals, such as *Beauty and the Beast* (1994), *The Lion King* (1997), and *Footloose* (1998.) It was around this time that Stigwood had an idea to properly resuscitate *Saturday Night Fever* for a new generation. He would bring it back to his first love—the stage.

CHAPTER 17

Stigwood's Last Dance

In the early 1980s, Stigwood had left the public eye, no longer feeling the joy in discovery and working. His picker was off, and he seemed to have lost his ability to predict new trends. The Bee Gees had gone on their own and he had no film productions on his slate. He shut down RSO Records in 1983 and laid off his staff except for domestics and one personal assistant. The former workaholic impresario spent his days in his various homes and yachts with a butler, gambling and drinking. Lots of drinking.

Kevin McCormick left RSO productions after the flop of 1978's *Moment by Moment* and never looked back. One of the biggest reasons for not keeping in closer contact with his former boss was Robert's excessive alcohol use. He told me, "He used to be incredibly instinctive and smart. When I left, I saw him a couple more times after that, but he was not in my life. I had friends who continued and were very much in his orbit. I didn't want to be around that world anymore because I'd outgrown it. He was a big alcoholic. And that just wasn't my life. I didn't know how to be half in and half out of it."

He continues, "And here's the other thing. The biggest takeaway for me after that was that here's a guy believing you can have anything you want in your career if you're willing to pay the price. And he'd gone broke a couple of times. He was determined to be so rich that he never had to worry about money again. He put vast amounts of money into Bermuda outside the tax structure.

Saturday Night Fever, the musical, was announced in London
in May 1998. *From left to right*: Maurice Gibb, Anita Louise Combe
(Stephanie), Adam Garcia (Tony), Robin and Barry Gibb.
PA Images/Alamy Stock Photo.

He had no incentive to take any risk. He only wanted to recycle
ideas that he'd already been successful with."

In 1997, Stigwood's longtime friend Paul Nicholas and his
production partner David Ian were involved in producing *Grease*
for the London stage using the songs from the 1978 soundtrack.
Owning the rights to so many musicals kept Stigwood solvent for
years. Watching the Bee Gees embraced by a whole new generation after their 1997 induction into the Roll & Roll Hall of Fame
gave him the idea that it was time to revive *Saturday Night Fever*.
Twenty years later, it was now considered a modern classic.

To bring it to the stage, Stigwood brought on writer Nan
Knighton, director and choreographer Arlene Phillips, and Nicholas to assist with the book (the script, in theater speak). The first
thing to figure out was how to present the show. Do we have the
actors sing? Do we have a band and singers onstage for the music
numbers? How do we make this family-friendly?

Nicholas explained, "I never really reconciled how to do it.
And I think at one point, we questioned if we should do it in

Las Vegas, with a band behind and have a group performer and actors act for the story? And I think it was me. I don't want to take credit, but I said, 'Why can't the actors sing the song?' All these songs kind of fit beautifully with the story."

Knighton, who had just completed *The Scarlet Pimpernel*, had known Stigwood for years through her husband, John Breglio, an entertainment lawyer who had the impresario as his client for years. She told me his instructions about shaping the story: "He specified that he wanted the musical to stick fast to the movie. A lot of the work I did in the adaptation was structural—creating transitions and segues, cohering long strings of movie sequences into fewer stage scenes."

Phillips is one of the top choreographers in the theater world (*Starlight Express, Annie*) and a fan of the movie. She told me, "Disco changed the world. I watched it change London overnight. Suddenly, partner dancing became the rage, and all the clubs and dance halls had disco contests.

"I remember being floored the first time I saw the movie and watching the dance club filled with young people dancing on that floor and the smoke machine. They were so beautiful, and the music was entrancing," she said. The challenge became to create moments onstage that were equal to the film. Remember that all the dancers needed to be excellent for the stage.

"John Travolta's solos are some of the best in movie dancing history. His partner's dancing is not as strong, but they were supposed to get beat by the Puerto Rican competitors. In the stage production, we made that clearer," she explained.

Knighton had to figure out how to move the action of several locations on one stage while also keeping the grit Stigwood wanted. "I did this sort of synthesizing throughout the show, often having to shift or rearrange dialogue, sometimes shorten, or add a new line for segues to work. Additionally, the dialogue placement could be crucial in understanding what was in the movie, which was only an expression in the eyes. For the most part, those segue changes and dialogue fixes were imperceptible, which was the best of my work," she remembers.

Phillips told me Barry Gibb also had sway over the production, "Robert Stigwood was passionate about bringing the show to the stage, and he and Barry Gibb were heavily involved in every aspect."

She and Knighton had watched the film dozens of times to get all the emotional beats down and found it a big challenge to translate onstage. "We discussed things such as my feeling the stage show would need a bit more humor, natural character humor. For example, there's a tiny moment in the movie when Tony shocks the little Italian grandmother who lives with them, and she hurtles off in embarrassment. I wanted to have her in the show and pop her in and out once or twice. Arlene liked the idea, but Robert nixed it."

Nicholas told Stigwood it would be important to workshop the show to get an honest reaction from the audience. "Nan did a great job in fleshing the whole thing out, but I wanted to make sure we do workshops here because if it doesn't work in a room with five people, you know, watching it, then it won't work at all. Plus, the fact that we needed a Tony Manero."

Adam Garcia was a twenty-four-year-old tap dancer from Australia who impressed Nicholas (and his teen daughter) with his charisma and star potential. With dark hair and blue eyes, he resembled Travolta, but his first audition for the West End's updated *Grease* did not go well. He was not used to projecting his voice, but eventually, he improved enough to play Doody. When it came time to find a new Tony, Nicholas made sure that Stigwood was at Garcia's audition.

Having spent time in Brooklyn working on his accent,

Garcia tried out for the part of Tony, and once again, his energy was low. After being coached by Nicholas and Phillips, Garcia changed his physique and upped his energy level to nail the part. But right up to previews, the show was still being worked out.

"For Arlene and me, previews were intense but also so much fun. We sat side by side each night, whispering our thoughts and taking notes. I particularly remember on preview nights how the two of us would dash from one side of the dress circle to the other to view any given scene from different points of view," says Nan Knighton.

She told me that during one of these previews, where they experimented with different dialogue, Stigwood had a full-throated temper tantrum. "At one point during previews, Robert did notice a few changes I had made and called a meeting directly after the performance, during which he hit the ceiling, letting Arlene and me know in no uncertain terms that the *Saturday Night Fever* onstage was to be from *Saturday Night Fever* the movie. Period. He must have known that changes had to be made while consolidating scenes, but he was very protective of the piece."

While he eventually apologized for his outburst (she told me, "I do tend to crumble in the face of anger") and Phillips forgave him, it was a sign that he was having difficulty adapting the material. He could not see further than his memories of the 1977 production, which made the task for his creators very trying.

Stigwood felt terrible for losing his temper with Knighton and Phillips. He normally preferred working with women (according to his nephew Ron) because he personally found them to be hardworking while not as aggressive or competitive as men could be. Knighton told me that years later, "He sent me a magnolia tree and I wondered if this was another apology. We planted it and it is still thriving. I refer to it as 'Robert's tree.'"

Also, making *Saturday Night Fever* stage-worthy meant taking out the foul language. "When we first created the musical, we were shocked to see how many parents brought their small children to the show. We quickly worked at eliminating much of the language from the film, and the violence had to be lessened," Phillips told me.

Regarding the location of the London show, following Stigwood's edict that everything be big and flashy, Nicholas told me, "Robert decided he wanted to put it at the London Palladium, one of London's bigger theaters, with over two thousand seats. It's a brand-new show, but that's typical Robert."

Also, changing the show's gender politics was important. The Annette rape scene is discarded (thankfully). Anita Louise Combe, who played Stephanie, wanted to add more texture to her character. She told me, "I wanted to make her a girl with a difficult background. To have a bit of a story behind her, maybe a very difficult upbringing, and just always aspiring and having a fantastic tenacity to become a better person."

She continues, "Even if she was a little bit pompous, sort of thinking she was better than you. I got into quite a few debates with Arlene about the character, because when you're doing a musical, you must tell the story sometimes through song. Stephanie was offered good moments to show another side of herself."

For the new stage show, the Bee Gees had written a song for Celine Dion called "Immortality," which became a hit in the UK. However, Combe felt another tune would work better from their catalog. "One day during our second workshop, I thought I'm going to see if I can take the bull by the horns here and see if I can convince Robert Stigwood, the producer, to ask Barry Gibb if I could sing 'What Kind of Fool' (the 1980 hit with Barbra Streisand and Gibb), a phenomenal song, and frankly anything that Barbra Streisand touches is gold as far as I'm concerned," she told me.

To Combe's delight, Stigwood called Barry and handed her the phone. "And he handed the phone to me, and he said, 'Well, you're going to have to ask Barry yourself.' Barry was in California."

She continues, "And I said, 'I know it's not a Bee Gees song, but it's one of your songs, and one of my all-time favorite songs. I know it's a duet, but I think the sentiment of that song could work for Stephanie.' And he said, 'Of course.' He's such a nice man."

Joanne Farrell eventually took over the role of Stephanie in London. It was important to her that a complicated power dynamic had been created from her character's affair with her boss. "I mean, I identified with it in the way that I'm from Manchester. It's two hundred fifty miles from London. I moved at sixteen to study because this is what I wanted to do. I wanted to take that step. And, talking about predatory men, I mean, it was rife. Obviously, that period would probably have been worse," she told me.

Opening night for the London show was a grand affair. "Robert Stigwood did everything big, and his opening-night parties were always a wonderful spectacle," says Arlene Phillips. Even though the reviews were mixed, most critics agreed that Adam Garcia was a top future talent. Stigwood brought his friend Sarah Ferguson as his plus one for the red carpet, and a glorious time was had by all.

Knighton remembers, "When we opened in London, we were a success. Even the semi-negative reviews were generous, and everyone acknowledged Adam Garcia's brilliant performance as an actor and a superlative dancer. I don't think there was ever any doubt that *SNF* would be an enormous crowd-pleaser, and audience members could hardly wait for the 'megamix' [a remix of a medley of songs] at the end of each show to leap up and finally be allowed to join in, dancing and singing along with the cast onstage."

She adds, "We used to worry that all that heavy foot stomping in the dress circle would simply cause it to crash down. This was always said with a laugh, but the dancing and cheering did get fairly wild from the stalls straight up to the highest balcony. Working in the Palladium is enormous fun, especially at such electric moments when sparks seem to fly through that huge venue."

Nicholas was relieved it was such a big hit (and that he made his investment back). "So, we opened it, and you could tell on the first night that the audience was just ready for it. Like *Grease,* when you start the overture about 'Summer Nights,' they all clap. The same thing happened with *Saturday Night Fever*; there was a buzz."

Stigwood was so eager to remind the world he was back that he gave a few eye-opening interviews. Now sixty-three and dealing with diabetes, he drank throughout his chat with Simon Fanshawe, a reporter for the *Sunday Times.* Fanshawe, speaking to me from London, offered me his private notes, clearly recalling all those years later his time spent with "Stiggy."

"He was sharklike. That was what I suggested, but the visit experience was extraordinary. He was the most conscientious and gracious host. I stayed the night at Barton on the Isle of Wight. And when I got there, the latest *Vanity Fair* was on my bedside table. And there was a novel. I don't remember what it was, but it was chosen because he'd found out about me," he begins.

"This is before Google, by the way. And so careful and clever—just beautiful hosting. That is what was extraordinary about him, and I think that shows a kind of sensibility and charm about that. I mean, it's also manipulation," he adds.

Stigwood saved his biggest reveal when he asked Fanshawe what his idea was for the perfect meal. "I mean, bringing the chef in and saying, 'What would you like for lunch?' and it was summer. And I said my perfect summer lunch has always been beef consommé with chives, poached salmon, new potatoes, frisée salad, and mayonnaise. Also, summer pudding with cream. That's what appeared. Wow."

Fanshawe also noticed Patrick Bywalski, Stigwood's longtime companion and business manager, "Who I think was French, married, and very handsome. And then the evening went on, and we had dinner, and he kept putting money on the horses during the afternoon. Soon, it was two o'clock in the morning, and we were drinking very good brandy, and that was how he was."

Stigwood never officially came out, but he was curious about Fanshawe, who has been open about his sexuality most of his life. "He was investigating my experience as a gay man. That is a very classic cross-generational thing. I am old enough to know men who were out and active adults when it was illegal. And I sensed that about him, that there was a sort of precarious kind of thing. I always wondered whether he ever had a love."

The show ran in London from May 1998 to February 2000, and it was mostly to full houses. Arlene Phillips was nominated as Best Choreographer and Adam Garcia for Best Actor at the Lawrence Olivier Awards in 1998. Nan Knighton received a Tony Award for Best Book of a Musical for *The Scarlet Pimpernel* at the same time. Knighton describes working on two popular shows simultaneously. "It was a very busy time, but also obviously thrilling."

It was time to take things to Broadway, bringing the story

back to its place of origin. The producers were concerned about the "Disney-fied" nature of New York City on the cusp of the millennium. This was no longer a city where you must fight to stay alive. Crime was down, the streets were cleaner, and, most important, Brooklyn was now the cool place to live.

Gentrification reached the outer boroughs. Brownstones that went for $50,000 in the 1970s were now selling for millions. Would theatergoers embrace this jukebox musical that had a toned-down Tony Manero?

The trouble began early during the casting of the show; Adam Garcia stayed in London and found the part too exhausting to continue beyond his contract. Plus, the Minskoff Theatre seated more than sixteen hundred people, which the producers worried might be too big. Stigwood wanted the largest theater available, which meant that *The Scarlet Pimpernel* was moved to the Neil Simon Theatre. *Saturday Night Fever* had a cavernous space to fill with disco nostalgia.

The first indication things that might not go smoothly was the multiple casting calls and auditions to cast the leads. James Carpinello, who played Tony, recalls, "It was a grueling audition process, but slowly it whittled down, and I got the job. And the work to get into stage shape started there. They flew me to London, and I saw the show. It was crazy. I mean, I was twenty-two years old. You know? I had just gotten out of college, and that process was nutty."

Paige Price was hired to play Stephanie after several auditions and callbacks. She remembers, "So when I first auditioned for the show, too, I wasn't sure which part I would go in for, Stephanie or Annette. And they had me do both materials for quite a while. I had eight auditions for that play, which is a lot!

"And they weren't just, like, come in and sing a song and do a scene. They were partner dancing from ten in the morning till four in the afternoon, and we would have a break in the middle. You would partner with dozens of different people. You would learn choreography. Then you would have a break, then you would be back, and then we would work on scenes. I mean, it was very, very extensive. It was shocking how many auditions we all went through," she recalls.

Nicholas believes this indecision and Stigwood's not listening to the show's producers are signs that he had lost some of his magic. "Well, that sounds to me like Robert wasn't paying attention. Robert was always a drinker and could always handle it. And Robert loved having a good time and was a lovely man. But I think by then, he was beginning to, you know, it was beginning to be more than it should be."

The part of Annette went to native New Yorker Orfeh, a powerful belter who once played Janis Joplin in an off-Broadway production of *Love, Janis*. She and choreographer Phillips have remained friends all these years. Arlene told me, "When Orfeh sings, you can feel deep into the pores of your skin." She brought the house down every night with her version of "If I Can't Have You."

Orfeh liked how they upgraded her character. "I was very happy about that. I think it was more of a tug of war, and it began and ended with her love for Tony and how he treated her. And, you know, occasionally, she'd be like, 'All right. Well, then I'm just gonna go and mess around with Gus.' You know what I mean? It wasn't the other way around. They weren't manhandling her. It was more like Annette was constantly being forlorn and rebuffed by Tony to be the party girl."

Carpinello wasn't as highly trained a dancer as his costars and found the choreography exhausting, "Yeah, it was really hard. All of them are just exceptional dancers and have had incredible careers. I mean, Andy Blankenbuehler choreographed *Hamilton*!"

Like Adam Garcia, Carpinello found dancing and singing throughout the whole production draining. In the movie, Tony's first big solo doesn't happen until a third of the way into the movie. While onstage, the actor has to deliver from the very first scene.

Carpinello remembers, "If you think about the movie, you see him dance once with the girl in the club. I didn't leave the stage. It was like every number. Like my body, our bodies were broken. When I watch those videos of it, it's like I'm watching another person. I wasn't primarily a dancer. I was an actor and a singer, and I worked for months ahead of time to be able to do that show."

Orfeh feels that Phillips's choreography is one of the toughest she has ever performed. "I maintain that it was the most challenging, the most difficult, the most unbelievably glorious choreography. It was the hardest to learn, the most effective. We were at a time during our run when Broadway was just very unkind to us. And the fact that it did not only not win, but the fact also that we got shut out of all the nominations is something that we're all still severely pissed about."

In particular, the dance contest needed to be over-the-top to impress the audience in such a large theater. Price told me, "The Latin couples dancing on Broadway were spectacular, like, death-defying, jaw-droppingly great. It really made its point. It was just so good. It was unbelievably complex and hard and amazing."

The cast appeared in the 1999 Macy's Thanksgiving Day Parade, an annual event that features the current stars of music, Broadway, and TV as part of the entertainment. There are clips on YouTube where you can see the original New York crew perform

"Night Fever" and the dancing truly seems challenging. Orfeh told me, "Look at that performance. It was thirty-two degrees, and we were (basically) naked. It was four thirty in the morning. It's amazing. And that's the choreography and the staging."

Carpinello recalls, "I remember being very cold and very wet. I was dancing in puddles. We wore the shoes that you wear just for the stage. All of our feet were wet and frozen. Still, to this day, every Thanksgiving morning, I turn on the parade. I mean, honestly, if we're to talk about highlights of that whole experience, that would have been one."

To prepare for the Broadway opening, Stigwood granted an interview with Lisa Gubernick of the *Wall Street Journal* (August 24, 1999), where she noticed that even though he told her about his diabetic condition, he was drinking rum and Cokes throughout their chat. She describes him as "sixty-five. Rheumy-eyed and raspy-voiced with thinning sandy hair, he dresses like an aging lord of leisure." And at one point, she tells us, "He tells the same anecdote three times over." He was a long way from his glory days of RSO.

On opening night, October 21, 1999, Nan Knighton remembers how late they were to start the show due to Stigwood's drinking, "There was a courtesy room at the Minskoff where Arlene, I, and a few others sat with Robert and the Bee Gees while the audience waited. Robert ordered another round of drinks for all of us, which made us nervous, because the crowd was waiting. And waiting. When Robert finally did give the signal, the Bee Gees entered, walking down the aisle for all to see, but the moment was not quite what one would have anticipated. Sitting there, waiting, the audience had simply become annoyed."

The opening night was special, as some of the cast from the movie were in attendance. Orfeh describes meeting Pescow for the first time. "They brilliantly doppelganger me [to look like

Annette from the film] and it was kind of frightening. When Donna Pescow came to the show, she and I, for about five long minutes, just stared at each other, didn't say a word, and kept screaming and hugging. Oh, my gosh. Everyone [from the original movie] came. Unfortunately, John Travolta did not. But it was still wonderful!"

The press was vicious in its reviews: The *New York Post's* Donald Lyons wrote, "It jettisons everything exciting in the movie and lovingly preserves everything mediocre." Ben Brantley of the *New York Times* called it "dreary."

But it made over $300,000 in its first week and gave over five hundred performances. Everyone involved in the show that I spoke to absolutely loved the experience. Knighton said, "I loved Robert before, during, and after, despite his scaring me right down to my shoes during the West End previews. He was a business wizard—brilliant, savvy, a master of whatever he touched, the tycoon displayed on the cover of *Newsweek* who, as he once told me, loved "playing the game." But there was also quite a warm side to Robert, almost a vulnerability. He had a truly generous heart."

Orfeh still maintains a close friendship with Carpinello and Price, and she told me this show is her favorite in her entire career: "One hundred percent. And I've done some popular musicals. Right before that pandemic, we all had our twentieth anniversary reunion in Times Square. We did that flash mob. So, you know, it was like a big love fest."

Phillips told me, "This was by far my favorite project of my career. I was obsessed with the movie and could not believe how lucky I was to have Robert Stigwood believe I could do it justice."

Carpinello recalls Stigwood's generosity. "One of the things Stigwood did on the night I got the part, my dad was in town, and he, my dad, and I went to the Waldorf Towers, where

Stigwood stayed every time he came to New York. And he had champagne cocktails, these massive lobsters. Just celebratory and wicked over-the-top."

He continued, "And he had us picked up in a limousine and taken there, and I was, like, 'What on earth is happening?' Then he says, 'You can keep the car. Go out for the night. Do whatever you want.' I remember picking up my two friends in the limo and just driving around New York City, hanging out of the moon-roof. 'We made it!' It was crazy!"

In 2004, Carpinello had a "full circle" moment playing John Travolta's son in *The Punisher*. "It was surreal that not long after I played Tony on Broadway, I mean, he's John Travolta, and it was awesome. Just to be in his presence was remarkable," he remembers.

Currently, multiple productions of the musical are being produced worldwide, which fits Stigwood's style of being critically roasted but ultimately winning over an audience. Over the years, he and Patrick Bywalski would attend premieres throughout Europe and Asia for new productions, but his health was failing, and eventually he was homebound.

Robert Stigwood died of a heart attack on January 4, 2016, at the age of eighty-one. According to *Mr. Showbiz* author Stephen Dando-Collins, he was found alone by his houseboy. Bywalski and his family, after working for Robert for over thirty years, received the bulk of his estate.

CHAPTER 18

Nik Cohn's Long, Strange Trip with the Fever

Writer Nik Cohn had a wild time after the success of *Saturday Night Fever*. Like many people in the 1970s and 1980s, he had developed a drug habit. He still worked for *New York* magazine but was not inspired by the music or the nightlife anymore without feeling high. Chronically shy, now divorced, and insecure about aging out of his career, he turned to cocaine to numb his feelings.

The problem is, when you have an illegal habit, you need to deal with seedy people to maintain your supply. Your life becomes about getting your next fix, and your morals can get pushed to the side, due to the stranglehold of addiction.

Lord Earl John Jermyn, the seventh marquess of Bristol, known alternately as John Jermyn and John Bristol (I will refer to him as John Jermyn), was born to English nobility in 1954. He grew up in a ludicrously wealthy family in the suburbs of Suffolk and had a distant relationship with his parents due to their multiple marriages, leaving him feeling a lack of stability.

When Jermyn was sixteen, he inherited £1 million and another £4 million more five years later. As a closeted gay man, the money allowed him to live more freely, and after eventually inheriting a $35 million fortune in the late 1970s, he moved to

Nik Cohn at a reading in 2014 in Deauville, France.
User RZOM/Wikimedia Commons.

New York City. With money no longer an issue, he indulged himself in drugs and parties.

Cohn found himself in the same social circle as Jermyn, who was known for his wicked sense of humor and irrational behavior. Jermyn reportedly would fly his helicopter to Long Island while snorting cocaine or would randomly shoot guns at his guests for a laugh. Unfortunately, he had also developed an addiction to heroin at this time and needed a special Indian supply to maintain his habit.

In May 1983, Cohn was arrested in a raid along with Jermyn and eighteen other people as part of a conspiracy to traffic Indian heroin to New York. Cohn's attorney stated that the writer had a drug habit but was not a part of any conspiracy to smuggle heroin. Cohn refused to give testimony, and the charges were eventually dropped. He served five years' probation and paid a $5,000 fine for cocaine possession for personal use.

According to the Associated Press, on November 18, 1983, Cohn's town house at 24 West Seventy-Sixth Street was where the raid had taken place, and his neighbor Frances Mullin confessed to being the "leader of a drug ring." Interestingly, the apartment to which the character Stephanie moved was located just a few feet away, at 34 West Seventy-Sixth Street.

According to the *Daily News*, on October 7, 1983, in her first appearance at Brooklyn Federal Court, the thirty-two-year-old London-born Mullin admitted to being a supplier. When Judge Henry Bramwell asked her if she was under the influence of any intoxicant or drug while making her plea, she reportedly said, "No, Your Honor," then whispered to her lawyer, "Unfortunately!" She was sentenced to ten years.

Jermyn fled back to England and married a woman in 1984 to escape the gossip. That marriage ended in 1987 and he eventually lost all of his fortune, dying penniless in 1999, at the age of forty-four, due to multiple organ failures brought on by his decades-long drug addiction.

About the arrest, Cohn told the *New York Times* on June 8, 1997, "There's a tremendous self-absorption that comes with drugs. And there comes a point where you either let the thing take over or you rid yourself of it. I didn't have to go through any huge thing of getting clean, I just got bored. When you get bored, you are boring."

The *Guardian* on June 16, 2016, reprinted much of a 1996 article written by Cohn admitting to conjuring up many of his characters in the *New York* 1976 cover story based on his years worshipping teddy boys and mods. He wrote, "Taking all I knew about the snake-charmer in Derry and, more especially, about Chris the mod in London, I translated them as best I could to Brooklyn. Then I went back to Bay Ridge in daylight and noted the major landmarks. I walked some streets, went into a couple of stores. Studied the clothes, the gestures, the walks. Imagined how it would feel to burn up, all caged energies, with no outlet but the dancefloor and the rituals of Saturday night. Finally, I wrote it all up. And presented it as fact."

The *Guardian* reporter Nadia Khomami, in the same article, asked him why he went to the trouble of presenting it as fact when it was not. He told her, "Magazine writing then was basically a boys' club. There was a lot of wretched excess. Along with some great writing came reams of self-indulgent bollocks. Tribal Rites being fiction was never a great secret. I remember once, at the end of a long night, blurting out to a publisher that the story was made up. 'You don't say,' the publisher drawled. 'And Liberace is gay.'"

When asked why he believes the story still resonates, he said, "Tribal Rites is about identity. Finding a place in the world where you can shine. What still resonates, to me at least, is the sense of yearning. If I was writing the story today, Vincent might be trans . . ."

In 1992, Cohn wrote *The Heart of the World*, a history of Broadway and the theater scene in New York City, after spending two months walking eighteen miles along the center of Manhattan collecting stories.

In the early 2000s, when looking to recuperate from hepatitis C, Cohn took his interest in hip-hop and matched it with his longtime affection for New Orleans. Deciding, after decades of writing about music, to try his hand at music production, he took an advance from DreamWorks of $20,000 to create a mini record label.

He called himself "Triksta" and spent over a year searching for talent in bars and clubs and walking around the city trying to find out the secret sauce to creating hip-hop magic. In 2005's *Triksta: Life and Death and New Orleans Rap*, Cohn makes himself a part of the story, and in the process of failing at becoming a rap mogul he confronts his own racism and how he sees Black people.

In his 1969 *Rock: From the Beginning* (his second book discussing rock and roll history) he makes some truly cringy observations. Cohn describes Tina Turner as "A great big woman (she was five feet four) with long black hair right down her back and a beautiful snarling animal face with a truly cosmic ass." Then he spends several pages stating he cannot find a record label Black enough for his aesthetics.

In New Orleans, pushing sixty and feeling his age, he seems to finally see his privilege and realizes that his English accent and his opinions on what needed to be recorded no longer have the value he thought.

As Ben Brantley observes in an interview with Cohn in the *New York Times* November 6, 2005, "Mr. Cohn owns up to his blarney, almost batters himself with the realization of it. Gradually moving out of a life of exaggerations and deceptions, he learns one rugged truth after another: that New Orleans hip-hop is deeply conservative and resistant to change; that it has little musical connection to the New Orleans music he has known and loved; that most hip-hoppers are uninterested in him and his ideas, unless he's got money to back them."

Now in his seventies, Cohn is still writing and conjuring. The red-haired, half-Jewish kid from Derry who has lived a dozen lives, made a fortune, lost a fortune, and has the best stories to tell married the children's author Michaela Munteen in 1985, and they live a quiet life outside of New York City.

CHAPTER 19

Norman

After the embarrassment of *Staying Alive*, Norman Wexler tried one more Hollywood script. *Raw Deal*, the 1986 film starring Arnold Schwarzenegger, was yet another unhappy experience, and he decided to live off his *Saturday Night Fever* money while figuring out new ideas to write about. Bob Zmuda talked about his experience of being an assistant to Norman on episode 274 of Marc Maron's podcast *WTF* in 2020.

Zmuda, who would go on to be a Comic Relief cofounder, talks about Norman taking thousands of dollars from the bank each day and insisting Zmuda record all his conversations. He was a provocateur who would instigate arguments with people just to get ideas for dialogue. Zmuda did not last long at the job. Norman tended to wear people out.

His daughter Erica told the *Telegraph* in London in 2013, "When not insane, my father was an extraordinarily magical and charismatic person who lavished me with love. My father's sudden explosions into madness were a recurring nightmare, happening every two years or so and lasting three to five months."

When she and her sister, Maren, were in their twenties, during one of these breakdowns, the daughters created "a complex sting operation called 'lock Daddy in the loony bin.'" With his multiple gun charges and his propensity to threaten violence, they found it necessary to take power of attorney over his ability to access his money.

At some point, Norman was living with an artist and hiding from his daughters. When they found him, the artist answered the door, saying, "He's holding me hostage." The police helped break down the door, and Erica describes him as "standing naked with a gaze of transcendent euphoria on his face, as if he were an omnipotent god in a cosmic drama."

Erica described for me some of his early trauma. "He was in mental institutions since he was seventeen. Supposedly, he went to Harvard on a scholarship because there was a Jewish quota, and he was always a very brilliant person. And he took his exams in a mental institution."

While in college, Norman's mother died by suicide, activating his mania to new levels. Erica describes what this was like for her. "He was so vicious when he was manic. Oh, man. He had a huge brain. You know? Like, his ability to assess your character and your psyche."

Eventually Erica and Maren had him committed to Silver Hill psychiatric hospital for twelve weeks. They mistakenly thought he would be grateful for their care, but he was furious instead, and it caused a rift for the rest of his life. He wanted to live with his manic depression no matter the cost.

Norman died of a heart attack on August 23, 1999, at the age of seventy-three. His play *Forgive Me, Forgive Me Not* was the last work of art produced in his lifetime. It won the Julie Harris Playwright Award in 1996.

Six weeks after his death, Erica and Maren went to the Broadway opening of *Saturday Night Fever.* "Norman was thrilled it became a piece of theater. He was a huge fan of theater, even musical theater. Film was secondary," Erica remembers.

CHAPTER 20

Lester

Lester Wilson continued choreographing for motion pictures and television, with one of his proudest achievements the Motown 25th Anniversary Special (*Motown 25: Yesterday, Today, Forever*) which aired May 16, 1983. It featured Michael Jackson's famous moonwalk, the reunion of Diana Ross and the Supremes, Smokey Robinson and the Miracles, and Marvin Gaye, among the musical geniuses honored in the two-hour special. With Wilson's ode to the painter Ernie Barnes (of *Good Times* fame) and Gaye's "I Want You," the Lester Wilson Dancers create a breathtaking piece of art. (It is a must-see on YouTube.)

His reputation as a professional who was beloved to all who worked for him is exemplified by the many friends and acquaintances who reached out to me while I was writing this book. His partner, Zack Reed, told me that people attending his work on specials as diverse as *Comic Relief*, *Solid Gold*, and *Scrooged* were always relieved to see him.

"I used to hear when we were doing something like the Soul Train Music Awards, in which he was either collaborating with an artist who was performing on the show or he was the choreographer and working with a dance sequence that was specific, 'It's gonna be okay. Lester's here,'" said Reed.

Wilson's friend, dancer Larry Vickers, credits his work on the 1975 *Funny Lady* movie for Wilson's ability to rise above the material. "Herb Ross directed it, and they hired thirty Black dancers, and I was one of those. Lester choreographed that. And that was the only number in the film that worked. All the other numbers did not work."

There was also a section in the film that Ross could not figure out, a number where an all-Black cast and Barbra Streisand clapped to a beat. After rehearsal, Ross decided to have his star remain still while the background did the routine. "After they saw the number, her boss said, 'Barbra, stay on the top. Do not move.' They took her out of the number so that she would not be with us," Vickers told me.

He continues, "We were supposed to be these little these little black fireflies, and she was the guardian angel, I guess. They wanted us to look like slaves. When I told you that they separated us from the white dancers, that is one of the reasons. It was all in segregation."

Richard Montoya is a dancer and longtime friend of Wilson's. He explained to me how Wilson was able to get people to move. "Whether it was his choreography or how he was as a human being to a fellow human being. His gift was relating to people at their level. You know? And his energy matched along with his personality."

Wilson was a huge Bugs Bunny fan and often quoted his favorite lines from those cartoons. Montoya told me about the favorite prank he played on his friend. "I found a six-foot stuffed Bugs Bunny and gave it to him for Christmas one year. I put it at his front door, knocked, and ran. When he opened the door, he fell on the floor laughing. We put Bugs through a lot. He was in the car, in the house with house parties. It was everywhere. So, yeah, that was our humor. He was a very magical human being."

Illustrative of Deney Terrio's referring to dancers as a hyper-competitive bunch, Wilson had a beef with one of his longest associates over Michael Jackson's "Beat It" video. In the 1970s,

Lester worked on several Lola Falana specials, and one in particular was called the "Money Medley," with the opening song
being "For the Love of Money," made famous by the O'Jays.

Michael Peters was in the segment (he and Lester went to
the Bernice Johnson Dance Studio together), and if you watch
the first few minutes, you will find the arm movements look
remarkably similar to what appears in Michael Jackson's "Beat
It" video. According to Reed, "MTV was showing videos, and
there was this video 'Beat It,' and Lester said he looked at a
sequence of movements which was a direct lift of a choreography piece that he had done, and I think he felt very betrayed
and very hurt by that."

Peters had apparently become friendly with Jackson and
had shown him a tape of his latest work, which included the
Falana special. Jackson specifically wanted the arm movements,
which apparently Peters claimed to be his own invention. Wilson and Peters eventually made up their differences later in the
1980s but it remained a sore point for Lester. (Michael Peters
died in 1994, at the age of forty-six.)

Wilson was notorious for having fun and making people
laugh. His friend costume designer Pete Menefee told me about
the time he choreographed a number with Goldie Hawn for a
TV special. "At one point, the producer called me aside and he
said, 'There's a rumor going around the set that you and Goldie
and Lester are doing drugs,' because we laughed all the time. I
mean, Lester made Goldie laugh so hard that they would not
allow him to stand next to the camera while she was working."

Menefee attempted to explain to me why so many people
loved Wilson. "Well, first, he was a character. His persona was
so electric, bizarre, and wonderful. And then, of course, when
you found out how talented he was, that all this fooling around
was not just noise, there was a talented man behind all the jokes.

That was very special. You can find people that are incredibly gifted but kind of boring or sour. Or vice versa. If they are fun, they are not necessarily talented."

Geneva Vivino, whom Wilson hired for *Saturday Night Fever*, loves seeing him in the movie *Scrooged*, where he plays the part of the Solid Gold Dancers choreographer. "It was so typical of him. He is just walking on, taking control, and then he is gone."

The producers of *Solid Gold* hired Wilson in 1986 to update the show, which was starting to lose its luster with the audience. He told the *Shreveport Times* at the time, "I've noticed the whole fashion mode is getting back to the luxurious look." His plan was to eschew the tiny leotards and have the women wear dresses, suits, and hats to play characters—in his words, "to sell sensuality as opposed to sexuality."

Former *Solid Gold* dancer Betsy Harris explained to me that, unlike previous seasons, when the show had become a "grind," with Wilson the mood on the set improved. "[*Solid Gold*] was not a creative place. We are doing pop songs. Every week, you must crank it out there. But [with Lester] we really had a lot of fun, and everybody appreciated that he just let us all be ourselves."

Darrell Wright worked with Wilson as a dancer on *Solid Gold*; *Motown 25: Yesterday, Today, Forever*; *Beat Street*; and *Comic Relief*. What he remembers best about Wilson's approach to choreography is "just the feeling of it, how musical it was, how it set in the pocket, how much sense it made, how it flowed from moment to moment. And just the accents, the sensuality of it." He also noted to me, "Everyone stole [moves] from Lester."

Wilson pushed himself even though he had had several bypass surgeries in his life. Vivino recalls noticing a scar on his leg. "Because my mother was a nurse, I was telling her he had this huge scar on the back of his leg. I knew he had heart surgery, so

I saw that. Everyone knew about that. But this thing was on his leg, and my mom said, 'Well, they took that vein.' Wow!"

Diane Day Crump-Richmond, who worked with Wilson many times in her dance career, told me, "It was scary, but he kept those nitroglycerin pills in his top pocket all the time. He would pop those things when he started feeling faint, and it made me so nervous."

She also told me about his notoriously difficult rehearsals. This was especially true in May 1980 for the *Uptown: A Tribute to the Apollo Theatre* TV special. "For the Apollo special, he decided that he wanted us to do this number straight through. He said, 'I don't want to lose the energy and do lot in editing.' I have a picture of Lorraine Fields, myself, and our friend Michelle sitting on the side of the stairs with our toes pointed in and the worst look on our faces and tears in our eyes. In fact, we have used it as a Christmas card because it was so funny."

Macarena Gandarillas worked with Wilson on *Solid Gold* and is also a dance instructor. She believes in passing on Wilson's tough rehearsals. "One of my students, Rubén J. Carbajal, played Hamilton's son. He told me that during the rehearsal process, he thought he was gonna die. He said if it were not for him staying up for hours in rehearsals [with me], then he probably would not have been able to do it. It is so important, because people really do not want to work with you again if you are not prepared and do not know your material."

Eventually, Wilson's heart condition became more than his body could handle. His partner, Reed, explains, "He had five bypasses. Basically, a congenital small vein and probably lifestyle. Right? So, yes; his diet, smoking, drinking, you know, the ways of living."

Montoya describes what happens next in 1993. "It was interesting because, my birthday is on January 29. And that day,

Lester said, 'I want to cook for your birthday. And so we went shopping, and he was not looking well. And he says, 'I'm just gonna go home.' I later saw him walking down a long corridor to my door carrying packages. People started to come over, and he cooked, and then he seemed to be fine."

According to Reed, "He was being monitored. He was on medication before that, up until, you know, when I found him. And it was just the lifespan of bypass surgery, I think I have heard is ten years. You are good if you get ten years. And that is ultimately . . . the cause of his death was just a coronary attack."

Lester Wilson died on Wednesday, February 14, 1993, of natural causes, according to his death certificate. He had cardiovascular disease, and it became just a matter of time before his heart gave out. He was at home doing laundry when Reed found him.

His friends were in complete shock. Ann-Margret, his longtime friend and advocate, paid for his funeral expenses and brought his family out for his funeral.

In 2000, the sixth American Choreography Awards on Broadway honored Lester Wilson's contribution to dance. Lewis Segal, the dance critic for the *Los Angeles Times*, wrote, "Lester Wilson generated high emotion through the reactions and reminiscences of performer Ann-Margret and the remarkable restraint of Wilson's mother Wilhemina Ana Bosley." His sister Julie tells me, "Lester lived a full life and did what he loved."

CHAPTER 21

Fever at Fifty

Ten years after the film's opening, there were only a few articles discussing *Saturday Night Fever* on its tenth anniversary, as it was still caught in a bit of backlash against the 1970s disco era it represented. Barry Miller told Gannett News on December 16, 1987, "I think it would be very damaging to the movie in a nostalgic sense for disco or the fashions. What really made the movie a valuable piece of filmmaking was that it emphasized the emptiness of that lifestyle. It's a tremendously ugly movie."

Miller would go on to star in 1980's *Fame* and in Francis Ford Coppola's *Peggy Sue Got Married* and won a Tony Award for Best Actor in 1985 as Arnold Epstein in *Biloxi Blues*. His performance was such an audience favorite on Broadway that it was rumored that Matthew Broderick forbade him from working on the 1988 Mike Nichols film adaptation.

Later on, Miller had a more sanguine opinion about the film. In the documentary *Saturday Night Fever: A 30-Year Legacy*, he states, "I think a sixteen-year-old of 2007 could watch *Saturday Night Fever* and see that its themes are resonant today." The talented actor has kept a low profile with his latest IMDb credit being 2003's *Shortcut to Happiness*.

Director John Badham would go on to big successes in the 1980s including *WarGames*, *Short Circuit*, and *Stakeout*. He is still directing in film and television, with more than a hundred credits to his name, and recently retired as a professor of film and

Saturday Night Fever poster, 1977.
Allstar Picture Library Limited/Alamy Stock Photo.

media at Dodge College of Film and Media Arts at Chapman University in Orange, California.

The Bee Gees released their album *E•S•P* in 1987 but found resistance to getting their work played on American radio. Barry Gibb told the *Boston Globe* reporter Steve Morse on October 9, 1987, "American radio has a hard time accepting us today. It can't seem to get *Saturday Night Fever* out of its hair. We didn't expect such a stone wall." The band did continue to write hit songs for Barbra Streisand, Donna Summer, and Kenny Rogers, and with constant touring they became very strong musicians.

The celebration of *Saturday Night Fever* as a film classic doesn't really begin until after its twentieth anniversary, with several documentaries including VH1's 2001 *Behind the Music* series, which covered the making of the film, to high ratings.

By 1997, the Bee Gees had had a huge resurgence, and were inducted into the Rock & Roll Hall of Fame. John Travolta introduced their reel at the ceremony, using the famous finger point pose to great effect with the crowd.

Brian Wilson of the Beach Boys was given the honor of giving a speech about the band. The famously reclusive genius praised their harmonies and musicianship. He also noted the importance and challenges of working with family in creative endeavors.

Sadly, Barry Gibb has outlived most of his siblings, with Andy passing away in 1988 at age thirty to heart failure, Maurice in 2003 at the age of fifty-three due to complications of a bowel obstruction, and Robin in 2012 due to cancer at the age of sixty-two. His older sister, Lesley, has lived a private life with her family in Sydney. Gibb tours occasionally as a solo act but is more focused on a Bee Gees biopic. Director Ridley Scott has attached himself to the project. He lives in Miami with his wife of over fifty years, Linda.

Travolta's movie career in the 1980s (besides *Staying Alive*) was a mixture of earnest dramas (*Urban Cowboy*), thrillers (the underrated *Blow Out*), and some truly baffling choices like *Two of a Kind* with former *Grease* costar Olivia Newton-John, and the trendy aerobics-centric of *Perfect* with Jamie Lee Curtis. The end of the decade would bring two blessings for him, when he met his future wife, Kelly Preston, in the not-so-great *The Experts* and the certified hit *Look Who's Talking*, which would celebrate a return to his comedy chops.

Travolta's career in the 1990s was exceptional, with his starring role in 1994's Quentin Tarantino classic *Pulp Fiction*. He would go on to make classics like *Get Shorty*, *Face/Off*, and

Primary Colors. In the December 28, 1995, issue of *Rolling Stone*, David Wild asked John Travolta what he was like during his *Fever* heyday and if he was aloof or had a "star attitude." Travolta replied, "Oh, no, never. Life was too humbling. I had a lot of losses: My girlfriend Diana Hyland, my mother, my manager died. Life was very real to me, if you know what I mean."

In 2010, Travolta spoke in the documentary *Saturday Night Fever: The Inside Story* about how he felt about Tony Manero as a legacy. "I'm asked often, does it upset you that often you're remembered for *Saturday Night Fever*. My immediate thought is, well, would it have upset Jimmy Stewart for being remembered for *It's a Wonderful Life* or Jimmy Cagney for *Yankee Doodle Dandy?* I mean, they were as closely identified with those roles as I am with *Saturday Night Fever* and who wouldn't want that?"

Sadly, he has experienced even more losses since then, including his son Jett, who passed away in 2009, at the age of sixteen, due to longtime health issues; Kelly Preston, at fifty-seven, in 2020; and his good friend Olivia Newton-John, at seventy-three, in 2022. The last two were due to breast cancer. At seventy, Travolta continues to act but prefers to spend time with his two children, Bella (twenty-four) and Ben (thirteen).

"The Faces," including Barry Miller, Paul Pape, Joe Cali, and Bruce Ornstein, continued acting on both coasts. Pape told me how he started his career in voice-over work. "I had the very good fortune of becoming friends with a senior VP of Paramount when I was doing promotion for *Fever*, and his name was Don LaFontaine. He became the biggest voice-over guy in the business over time. I was getting a lot of interest, but not enough work. So, I looked at it to make extra money at first." He continues to this day to succeed in a very competitive profession.

Cali had a few TV series and films in the 1980s but he soon grew bored of the grind of auditions. He started his own audio/video company—Joseph Cali Systems Design Inc.—and he works with an A-list clientele. He is married to Lori Lieberman, a singer-songwriter who composed the song "Killing Me Softly with His Song," which has been covered to great acclaim by Roberta Flack and the Fugees.

Bruce Ornstein is an actor and acting coach who holds workshops in New York City. He said in the 2010 documentary *Saturday Night Fever: The Inside Story* about the film's legacy, "There are things like a piece of music that you remember that really move you and take you back to a particular time. And I think people experience *Saturday Night Fever* like that. It takes them back now to a time where they once were and that meant something to them. And I think the film resonates in people because of that."

In 2023, Donna Pescow and her former costar Travolta were featured in a holiday-themed Capital One commercial with Travolta being a disco version of Santa. She told me the lengths they went to to re-create Tony's famous walk in Bay Ridge. "It was adorable. It was amazing. And you know what? They literally did frame for frame of the opening of him walking down Eighty-Sixth Street. There was a storyboard of every single shot that matched the movie. It was unbelievable. And they filmed it, at Paramount, and they redressed, I think it was a New York street, you know, one of those sorts of . . . it could be anywhere in New York."

She and Travolta found themselves going back to their original working personalities, with him making sure she was happy with her performance. She remembers, "I was already on set, and John was coming in. Just this whole vibe of *Saturday Night Fever* again. And it was just so sweet and touching and wonderful. I can't explain it other than I think everybody [on the set] felt that moment. Oh, my goodness."

Karen Lynn Gorney has kept busy with her music, art-work, and acting in film, television and stage, appearing on *The Sopranos, Clifford the Big Red Dog,* and *Law & Order.* She took up dance more extensively after *Saturday Night Fever* and was a ballet teacher for a time.

Deney Terrio had some struggles after *Dance Fever* went off the air in 1987. He sued Merv Griffin in 1991 for sexual harass-ment and endured a horrible, scathing interview with a cynical Geraldo Rivera. That suit was dropped and then he had a case against Hasbro for creating a character named Vinnie Terrio in 2015, which he later settled out of court. Terrio wrote for the *Financial Times* in 2012 that in the late 1980s he had "burned out on drugs and alcohol" and took some time to get his life together. In 2004, he cohosted the PBS special *Get Down Tonight: The Disco Explosion.* He currently runs his own events company, the Deney Terrio Dance Party, and tours with top disco acts like Tavares, the Trammps, and Bonnie Pointer.

Lisa Peluso lives with her family in New Jersey. In spite of making sure to raise her children in a show business–free home, her son has decided to be a musician. She told me, "He we went to school for computer science cybersecurity, but music is his pas-sion. So, what am I gonna say?"

Barry Diller was inducted into the Television Hall of Fame in 1994 and is currently the chairman of IAC and Expedia Group. Michael Eisner was the chairman and CEO of the Walt Disney Company from 1984 to 2006. He received a star on the Hollywood Walk of Fame in 2008 and is retired.

Kevin McCormick is a successful executive producer who has worked on dozens of top projects in television and film, including *Elvis, In the Heights,* and *Gangster Squad* but still con-siders *Saturday Night Fever* his best work experience.

Saturday Night Fever was inducted into the Library of

Congress in 2010 for being "culturally, historically, or aesthetically significant." It was also selected for preservation in the United States National Film Registry. Adjusted for inflation, it was one of the highest-grossing R-rated films released in the United States in the 1970s, with a total box office gross of $673,899,098. Officially, the number of "fucks" in *Saturday Night Fever* is seventy-seven.

Interview Biographies

I was incredibly fortunate to speak with so many interesting and creative people associated with *Saturday Night Fever*. As a mega-fan of the movie, I often asked my subjects about their personal favorite song from the soundtrack. A few demurred but most quickly gave me their response. I want to thank them for their time and generosity. You are all exceptional!

Julie Anderson: Sister of Lester Wilson, she resides in South Carolina and keeps his memory active in the arts community. Favorite song from the soundtrack: "Stayin' Alive."

John Badham: Director John Badham is a veteran of more than thirty films and fifty television episodes. His biggest films are *Saturday Night Fever*, *WarGames*, *Short Circuit*, and *Stakeout*. In television, he has worked on *Heroes*, *Supernatural*, *12 Monkeys*, and *Nikita*. His favorite song from the soundtrack: "Stayin' Alive."

Jospeh Cali: Cali is an actor with a lengthy list of credits that includes *Saturday Night Fever*, *Suicide Kings*, and *Melrose Place*. For more than thirty years, he has worked as one of the top home theater/audio creators and runs Joseph Cali Systems Design Inc. with an A-list clientele. Favorite song from the soundtrack: "Stayin' Alive."

James Carpinello: Tony Manero in the 1999 Broadway musical *Saturday Night Fever*, also starred in *Rock of Ages* onstage and in *The Punisher* with John Travolta. He is co-producing the musical stage version of *The Lost Boys* for Broadway which is scheduled to open in the Spring 2026 Favorite song from the soundtrack: "Night Fever."

Ed Cermanski: The Trammps piano player since 1975. Favorite song from the soundtrack: "Disco Inferno."

Anita Louise Combe: Played Stephanie in the West End premiere of *Saturday Night Fever* and appeared as well in *Cats, Evita,* and *Sunset Boulevard.* Favorite song: "Nights on Broadway" (from the stage musical).

Robert Costanzo: The Brooklyn native is a longtime character actor who plays a paint store customer in *Saturday Night Fever* and had memorable roles in *Total Recall, Die Hard 2,* and *City Slickers.* Favorite song from the soundtrack: "Stayin' Alive."

Erica Damsky Loiacano: As a ten-year-old, she was lucky enough to be on set when *Saturday Night Fever* was filmed in her neighborhood in March 1977. Favorite song from the soundtrack: "If I Can't Have You."

Dennis Danehy: The son of Don Campbell of the Lockers. Dennis is an artist, dancer, teacher, choreographer, and performer. Favorite song from the soundtrack: "If I Can't Have You."

Diane Day Crump-Richmond: A dancer best known from *Dance Fever* and *History of the World, Part I;* she was a longtime friend of choreographer Lester Wilson and performed on *Motown 25: Yesterday, Today, Forever.* Favorite song from the soundtrack: "You Should Be Dancing."

Denny Dillon: Tony Award–nominated actor who played Doreen in *Saturday Night Fever.* With a fifty-plus-year career, she also starred in *Saturday Night Live, Dream On,* and *Servant.* Favorite song from the soundtrack: She will reveal in her upcoming memoir!

Yvonne Elliman: Singer and songwriter who is best known for playing Mary Magdalene in *Jesus Christ Superstar,* her work with Eric Clapton, and the song "If I Can't Have You."

Simon Fanshawe: An English writer, activist, and broadcaster; he interviewed Robert Stigwood for the *London Times* in 1998 and is on the board for Edinburgh Fringe Festival. Favorite song from the soundtrack: "Stayin' Alive."

Joanne Farrell: Singer and actor who played Stephanie in the 1999 West End musical *Saturday Night Fever* and starred in many stage productions, including *Smokey Joe's Café, Showboat,* and *The Rocky Horror Picture Show.* Favorite song from the soundtrack: "Stayin' Alive."

Lorraine Fields: An assistant to choreographer Lester Wilson for *Saturday Night Fever,* she has performed as an actor and dancer in *Moonwalker, The Best Little Whorehouse in Texas,* and *Motown 25: Yesterday, Today, Forever.* Favorite song from the soundtrack: "You Should Be Dancing."

Jimmy Gambina: Born in Hollywood in 1943; actor, boxer, and expert coordinator; Gambina is featured in *Rocky* and *Snake Eyes* and trained John Travolta for *Saturday Night Fever*. Favorite song from the soundtrack: "How Deep Is Your Love."

Macarena Gandarillas: A professional dancer who has worked on *Solid Gold* and *The Love Boat* and was a longtime friend of the choreographer Lester Wilson. She is now an instructor. Favorite song from the soundtrack: "More Than a Woman."

Freddie Gershon: An entertainment attorney, a former president of the Robert Stigwood Group, and the author of *Sweetie, Baby, Cookie, Honey*. Since 2018, Gerson has been co-chair of Musical Theatre International (MTI), where he developed the Broadway Junior Program, which brings art, theater, dance, and music to children.

Kristian Gravenor: A Montreal-based journalist, author of *Montreal: The Unknown City*, and the nephew of Pamela "Arfur" Marchant. Favorite song from the soundtrack: "How Deep Is Your Love."

Noel Hankin: A longtime marketing expert, author of *After Dark: Birth of the Disco Dance Party*, and the founder of The Best of Friends (TBOF), a pioneer empire of Black-owned business that owned several nightclubs in New York City in the 1970s. Favorite song from the soundtrack: "More Than a Woman."

Betsy Harris: Dancer and choreographer who worked on *Solid Gold*, *Scrooged*, and *Man on the Moon*. Friend of Lester Wilson. Favorite song from the soundtrack: "You Should Be Dancing."

Michael Hausman: Producer and assistant director known for his work on dozens of films, including *Saturday Night Fever*, *Amadeus*, and *Brokeback Mountain*. Favorite song from the soundtrack: "Stayin' Alive."

Shawn Hausman: Worked as a production assistant on *Saturday Night Fever*, a former co-owner of the Area nightclub in New York City, and currently an in-demand design expert at Shawn Hausman Design. Favorite song from the soundtrack: "Stayin' Alive."

Adrienne King: Actor best known for playing Alice Hardy in the *Friday the 13th* movies, she is also a dancer, with her first screen credit being from *Saturday Night Fever*. Favorite song from the soundtrack: "Stayin' Alive."

Randal Kleiser: An actor, director, screenwriter, and producer known for *Grease*, *The Blue Lagoon*, and *The Boy in the Plastic Bubble*. Favorite song from the soundtrack: "Stayin' Alive."

Nan Knighton: A poet and Tony Award–nominated playwright best known for the musicals *The Scarlet Pimpernel* and *Saturday Night Fever.*

Shanta Kumari: A longtime Brooklyn resident whose home interiors for the Manero family household are featured in *Saturday Night Fever.*

Alex Marchak: Dancer from 2001 Odyssey, he is the owner and funeral director at Bay Ridge's Herbst-Trzaska-Waldeck Funeral Home. His business has been in many TV productions, including *Law & Order* and *The Sopranos.* Favorite song from the soundtrack: "More Than a Woman."

Kevin McCormick: Executive Producer for *Saturday Night Fever,* he started his career with RSO and has worked on dozens of projects in a similar capacity including *Elvis, Wonka, In the Heights,* and *Doctor Sleep.* Favorite song from the soundtrack: "How Deep Is Your Love."

Joy McMillan: A former assistant to Robert Stigwood, she left the music business and is happily retired.

James McMullan: An artist and illustrator who worked for *New York* magazine when he created the artwork for the original "Tribal Rites of the New Saturday Night" article. He has won several awards for designing theatrical posters and has co-authored children's books with his wife, Kate McMullan. Favorite song from the soundtrack: "Stayin' Alive."

Pete Menefee: An artist, dancer, and costume and stage designer with several Emmy nominations to his credit. He has worked with Ann-Margret, Lester Wilson, and Dita Von Teese, and created the costumes for *Motown 25: Yesterday, Today, Forever.*

Richard Montoya: Dancer and choreographer who worked with Lester Wilson and has performed in *Chita Rivera: The Dancer's Life, Motown 25: Yesterday, Today, Forever,* and *Kiss of the Spider Woman.* Favorite song from the soundtrack: "Stayin' Alive."

Charonne Mose: An Emmy-winning choreographer (1995's "Miss America Pageant"), dancer, and Webby Award–winning designer. Worked with Lester Wilson and is currently living in Washington, DC. Favorite song from the soundtrack: "Disco Inferno."

Paul Nicholas: Actor, singer, and producer who began his career at the West End as the lead in *Jesus Christ Superstar.* Worked with Robert Stigwood on *Tommy, Sgt. Pepper's Lonely Hearts Club Band,* and the musical *Saturday Night Fever.* Favorite song from the soundtrack: "Stayin' Alive."

Orfeh: A Tony-nominated actor, singer, and songwriter who played Annette in the Broadway debut of *Saturday Night Fever* as well as onstage with *Pretty Woman*; *Love, Janis*; and *Legally Blonde.* Favorite song from the soundtrack: "If I Can't Have You."

Bruce Ornstein: Actor and director who played Gus in *Saturday Night Fever* and appeared in various TV roles, including *L.A. Law* and *Law & Order.* He runs his own acting workshops in New York City. Favorite song from the soundtrack: "Night Fever."

Paul Pape: Actor and voice-over artist who plays Double J. in *Saturday Night Fever.* His work has been featured in *Frozen*, *Shrek*, and *Tangled.* President and CEO of New Trails Productions. Favorite song from the soundtrack: "Stayin' Alive."

Lisa Peluso: Linda in *Saturday Night Fever* and later starring in the soap operas *Loving* and *Another World.* She started her Broadway career at the age of nine in *Gypsy* with Angela Lansbury. Favorite song from the soundtrack: "More Than a Woman."

Donna Pescow: Annette in *Saturday Night Fever.* A busy actor, she was also lead on television with *Angie*, *Out of This World*, and *Even Stevens.* Favorite song from the soundtrack: "If I Can't Have You."

Arlene Phillips: Director and choreographer for the musical *Saturday Night Fever* who has also worked on *Starlight Express*, *Annie*, and *We Will Rock You.* Also a judge on Britain's *Strictly Come Dancing.* Favorite song from the soundtrack: "If I Can't Have You."

Paige Price: Played Stephanie in the Broadway debut of *Saturday Night Fever.* She has also worked in *Smokey Joe's Café* and *Beauty and the Beast* in New York. Her favorite song from the soundtrack: "Night Fever."

Zack Reed: Former partner of Lester Wilson (personally and professionally) and now a resident of New Zealand in financial and insurance services. His favorite song from the soundtrack: "If I Can't Have You."

Denise Rusinak: Her father, Charlie Rusinak, owned 2001 Odyssey (the original club featured in the *New York* magazine article and the movie). She is the owner and artistic director of the Brooklyn Dance Centers and is a dancer in *Saturday Night Fever.*

Martin Shakar: Plays Frank Jr. in *Saturday Night Fever* and is a longtime actor of stage, film, and TV. He has appeared on *Law & Order, Uptown Girls,* and *Fresh.*

David Shire: The composer of the score for *Saturday Night Fever*, he has also worked on *The Conversation, All the President's Men,* and *Zodiac* and is married to actor Didi Conn. His favorite song from the soundtrack: "Stayin' Alive."

Yelena Sionova and Michael Grazidei: The lucky owners of the original Tony Manero home (exteriors). Grazidei is a longtime resident of Brooklyn and a huge fan of the movie. Favorite song from the soundtrack: "Night Fever."

Sue Samuels: Former spouse of JoJo Smith; a teacher, choreographer, and dancer who helped train John Travolta and Karen Lynn Gorney in *Saturday Night Fever*. She was named a "Legendary NYC Dance Instructor" by *Backstage* magazine. Favorite song from the soundtrack: "Stayin' Alive."

Jason Samuels Smith: Dancer and choreographer. The son of JoJo Smith has dozens of film, stage, and television credits and has won an Emmy for Best Choreography for the 2003 Jerry Lewis Telethon. Favorite song from the soundtrack: "You Should Be Dancing."

Peter Stanfield: A professor of film at the University of Kent in Canterbury, England, and an author and journalist with expertise in the 1960s and 1970s music scene in London. Favorite song from the soundtrack: "Boogie Shoes."

Ron Stigwood: Nephew of Robert Stigwood who worked as his assistant on *Saturday Night Fever*. Worked on several projects in the US and Australia, including *Gallipoli* and *Paradise Beach*. Favorite song from the soundtrack: "How Deep Is Your Love."

Ann Travolta: Appearing as the "Pizza Girl" in the opening scene, she is an actor who has worked for more than fifty years on stage, in film, and on TV, with credits for *Swordfish* and *Two of a Kind*. Favorite song from the soundtrack: "How Deep Is Your Love."

Robert Upchurch: Singer for the Trammps who performed on the original recording of "Disco Inferno," which also his favorite song from the soundtrack.

Alberto Vasquez: He started his acting training with Julie Bovasso and got a stunt job working on *Saturday Night Fever*. He has dozens of credits in film, stage, and television. Favorite song from the soundtrack: "Night Fever."

Ben Vereen: An actor and dancer who trained with Lester Wilson at the Bernice Johnson Dance Studio in Queens. Nominated for a Tony Award for 1973's *Pippin*. Also known for *All That Jazz, Roots,* and *Jesus Christ Superstar*.

Frankie Verroca: An actor who was at 2001 Odyssey for the entire shoot. More than fifty years of experience in entertainment as an actor, a background artist, and a cruise director. Favorite song on the soundtrack: "Night Fever."

Larry Vickers: Now based in France, Tennessee native Vickers started dancing with Lester Wilson and has worked with Barbra Streisand, Goldie Hawn, Shirley MacLaine, and Cher, and on the *Motown 25: Yesterday, Today, Forever*. Favorite song from the soundtrack: "Disco Inferno."

Geneva Vivino (aka Karen Burke): A dancer who has performed in multiple Broadway shows, including *Raisin, Dancin'*, and *Chicago*, and was an assistant choreographer for *Dreamgirls* and *Leader of the Pack*. Favorite song on the soundtrack: "More Than a Woman."

Patrizia von Brandenstein: The creator of "the white suit," she is one of the most celebrated art directors and production designers, with an Academy Award for *Amadeus*. She has also worked on *The Untouchables*, *Ragtime*, and *Julia* for HBO. Favorite song on the soundtrack: "How Deep Is Your Love."

Erica Wexler: Actor, writer, singer, and musician. Her latest album, *Sunlit Night*, was produced by XTC's Andy Partridge. As the daughter of the screenwriter Norman Wexler, she was often on the set of *Saturday Night Fever*. Favorite song from the soundtrack: "How Deep Is Your Love."

Darrell Wright: A dancer who appeared in *Solid Gold*, *Beat Street*, *Boogie Nights*, *13 Going on 30*, and *The Princess Diaries 2*. Worked with Lester Wilson on *Motown 25: Yesterday, Today, Forever*. Favorite song from the soundtrack: "Stayin' Alive."

Jeff Zinn: A director and actor who worked on stage and screen in New York and was John Travolta's double for *Saturday Night Fever*. He is the author of *The Existential Actor: Life and Death, Onstage and Off* (2015). Favorite song on the soundtrack: "Stayin' Alive."

Acknowledgments

There is no way possible for me to properly show my appreciation to the more than seventy people who agreed to speak with me about their experiences with *Saturday Night Fever* in all its iterations. Your generosity and the trust you had in me to tell your stories were a gift. I welcome all the new friendships and look forward to our future journeys. Writing this book was a longtime dream, and meeting you all from all over the world filled my heart with total joy.

Julie Anderson, John Badham, Joseph Cali, James Carpinello, Ed Cermanski, Anita Louise Combe, Robert Costanzo, Erica Damsky Loiacano, Dennis Danehy, Diane Day Crump-Richmond, Denny Dillon, Yvonne Elliman, Simon Fanshawe, Joanne Farrell, Lorraine Fields, Jimmy Gambina, Macarena Gandarillas, Freddie Gershon, Kristian Gravenor, Noel Hankin, Betsy Harris, Michael Hausman, Shawn Hausman, Adreinne King, Randal Kleiser, Nan Knighton, Shanta Kumari, Joy McMillan, Alex Marchak, Kevin McCormick, James McMullan, Pete Menefee, Richard Montoya, Charonne Mose, Paul Nicholas, Orfeh, Bruce Ornstein, Paul Pape, Lisa Peluso, Donna Pescow, Arlene Phillips, Paige Price, Zack Reed, Denise Rusinak, Martin Shakar, David Shire, Yelena Sionova and Michael Grazidei, Sue Samuels, Jason Samuels Smith, Peter Stanfield, Ron Stigwood, Ann Travolta, Robert Upchurch, Alberto Vasquez, Ben Vereen, Frankie Verroca, Larry Vickers,

Geneva Vivino, Patrizia von Brandenstein, Erica Wexler, Darrell Wright, and Jeff Zinn. THANK YOU! A special shout-out to all the dancers and choreographers who patiently taught me the ins and outs of the business. I have developed an immense appreciation and awe of what you create for the universe.

I could not imagine a better publisher to work with than Kensington Books: Ann Pryor, John Scognamiglio, and all the marketing and sales crew—you are amazing and inspiring!

My agent, Mitchell Waters, at Brandt and Hochman is a true gem.

For their friendship and support I thank, Deborah Cota, Candy Cota, Sonia Mansfield, Michelle Mansfield, Adam Riske, Rob DiCristino, Erika and Patrick Bromley, Kim and David Hicks, Patty Berg, Barry Berg, Stacy Mar, Michelle Cramer, Deborah Schutt, Cristina and Tom Rasmussen, Margo Porras, Kristen Meinzer, Kristen Lopez, Lisa Mack, Bill and Kristen Stahl, Susannah Davis, Martin White, Marrilee Wilson, Julietta Wright and Nick Kujawski, Jenny Rodriguez and Josh Rodriguez, Laura Goldberg, Kim Small, Stephen Dolginoff, Jill Rosen, Trisha Choate, JB and Jan Bottiglieri. I am not sure why I am lucky enough to call you my friends and family, but I am very grateful.

To the best writing group—the "TSBs"! Thank you, Becky Randall, Laura Kindred, Mary Lukasiewicz, Salma Kahn, Katya Lidsky, Angelica Florio, and Alisha Gaddis.

I could not have done extensive research without IMDb Pro, eBay, and Newspapers.com. This is your free plug! Worth. Every. Penny.

For the inspiration—Sirius XM's *70s on 7* kept me motivated with the help of their DJs Lisa Evans, Jaybeau Jones, Bobby

Watman, Ron Parker, Jonathan Hanst, and the late great Casey Kasem—y'all are the best!

To all of my listeners at *Book vs. Movie, What a Creep, Dorking Out,* and *Not Fade Away* podcasts: You make all the work not only worthwhile but also so much fun. Thank you for your continued support!

My podcast peeps: Anneleis and Neil, Deanna Marie, Juliette and David, *Trashy Divorces, Twisted Philly, Daily Fail, Fixing Famous People, F! This Movie, Crime Writers On,* and *Sam Pancake Presents the Monday Afternoon Movie.*

RIP: Norman, Robert, Julie, Lester, Val, JoJo, Don, Maurice, Robin, and Andy.

Though you did not grant an interview, I still appreciate all that you do, Nik Cohn, John Travolta, and Barry Gibb. We're good! Thank you for all the beauty you bring to the world.

My favorite song from the soundtrack: "You Should Be Dancing."

For fulfilling my dream of being a "Brooklyn spinster"—much love to my kitties, T and Sadie.

To ten-year-old Margaret: "You did it!"

Bibliography

Books, Magazines, and Online Media Sources

Abele, Robert. "Gotta Dance." *DGA Quarterly Magazine*, Summer 2013.

Aletti, Vince. "Dancing Madness." *Rolling Stone*, August 28, 1975.

Anderson, Melissa. "The Last Days of Disco: '*Saturday Night Fever*' and the Politics of Dancing." *Village Voice*, May 9, 2017.

Ansen, David. "The Boogie Man." *Newsweek*, December 19, 1977.

Agrest, Susan, Katrine Ames, David Anson, and Janis Huck. "Rock Tycoon." *Newsweek*, July 31, 1978.

Armstrong, Lois. "Sweathog John Travolta Treads Where Fonzie Never Dared: Out of Prime Time." *People*, November 29, 1976.

Badham, John. *On Directing*. Studio City, CA: Michael Wise Productions, 2013.

Badham, John, and Craig Modderno. *I'll Be in My Trailer: The Creative Wars Between Actors & Directors*. Studio City, CA: Michael Wise Productions, 2006.

Baird, Barbara. "Disco Dynamo Riding Crest of Disco Wave." *Los Angeles Times*, August 26, 1979.

Bilyeu, Melinda; Hector Cook, and Andrew Mon Hughes. *The Ultimate Biography of the Bee Gees: Tales of The Brothers Gibb*. London, England: Omnibus Press, 2004.

Bowles, Pete. "Jet-Set Drug Ring Broken." *Newsday*, May 20, 1983.

Bream, Jon. "'Dancing Madness'—It Goes Bump in the Nightlife." *Minneapolis Star*, October 13, 1976.

Britt, Karen. "The Disco Phenomenon." *Sentinel* (Winston-Salem, North Carolina), December 9, 1976.

Brown, Mick. "A Brit on Broadway." *Daily Telegraph*, March 21, 1992.

Burke, Tom. "Struttin' His Stuff." *Rolling Stone*, June 15, 1978.

Burns, Cherie. "'We Knew It Was Hot,' Says Karen Lynn Gorney, but Was Her Fever Over the Film or John Travolta?" *People*, January 9, 1978.

Chiu, David. "*Saturday Night Fever* at 45: Music Producer Bill Oakes Explains the Soundtrack's 'Staggering Success.'" *Billboard*, November 14, 2022.

Clarkson, Wensley. *John Travolta: King of Cool*. London, England: John Blake Publishing, 2005.

Cohn, Nik. *Arfur*. New York: Simon & Schuster, 1970.

———. "Arfur: The Teenage Pinball Queen." *Eye*, February 1969.

———. *Awopbopaloobop Alopbamboom: The Golden Age of Rock*. New York: Grove Press, 1996 (originally published 1968).

———. *Rock from the Beginning*. New York: Pocket Books, 1970.

———. "This Is Arfur. She Is on the Cover. She Is Fifteen. She Shoots Pinball." *Queen*, October 23, 1968.

———. "Tribal Rites of the New Saturday Night." *New York*, June 7, 1976.

———. "Triksta, Licensed to Rap." *The Guardian*, February 3, 2003.

Colacello, Bob, and Ian Schrager. *Studio 54*. New York: Rizzoli, 2017.

Collins, Nancy. "John Travolta: Sex and the Single Star." *Rolling Stone*, August 18, 1983.

Crockett, Lane. "Wilson Keeps 'Solid Gold' Dancers on Their Feet." *Shreveport Times*, November 8, 1986.

Dahl, Steve, and Dave Hoekstra. *Disco Demolition: The Night Disco Died*. Chicago: Curbside Splendor Publishing, 2016.

Dando-Collins, Stephen. *Mr. Showbiz; The Biography of Robert Stigwood*. Random House Australia, 2017.

Drescher, Fran. *Enter Whining*. New York: HarperCollins, 1996.

Drew, Bernard. "Screen's Newest *Rocky*." *Mount Vernon Argus*, December 16, 1977.

Echols, Alice. *Hot Stuff: Disco and the Remaking of American Culture*. New York: W. W. Norton, 2010.

Ellis, David. Lester Wilson profile. *Black Elegance*, March 1988.

Fanshawe, Simon. Original 1998 profile of Robert Stigwood, appeared in the *Sunday London Times*, published at SimonFanshawe.com in 2006.

Farber, Stephen. "New Travolta Leaner, Sexier, Still Awed by Fame." *New York Times*, July 10, 1983.

Frank, Al. "*Saturday Night Fever*: Only Teens Will Want to Give Up a Saturday Night for This One." *Daily Record* (Morristown, NJ), December 18, 1977.

Garret, Tom, and Larry Powell. *The Films of John G. Avildsen*. Jefferson, NC: McFarland & Company, 2013.

Gilmore, Joan. "Travolta's Dance Teacher Says John's Only Good." *Daily Oklahoman*. August 13, 1978.

Gold, Mike. "Titusville Dance Expert Put Travolta on Step to Oscar." *Orlando Sentinel*, March 1, 1978.

Goldman, Albert. *Disco*. New York: Hawthorn Books, 1978.

Gorman, Collen. "Fond du Lacs Nightlife Spins to Tune of Disco Mania." *The Reporter* (Fond du Luc, Wisconsin), December 10, 1976.

Gravenor, Kristian, and John David Gravenor. *Montreal: The Unknown City*. Vancouver: Arsenal Pulp Press. 2002.

Grizzuti-Harrison, Barbara. "John Travolta: His Mother's Story." *McCall's*, July 1978.

Gubernick, Lisa. "Has Starmaker's 'Fever' Broken?" *Wall Street Journal*, August 24, 1999.

Hays, Daniel. "She Admits Keeping Jet Setters on High." New York *Daily News*, October 7, 1983.

Hackett, Pat. *The Andy Warhol Diaries*. New York: Hachette Book Group, 2014.

Hankin, Noel. *After Dark: Birth of the Disco Dance Party*. East Hampton, NY: Leon Niknah Publishing Company, 2021.

Hendrickson, Paul. "Bobby Zarem's the Name, Celebrities Are His Game, Bobby Zarem's the Name and Celebrities Are His Home." *Washington Post*, October 30, 1978.

Hsu, Hua. "The First Days of Disco." *New Yorker*. January 29, 2019.

Hughes, Andrew Mon; Mark Croham, and Grant Walters. *The Bee Gees in the 1970s*. Manchester, England: Sonicbond, 2023.

Hunt, Dennis. "Disco 1976—Where Do We Go from Here?" *Los Angeles Times*, February 8, 1976.

Ingle, Schuyler. "Lester Wilson: Famous in Europe . . . Frustrated in Hollywood." *LA Weekly*, January 11–17, 1980.

Kashner, Sam. "Fever Pitch." *Vanity Fair*, December 2007.

Kennedy, Shawn G. "The New Discotheque Scene: 'Like Going to a Big House Party.'" *New York Times*, January 3, 1976.

Khrealing, Lorraine. "Writer Flies High: Then Tumbles but Gets Back Up Again." *New York Times*, June 8, 1997.

Khomami, Nadia. "Disco's Saturday Night Fiction." *The Guardian*, June 26, 2016.

Kurycki, Mary Rita. "A 'Good Little Kid' Turns Psychotic." *Rochester Democrat and Chronicle*, May 7, 1977.

Laufer, Kerry. "Deney Terrio—The Man Who Taught Travolta to Dance." *Rona Barrett's Gossip*, August 1979.

Leduff, Charlie. "Saturday Night Fever: The Life." *New York Times*, June 9, 1996.

Lopez, Sonia. "Who Is Tommy?" *Radio Times* (London, England), October 5–11,1974.

Lugen, Makala. "The Day Disco Died: Remembering the Unbridled Chaos of 'Disco Demolition Night'. EDM.com, July 12, 2021.

Manbeck, John B. *The Neighborhoods of Brooklyn*. New Haven and London: Yale University Press, 2004.

Marlowe, Jon. "Mirror. Mirror, Disco Deceiver . . . Who Taught Travolta to Dance in 'Fever'?" *Miami Herald*, September 27, 1978.

McCabe, Bruce. "Backstage at the Oscars." *Boston Globe*, March 29, 1977.

McLaurin, Preston. "Boogie—The Myrtle Beach Disco Whirl Is Spinning Round in High Gear." *Sun-News* (Myrtle Beach, South Carolina), June 12, 1977.

McLean, Keitha. "Yes! Arfur the Pinball Queen Lives!" *Montreal Star*, March 29, 1969.

McMurran, Kirstin. "Why No Blow Ups on 'Blow Out'? Because Travolta, Allen, and DePalma Are Just Friends." *People*, August 17, 1981.

Meyer, David N. *The Bee Gees: The Biography*. Lebanon, IN: Da Capo Press, 2013.

Michelson, Herb. "John Revolting." *Sacramento Bee*, August 4, 1983.

Milward, John. "Movie Music Fever Sweeps Audiences" *Chicago Daily News*, February 13, 1978.

Morse, Steve. "The Bee Gees Are Getting the Cold Shoulder." *Boston Globe*, October 9, 1987.

Mose, Charonne. "A Gift to Dance." *Dance Vibe*, October 1994.

Munshower, Suzanne. *John Travolta: An Illustrated Biography*. New York: Grosset & Dunlap, 1978.

———. *Meet John Travolta*. New York: Grosset & Dunlap, 1976.

Murphy, A. D. "Teenage Rock Music Cheapie: The 'R' Stands for Raunchy." *Variety*, December 16, 1977.

Nadel, Norman. "Waiting to See if Fever Catches." *Daily Herald* (IL), December 21, 1977.

New York Times. "Out of the Soaps and Into the Discos" (Profile of Karen Lynn Gorney), December 30, 1977.

Nicholas, Paul. *Musicals, Marigolds & Me*. Croydon, England: Fantom Publishing, 2021.

Nicholson, Jacquelyn. "Disco Fever: It Just Won't Go Away." *Rona Barrett's Hollywood*, August 1979.

Orth, Maureen. "From Sweathog to Disco King." *Newsweek*, December 19, 1977.

Peck, Abe (*Rolling Stone*). *Dancing Madness*. New York: Anchor Books, 1976.

Prelutsky, Burt. "Million-Dollar Sweathog." *TV Guide*, January 1–7, 1977.

Radel, Chris. "The Disco Scene from Buster's to Trumps." *Cincinnati Enquirer*, January 16, 1977.

Ratliff, Ben. "Meet New Orleans Rap's Most Surprising Savior." *New York Times*, November 6, 2005.

Robins, Wayne. "Disco Pro: The Lockers" *Rolling Stone*, August 28, 1975.

Rose, Frank. "How Can You Mend a Broken Group? The Bee Gees Do It with Disco." *Rolling Stone*, July 14, 1977.

Rose, Frank. "Travolta Dominates New Disco Movie." *Chicago Daily News*, December 17, 1977.

Segal, Lewis. "A Step Up at Choreography Awards." *Los Angeles Times*, September 26, 2000.

Sharbutt, Jay. "High Flying *Dove*, Won't Keep It Out of Third." *Los Angeles Times*, February 10, 1989.

Silverton, Peter. "Groover and Shaker." *Sunday Telegraph Magazine*, May 1998.

Smilgis, Martha. "At 23, John Travolta Aims for the Stardom That Lover Diana Hyland Died without Sharing." *People*, June 13, 1977.

Smith, Liz. "Martin Shakar: On the Ascend." New York *Daily News*, February 16, 1978.

——."Other Fragments." New York *Daily News*, January 13, 1978. A shout-out for Lester Wilson's work.

——. "Without a Program." New York *Daily News*, February 15, 1977. The announcement of Avildsen's being fired.

Stanfield, Peter. *A Band with Built-In Hate: The Who from Pop Art to Punk.* London: Reaktion Books, 2021.

——. *Pin-Ups 1972.* London: Reaktion Books, 2022.

Stock, Craig. "Disco—Alive and Thriving." *Wichita Beacon*, December 26, 1976.

Swertlow, Frank. "Cancer Victim Diana Hyland: Amazingly Brave." *Shreveport Journal*, July 19,1977.

Taylor, Clarke. "Ins and Outs of Saturday Night." *Los Angeles Times*, June 12, 1977.

——. "New York Alive with the Sound of Disco." *Los Angeles Times*, August 14, 1977.

Terrio, Deney, as told to John O'Connor. "First Person: Deney Terrio." *Financial Times*, June 29, 2012.

Thomas, Kevin. "Travolta: Welcome to Movies." *Los Angeles Times*, December 19, 1977.

Thompson, Simon. "Saturday Night Fever Director on Hollywood's $3 Million Gamble That Became Iconic." *Forbes*, May 13, 2017.

Time. "High Steppin' to Stardom," April 3, 1978.

Townshend, Pete. *Who I Am: An Autobiography.* New York: Harper Perennial, 2013.

Travolta, John. "You Should be Dancing." *Crawdaddy*, March 1978.

Van Gelder, Lawrence. "New Race: Donna Pescow." *New York Times*, January 6, 1978.

Ward, Christopher. "That's Why the Lady Is a Champ." *Daily Mirror* (London), September 5, 1968.

Welch, Andrew. "Disco Daddy Gives SLC Soul." *Daily Utah Chronicle*, January 17, 1977.

White, Timothy. "Earthly Angels." *Rolling Stone*, May 11, 1979.

Whitney, Karl. "Nik Cohn: I Was Right. The Stones, After the Age of 30, Didn't Create Anything Good." *Irish Times*, January 21, 2016.

Wild, David. "Q&A: John Travolta." *Rolling Stone*, December 28, 1995.

Recommended
Documentaries

Bee Gees: One Night Only & the Official Story: Double DVD with live performances and documentary telling the story of the band and featuring interviews with the boys (2007).

The Godfather of Disco, directed by Gene Graham (2007).

How Can You Mend a Broken Heart: HBO Documentary about the Bee Gees, directed by Frank Marshall (2020).

King of the Underdogs: A documentary about the career of John G. Avildsen, directed by Derek Wayne Johnson (2017).

Mr. Saturday Night: HBO Documentary about Robert Stigwood, directed by John Maggio (2021).

Saturday Night Fever: A 30-Year Legacy: Available in the 45th Anniversary Blu-Ray of *Saturday Night Fever* (2007).

Saturday Night Fever: The Ultimate Disco Movie: Hosted by Bruno Tonioli (*Dancing with the Stars*), directed by Ian Denyer (2017).

Saturday Night Fever: The Inside Story: A&E Network, directed by Anthony Uro (2010).

The Secret Disco Revolution: Directed by Jamie Kastner (2012).

Studio 54: A&E Indie Films, directed by Matt Tyrnauer (2019).

VH1's *Behind the Music: The Making of Saturday Night Fever*, directed by Jill Modabber (2001).

The War on Disco: The American Experience: PBS, directed by Rushmore DeNooyer (2023).

When Disco Ruled the World: BBC, directed by Stephen Franklin (2002).